# COLERIDGE AND THE GEOMETRIC IDIOM

When Coleridge described the landscapes he passed through while scrambling among the fells, mountains, and valleys of Britain, he did something unprecedented in Romantic writing: to capture what emerged before his eyes, he enlisted a geometric idiom. Immersed in a culture still beholden to Euclid's *Elements* and schooled by those who subscribed to its principles, he valued geometry both for its pragmatic function and for its role as a conduit to abstract thought. Indeed, his geometric training would often structure his observations on religion, aesthetics, politics, and philosophy. For Coleridge, however, this perspective never competed with his sensitivity to the organic nature of his surroundings but, rather, intermingled with it. Situating Coleridge's remarkable ways of seeing within the history and teaching of mathematics and alongside the eighteenth century's budding interest in non-Euclidean geometry, Ann C. Colley illuminates the richness of the culture of walking and the surprising potential of landscape writing.

ANN C. COLLEY is SUNY Distinguished Professor Emerita at SUNY Buffalo State University. She has taught in Ukraine and Poland as a Fulbright Scholar and has been a Visiting Fellow at Wolfson College, Cambridge. She has written extensively on nineteenth-century British literature and culture.

# CAMBRIDGE STUDIES IN ROMANTICISM

*Founding Editor*
MARILYN BUTLER, *University of Oxford*

*General Editor*
JAMES CHANDLER, *University of Chicago*

*Editorial Board*
CLAIRE CONNOLLY, *University College Cork*
PAUL HAMILTON, *University of London*
CLAUDIA JOHNSON, *Princeton University*
ESSAKA JOSHUA, *University of Notre Dame*
NIGEL LEASK, *University of Glasgow*
ALAN LIU, *University of California, Santa Barbara*
DEIDRE LYNCH, *Harvard University*
JEROME MCGANN, *University of Virginia*
DAVID SIMPSON, *University of California, Davis*

This series aims to foster the best new work in one of the most challenging fields within English literary studies. From the early 1780s to the early 1830s, a formidable array of talented men and women took to literary composition, not just in poetry, which some of them famously transformed, but in many modes of writing. The expansion of publishing created new opportunities for writers, and the political stakes of what they wrote were raised again by what Wordsworth called those "great national events" that were "almost daily taking place": the French Revolution, the Napoleonic and American wars, urbanization, industrialization, religious revival, an expanded empire abroad, and the reform movement at home. This was an enormous ambition, even when it pretended otherwise. The relations between science, philosophy, religion, and literature were reworked in texts such as *Frankenstein* and *Biographia Literaria*; gender relations in *A Vindication of the Rights of Woman* and *Don Juan*; journalism by Cobbett and Hazlitt; and poetic form, content, and style by the Lake School and the Cockney School. Outside Shakespeare studies, probably no body of writing has produced such a wealth of commentary or done so much to shape the responses of modern criticism. This indeed is the period that saw the emergence of those notions of literature and of literary history, especially national literary history, on which modern scholarship in English has been founded.

The categories produced by Romanticism have also been challenged by recent historicist arguments. The task of the series is to engage both with a challenging corpus of Romantic writings and with the changing field of criticism they have helped to shape. As with other literary series published by Cambridge University Press, this one will represent the work of both younger and more established scholars on either side of the Atlantic and elsewhere.

*See the end of the book for a complete list of published titles.*

# COLERIDGE AND THE GEOMETRIC IDIOM

*Walking with Euclid*

ANN C. COLLEY
*SUNY Buffalo State University*

Shaftesbury Road, Cambridge CB2 8EA, United Kingdom

One Liberty Plaza, 20th Floor, New York, NY 10006, USA

477 Williamstown Road, Port Melbourne, VIC 3207, Australia

314–321, 3rd Floor, Plot 3, Splendor Forum, Jasola District Centre, New Delhi – 110025, India

103 Penang Road, #05–06/07, Visioncrest Commercial, Singapore 238467

Cambridge University Press is part of Cambridge University Press & Assessment, a department of the University of Cambridge.

We share the University's mission to contribute to society through the pursuit of education, learning and research at the highest international levels of excellence.

www.cambridge.org
Information on this title: www.cambridge.org/9781009271745

DOI: 10.1017/9781009271769

© Ann C. Colley 2023

This publication is in copyright. Subject to statutory exception and to the provisions of relevant collective licensing agreements, no reproduction of any part may take place without the written permission of Cambridge University Press & Assessment.

First published 2023
First paperback edition 2025

*A catalogue record for this publication is available from the British Library*

ISBN 978-1-009-27175-2 Hardback
ISBN 978-1-009-27174-5 Paperback

Cambridge University Press & Assessment has no responsibility for the persistence or accuracy of URLs for external or third-party internet websites referred to in this publication and does not guarantee that any content on such websites is, or will remain, accurate or appropriate.

This book is dedicated to the landscape of my childhood walking in Britain.

# Contents

| | |
|---|---|
| *List of Figures* | *page* viii |
| *Acknowledgments* | ix |
| *List of Abbreviations* | xii |
| Introduction | 1 |
| 1  Coleridge Walks: The Measure of the Landscape | 11 |
| 2  Lines of Motion | 51 |
| 3  A Geometric Frame of Mind | 78 |
| 4  Ars Poetica | 114 |
| 5  Youth and Age: Coleridge and the Shifting Paradigm of Geometric Thought | 145 |
| Afterword: An Organic Geometry | 176 |
| *Bibliography* | 181 |
| *Index* | 190 |

# *Figures*

| | | |
|---|---|---|
| 1 | Thomas Barker of Bath, *Travellers in a Landscape* | page 34 |
| 2 | Sir George Beaumont (1753–1827), *Keswick*, 3 July 1798 | 64 |
| 3 | Edward Lear's diagram of Miss Alderson's singing "The Last Rose of Summer," October 1869 | 72 |
| 4 | Samuel Taylor Coleridge's diagram of a triangle representing "wedded Love in its Ideal" | 99 |
| 5 | Samuel Taylor Coleridge's diagram from an August 1807 letter to Mary Cruikshank | 139 |
| 6 | Author's diagram of an open triangle illustrating "This Lime-Tree Bower My Prison" | 139 |
| 7 | Author's diagram of a complete triangle illustrating "This Lime-Tree Bower My Prison" | 140 |
| 8 | Author's diagram of the sun's radiant orb encircling the complete triangle in "This Lime-Tree Bower My Prison" | 141 |
| 9 | Page from James Sharp(e)'s 1782 copybook | 156 |

## *Acknowledgments*

I would like to start by thanking those in Buffalo, New York, who have supported my work. I am especially grateful for the assistance of the late Dean Ben Christy, whose encouragement and resources made it possible for me periodically to leave my teaching duties and travel to libraries and archives relevant to my research. I miss your presence. One never succeeds without the help of librarians. In particular, I would like to extend my gratitude to the Interlibrary loan staff at the E. H. Butler Library. During the recent pandemic, I would not have been able to consult a number of texts if ILL had not extended its services. Similarly, I appreciate the technological assistance of Kaylene Waite, Senior Graphic and Web Designer at SUNY Buffalo State College, who willingly and repeatedly helped me, especially when her time was restricted because of Covid regulations. And thank you, Dr. Julian Cole, a philosopher and mathematician who patiently allowed me to understand a number of geometrical concepts. I also appreciate the interest shown in the book by my colleagues Lisa Berglund and David Ben-Merre. Moreover, I am grateful for the presence of Maureen Lougen and Gail M. Phillips, who printed out materials for me. Throughout the recent closings of college buildings, they have consistently been present for me.

   As always, I am especially beholden to the members of the Writing Group, who devoted many hours to reading through and commenting on each chapter. In this respect, I am indebted to Professors Carrie Bramen, Regina Grol, and Carolyn Korsmeyer. During the long periods of lockdown and a Buffalo winter, all of you, wrapped in down coats, scarfs, and woolen hats, persisted and met outside or online with me. The group's critique and belief in the project were immensely reassuring. I also cannot forget the encouragement of Charles and Irene Haupt who made it possible on October 20, 2017, in the Burchfield Penney Art Gallery, Buffalo, New York, to perform my *Cantata for Coleridge* based on the poet's notebooks. Tiffany DuMouchell, soprano, Paul Tadaro, actor, and Anthony Chase, narrator, were the artists who performed this piece.

During my research travels, I have met many who have offered and given me assistance. I begin by thanking Roma Kail and the staff of Special Collections, Victoria University Library, who, in December 2016, made it possible for me to access their collection of Samuel Taylor Coleridge's notebooks. Similarly, I wish to thank the staff of the British Library Manuscript and Rare Book Room. In addition, I am grateful for the generous welcome that the staff of Christ's Hospital Museum extended toward me. I am particularly indebted to Mike Barford, Laura Kidner, Amy Potter, and Clifford Jones, who offered me guidance and support. In addition, I appreciate the attention I received at the Special Collections in the library of the University of Leicester. I wish to thank Dr. Simon Dixon and especially Mike Price, who, representing the Mathematical Society, sat with me, suggested readings, and helped me understand what I was viewing. I also cannot forget the thoughtfulness of the staff at the Jerwood Centre in Grasmere. During the winter months when the library is usually shut, they accommodated me and brought out items I wished to see.

It goes without saying that I am grateful to Wolfson College, University of Cambridge, for making it possible for me as a visiting fellow to spend two half-year periods (in 2017 and 2019–20) so that I might research materials for the book. In particular, I want to express my gratitude to Christine Corton, Richard Evans, Michelle Searle, and the librarians of Wolfson College Library. While in Cambridge, I spent most of my time in the Rare Book and Manuscript Room of the Cambridge University Library as well as in the library stacks. The librarians in the University Library's Rare Book and Map Room were most accommodating and pleasant. While in Cambridge I also had the support of two nineteenth-century scholars, Kathleen M. Wheeler and Heather Glen. Their commentary, encouragement, and enduring, generous friendship are with me still.

Conferences also play a role in preparing a book. In this respect I am indebted to Tim Fulford, who helped organize the Friends of Coleridge Biennial Conference at Jesus College, University of Cambridge, in August 2018, and who with Kerri Andrews in April 2018 arranged a conference on "Romantic-Era Lakeland Walking" in Keswick. Moreover, in September 2019 Tim helped plan the Friends of Coleridge Halsway Weekend on "Coleridge and the Natural World." All these gatherings allowed me to be with other Coleridge scholars, present some of my ideas, and, in addition, meet members of the Coleridge family. I am especially grateful to one of the descendants, Sara Milne of Piddlehinton, Dorchester, Dorset, for her hospitality and kindness in taking me to places associated with Samuel Taylor Coleridge.

Family also plays a role. I would like to thank Rachel Ida Massey for her willingness to comment on drafts of chapters, and I am appreciative of her father's giving me books from his Coleridge collection. And finally thank you Gwen Hilary Colley for your understanding and attention.

# Abbreviations

CC     Samuel Taylor Coleridge, *The Collected Works of Samuel Taylor Coleridge*, 16 vols., General Editor Kathleen Coburn (Princeton, NJ: Princeton University Press, 1971–2002). References include volume and page numbers.

CL     Samuel Taylor Coleridge, *Collected Letters of Samuel Taylor Coleridge*, 6 vols., ed. Earl Leslie Griggs (Oxford: Oxford University Press, 1956–71). References include volume and page numbers.

CN     Samuel Taylor Coleridge, *The Notebooks of Samuel Taylor Coleridge*, 5 vols., ed. Kathleen Coburn (Princeton, NJ: Princeton University Press, 1957–2002). References include volume and entry numbers followed by British Library folio number.

CP     Samuel Taylor Coleridge, *The Complete Poetical Works of Samuel Taylor Coleridge*, 2 vols., ed. Ernest Hartley Coleridge (Oxford: Clarendon Press, 1957). References include volume and page numbers.

# Introduction

> About two miles from Bampton our road walled by the mountains – that on our left Walla Crag – a mountain whose constituent lines with infinite variety yet all in segment of Circles – the whole Crag a rude semicircle – the other Hills bare (save at their feet inclosed fields) the Walla's *Toes* run into the Lake in Lingulis Where the foot of the Walla runs with its distinct Toes into the Lake, there the inclosures too from the opposite mountains run into it – & these form that narrow part of the lake, which as you first approach appears the termination / But standing a hundred yards high you behold a second reach – where no inclosures are seen, but the bare Mountain on the right which alone we see, forms a bay / a beautiful Crescent /
>
> <div align="right">(<i>CN</i> 1:510; f. 52)</div>

This book began when I opened the first two volumes of Coleridge's *Notebooks* and started reading his descriptions of the landscape he passed through while scrambling among the fells, mountains, valleys, and hills of Britain between 1794 and 1804. The extraordinary rigor of Coleridge's walking as well as the mode in which he experienced his own passage through rough and rugged terrain immediately intrigued me. In particular, Coleridge's alertness to the lines of motion that run through and help define his surroundings caught my attention and alerted me to his calling upon what I came to term "the geometric idiom" to aid his capturing, and, at times, diagramming the shape of what he perceived. This recognition led me on a journey that commences with a description of his walking excursions, then discusses his idiosyncratic perspective when writing about what he saw or felt underfoot. Eventually this inquiry directed me to consider his indebtedness to his training in Euclidean geometry, an instruction that began at Christ's Hospital School and continued, in earnest, at the University of Cambridge. Studying this discipline not only gave him a groundwork by which to measure and comprehend what emerged while tramping from place to place but also offered him a means of understanding the natural world. Inevitably, Coleridge's sense of the tread and pace of his feet, his sensitivity to line, as well as his attention to geometry played a role when he composed his nature poetry.

That Euclid's *Elements* should have been such a basic text in the eighteenth and early nineteenth centuries in England is understandable. For centuries, Euclid – whose work first appeared in Greek during the third century BC – had been a means of working out the spatial arrangement of one's surroundings.[1] As Jacqueline Stedall, an historian of mathematics, points out, many manuscript translations from Arabic to Greek and to Latin would have been on the shelves of monastic libraries as well as in the libraries of fledgling universities in Paris, Oxford, and Cambridge during the twelfth and thirteenth centuries.[2] Indeed, the Bodleian Library owns the oldest extant copy, created in Byzantium in AD 888. Scholars would have been familiar with his work not only through these copies but also as a result of their reading Aristotle and Plato as well as their studying commentators like Proclus, who in 1533 annotated the first four books of Euclid's *Elements*. Of course, the reading of Proclus until the publication of Thomas Taylor's English translation at the turn of the eighteenth century would have been limited to those who knew Greek or Latin.[3]

In 1551, however, a change occurred. It was in that year that Robert Recorde (1510–58), a fellow of All Souls College, Oxford, and later associated with Cambridge, published *The Pathway to Knowledge*, a conceptual translation into English of Euclid's *Elements*. His desire was to make some parts of that work available to the "ordinary" Englishman.[4] Stedall suggests that he wanted to introduce geometry to a population that had hardly heard of such a subject so as to provide a practical geometrical knowledge for use in everyday life. Recorde had in mind those whose livelihood could be improved by a knowledge of geometry – such people as carpenters, joiners, masons, and farmers who measured the ground and

---

[1] It was not until the late nineteenth century that non-Euclidean mathematics was finally accepted in Britain.
[2] See Jacqueline Stedall's "*The Pathway to Knowledge* and the English Euclidean Tradition," in *Robert Recorde: The Life and Times of a Tudor Mathematician*, ed. Gareth Ffowc Roberts and Fenny Smith (Cardiff: University of Wales Press, 2012), 57–72.
[3] For an exhaustive study of early English publications of Euclid's *Elements* see Diana M. Simpkins's "Early Editions of Euclid in England," *Annals of Science* 22.4 (December 1966): 225–49.
[4] Interestingly, Stedall in "*The Pathway to Knowledge*" points out that when Recorde translated Euclid from Greek and Latin, he had some difficulty, for there were no natural equivalents in English to some of the geometric terms, such as "triangle," "trapezium," and "acute angle." He either had "to carry over Latin words into English, or he had to invent new English words to carry old meanings" (58).

calculated how to dig a ditch or build stacks of hay. But Recorde's perspective was not just limited to the pragmatic aspects of geometry; like many before and after him, he also recognized that geometry was not only useful for its practical applications but also valuable for its metaphysical insights – to "howe the divines also in their mysteries of Scripture doo use healpe of geometrie."[5]

It is as if Recorde's book set into motion numerous subsequent translations of Euclid into English. Years later there was not only Henry Billingsley's lavish 1570 *The Elements of Geometrie of the Most Aunciant Philosopher Euclide of Megara* that he considered helpful for "handy works" as well as "mind works"[6] but also, in centuries to come, multiple English editions of Euclid's *Elements* prepared for teaching geometry in schools and in universities. By the middle of the seventeenth century, there were, for instance, Thomas Rudd's *Euclide's Elements of Geometry* (1651), Isaac Barrow's 1660 *Euclide's Elements of Geometry*, written to appeal to Cambridge students, John Leeke and George Serle's *Euclid's Elements of Geometry* (1661), and William Allingham's *Epitome of Geometry* (1695). By the time Coleridge was in school and at university, the number of English editions of Euclid had proliferated. What is more, their contents had become an essential part of a man's education. For many, including Coleridge, geometry was not just a discipline to be applied to pragmatic needs but also a passageway, a means to reach higher truths. Continuing its ancient applications, a knowledge of geometry was deemed essential if one was to think philosophically. It is not surprising that Coleridge was attracted, though as we shall see, not exclusively, to the geometric idiom when considering his surroundings. The discipline was, as Recorde had once pronounced, *The Pathway to Knowledge*.

The following study of Coleridge's appreciation of landscape takes into account not only the context of his and his culture's attention to Euclid but also other factors that were influencing Coleridge's perception, such as his keen sensual appreciation for what he saw, felt, and heard as he wandered through the countryside on foot. Indeed, the point of the book is not only to examine the role of the geometric idiom in his descriptions but also to illustrate how his sensitivity to the organic, fluid, lush phenomena populating his surroundings intermingled with this perspective to

---

[5] As quoted by Stedall, "*The Pathway to Knowledge*," 65. Although Recorde did not devote many pages to the philosophical dimension of geometry, in the "Preface" to his translation, he stated that geometry was helpful in explaining "seemingly magical or unnatural occurrences" (Stedall, "*The Pathway to Knowledge*," 65).

[6] Stedall, "*The Pathway to Knowledge*," 70.

create such entries as the one that heads this Introduction and another that he hurriedly jotted down on November 11, 1799 in which he calls upon the figures of the wedge, the cone, the square, the circle, and the semicircle to help him describe the luminous, dynamic view of the "whole length of Basenthwait":

> From Ouse bridge, from the Inn Window, the whole length of Basenthwait, a simple majesty of water & mountains– / & in the distance the Bank rising like a wedge ◮ – & in the second distance the Crags of Derwentwater / What an effect of the Shadows on the water! / – On the left the conical Shadow, On the right a square of splendid Black, all the area & intermediate a mirror reflecting dark & sunny Cloud / – but in the distance the black Promontory with a circle of melted Silver & a path of silver running from it like a flat Cape in the Lake – The snowy Borrodale in the far distance / & a ridge, nearer mountains sloping down as it were to the faint Bank of the Basenthwaite. (*CN* 1:536; f. 43)

These passages resemble many others composed during his walking years that intermingle Coleridge's sensitivity to abstract, geometric forms with his keen appreciation for the shifting, sensuous particulars of his surroundings. For him the two modes of perception are not, as most might imagine, contradictory but complementary. Together they create a more complete sense of the world. This study acknowledges Coleridge's appreciation for Euclidean geometry, a dimension that tends to be overlooked in critical studies of his early work. Furthermore, it concludes by considering how he also tangentially participated in the various challenges to Euclidean geometry.

The chapters in *Coleridge and the Geometric Idiom: Walking with Euclid* explore Coleridge's use of the geometric figure while scrambling among the fells, mountains, valleys, and hills of Britain between 1794 and 1804 and when working out his ideas concerning religion, politics, literature, aesthetics, and philosophy. Coleridge periodically drew upon his mathematical training to help structure his thoughts. Immersed in a culture beholden to Euclid's *Elements*, he valued the discipline both for its pragmatic function, such as a tool with which to measure the landscape, and for its role as a conduit to abstract thought. Schooled by those who continued geometry's ancient applications and deemed a knowledge of geometry essential, he also valued it as a pathway to truth.

Coleridge's vital relationship to this geometric perspective has either been glossed over or virtually ignored by commentators, who have chosen to concentrate on his interest in the sciences and his involvement in metaphysical, religious, political, social, and aesthetic matters. As a result, Coleridge's pervasive attachment to the geometric idiom in his notebooks, prose, and poetry begs to be recognized and explored. Calling upon this orientation, *Coleridge and the Geometric Idiom* offers a fresh and enlightening approach to Coleridge's mode of perceiving and recording the landscape of his rambling, of his eliciting geometric shapes in his philosophic work as well as in the composition of his so-called nature poetry. This study examines his keen sensuous appreciation for what he saw, felt, and heard as he wandered through the countryside on foot. The book illustrates how his appreciation for the geometric idiom intermingled with his sensitivity to the organic, fluid, lush phenomena populating his surroundings so as to create living, breathing pieces of writing. Moreover, *Coleridge and the Geometric Idiom* occasionally ranges beyond Coleridge's work and refers to ancient and contemporary philosophers as well as to artists like Paul Klee and Wassily Kandinsky, for whom Euclidean principles were as essential in defining shape and creating patterns of meaning as they were for Coleridge. With this approach, this study will appeal to scholars, students, and a reading public interested in all aspects of the work and life of Coleridge as well as theories of Romanticism and the period's writers and thinkers. This book will also be attractive to those who take a particular interest in the culture of walking and ways of perceiving a landscape. Furthermore, it will engage an audience interested in interdisciplinary studies, especially those who are fascinated by the intersection between the arts and mathematics, including readers interested in the concept of line, pattern, and form.

To guide the reader through this study, an outline of the book's argument and sequence of chapters follows.

Chapter 1 of *Coleridge and the Geometric Idiom* describes the rough and tumble of Coleridge's rambles between 1794 and 1804, which reflect his unique power as an observer – a discussion that prefaces and prepares the reader for an exploration of his use of the geometric idiom. This chapter opens by placing these excursions within a culture of walking, depicts his various undertakings, and, in particular, dwells on his propensity to be his own path-maker rather than follow either the directives of the picturesque guides or the assigned routes of maps. Entries in the pocket notebooks he carried with him reveal that Coleridge's understanding of a landscape was not exclusively based upon what his eyes could see but also upon what his feet could register. His was an orientation not necessarily based upon fashionable, aesthetic ways of seeing. Rather, during his spatial exploration of his surroundings, he also paid particular attention to the tread (and condition) of his boots. In many respects, Coleridge emerges as a surveyor who measures the terrain with his feet. Often modeling his understanding of a landscape on the spirit of geometric exercises, Coleridge measured and counted his paces over a portion of ground and observed its lines and angles. Like the geometric caterpillar (*geometridae*) he once described in his book on logic, he periodically becomes the surveyor who walks out to plot the earth.

Taking its cue from this orientation, Chapter 2, "Lines of Motion," demonstrates in what ways Coleridge was alert to the tangible lines that run through and lend character to a landscape. As anticipated in the previous chapter, during the period of his walking excursions, Coleridge visually traced their presence in the areas through which he rambled and, consequently, repeatedly attended to what he termed a landscape's lines of motion. As a result, throughout his early notebook entries and letters, he plotted these lines to create diagrammatic sketches that recall the geometric idiom. Many critics tend to dismiss these sketches as being either extraneous or some scribbled afterthought. But, if one looks at Coleridge's original notebooks housed in both the British Library and Victoria University at the University of Toronto (instead of their published renditions in the edited notebooks), one discovers that they are not. Rather, these line drawings are crucial to his meaning; they interact with, traverse the path of, extend, or emerge from his handwritten words. Indebted to this sensibility, Coleridge also "translated" Sir George Beaumont's and Washington Allston's watercolors into diagrams by attending to the various lines that organize each painting's content – the intent was to transform these paintings into poems. Participating in a diagrammatic culture that was indebted to a culture of geometric modeling and one that influenced writers like Laurence Sterne to chart the motion of the corporal's walking stick as it wafts through the air, Coleridge liked to capture the defining lines of a place and integrate them into his verbal descriptions. This habit reflects his obligation to the geometric spatial imagination. Indeed, his sense of the active lines that trace movement in a landscape has much in common with Klee's and Kandinsky's concept of line – a focus that reflects these artists' own training in a Euclidean perspective. As Klee, thinking of Euclid's definitions, once remarked, the point sets itself in motion, "moves off," and a line comes into being – "it goes out for a walk."[7] In all these instances, there is a geometric underpinning, a memory of geometric diagrams that utilize line to organize space and recall a

---

[7] Paul Klee, *The Thinking Eye*, ed. Jerry Spiller (London: Lund Humphries, 1961), 24, 105.

mathematical set of relations. Far more than in the work of his fellow poets and writers, this groundwork is very much at play in Coleridge's landscape descriptions.[8]

Chapter 3, "A Geometric Frame of Mind," discusses the extent to which Coleridge relied upon geometric forms to describe his surroundings and to construct aspects of his abstract thoughts. The chapter opens with a discussion of his use of these in his landscape descriptions when he would fill his notebooks with references to triangles, perpendiculars, ellipses, parallelograms, convex semicircles, squares, ovals, and spheres. These helped him record the shapes of the mountains, streams, rivers, and clouds he passed by. But the question arises: Given Coleridge's fascination with the irregular and wild scenery of his rambles, why would he utilize the fixed, abstracted geometric idiom, removed from time? This chapter addresses this seeming contradiction by suggesting that his attraction to the geometric figure in his descriptions is neither incongruous nor paradoxical, but rather an expression of being immersed in a culture that nurtured such a frame of mind and believed in a mathematical ordering of the entire universe. Beginning with his training both at Christ's Hospital School and at the University of Cambridge, Coleridge inherited a deeply ingrained conviction that one should take Euclid seriously. Moreover, he recognized that a knowledge of Euclid's *Elements* was a prerequisite to comprehending both the phenomenal world and intellectual thought. As a result, he often used a geometric shape as a scaffolding and as a process of reasoning by which to work out his ideas about marriage, faith, aesthetics, and other metaphysical matters. It was the vestibule of thought. Most particularly, Coleridge respected a geometrical perspective not only because of his training but also because the discipline sharpened the powers of attention, abstraction, and an *a priori* intuition, all of which increased his ability to see and organize what engaged him.

Ultimately, in spite of its conceptual character, Coleridge's attachment to a geometric perspective did not contradict his attraction to the sensual details of his surroundings. For him, there was little disparity between the realm of geometric abstraction associated with the pure, non-sensible Platonic idea or Kant's understanding of intuited knowledge and the sensory, experiential world. Rather than accepting, as so many of his

---

[8] There has been the occasional study that acknowledges William Wordsworth's indebtedness to his geometrical training. See, for instance, L. M. Johnson. *Wordsworth's Metaphysical Verse: Geometry, Nature, and Form* (London: University of Toronto Press, 1982). This study, however, dedicates itself to Wordsworth's symbolic use of geometrical patterns and the abstract notion of form.

contemporaries did, the differences between these seemingly dissimilar ways of regarding one's surroundings, Coleridge intertwined the two. He entangled the movements, sounds, and colors of his natural surroundings with the geometric so that neither detracted from nor competed with the other. Neither precluded nor sullied the other but rather, in their intermingling, the two created a more complex and richer sense of the surrounding world.

With this context in mind, Chapter 4, "*Ars Poetica*," turns to Coleridge's nature poetry and examines what remnants of his sensitivity to the tread and feel of his feet as well as to his lineal and geometric orientation – all discussed in the previous chapters – helped sculpt these verses.

This chapter begins by focusing on how the imprint of his feet moving through a landscape, discussed in Chapter 1, significantly contributed to the ways in which Coleridge shaped the contours of his nature poems and bestowed upon them a feeling of immediacy. Their uneven, erratic rhythms suggest the stride of his walking and, thereby, introduce a sense of sequential immediacy to the poetic line. Little attention has been directed to this aspect of his art. The progress of these peripatetic poems, such as "Lines Composed while climbing the Left Ascent of Brockley Coomb, Somersetshire, May 1795,"[9] brings to mind his reference to a serpent that makes it way along a path by pausing and half retreating so as to collect the force with which to carry itself forward. So, as well, do the irregular, back and forth, here and there movements of Coleridge's footsteps propel him and his ideas along his poetic lines.

When composing his nature poetry, Coleridge, as if extending the path made by the tread of his feet, also occasionally resuscitated his keen sensitivity to the lines of motion, examined in Chapter 2, that run through and diagram the landscapes described in his notebooks. As a result, he often paid close attention to the pattern of a poem's lines – to their arrangement on a page. Taking a cue from Euclidean geometry and appreciating that lines are essential to the shaping and construction of a poem, he carefully considered how each poetic line emerged from one point and traveled to another. Together they generate the surface of the poem.

Coleridge's attention to line in his verses connects to a larger understanding that a poem, like a geometric figure, is basically an arrangement of

---

[9] The capitalization and punctuation in titles of Coleridge's poems are taken from *The Complete Poetical Works of Samuel Taylor Coleridge*, ed. Ernest Hartley Coleridge, 2 vols. (Oxford: Clarendon Press, 1957).

lines in space – a circumstance that prompts a consideration of the relationship between the two. Acutely aware that an understanding of the phenomenal world can be enhanced by geometric reasoning and that mathematics is the natural language of pattern and form – an orientation discussed in Chapter 3 – Coleridge was not always averse, when composing his verses, to thinking geometrically. To reach a better understanding of how this inclination works, this chapter turns to "Frost at Midnight" and then to "This Lime-Tree Bower My Prison" to illustrate how circular and triangular forms ultimately shape and unite what initially seems separated or disconnected.

The chapter concludes by recognizing that the topography of Coleridge's nature poetry is not just determined by the geometric outline of its structure but rather finds its vibrancy in the selection of its sensual details – a condition that recalls the potency of his notebook entries that intermingle the geometric figure with the surrounding sights, movements, sounds, and colors to create a fuller sense of the landscape that emerges before his consideration. In the end, even though alert to abstract geometric figures, Coleridge's nature poetry primarily grounds itself within the realm of the poet's physical contact with the earth. These poems dwell among the emerging shadows created by the shifting light and find some semblance of order within the timeless geometric form. Both perspectives work together to create one graceful and intelligent whole.

Chapter 5 of *Coleridge and the Geometric Idiom*, "Youth and Age: Coleridge and the Shifting Paradigm of Geometric Thought," examines the changes through time in Coleridge's indebtedness to the Euclidean idiom. In particular, this chapter explores the challenges to Euclid's tenacious hold on the British imagination in the late eighteenth and early nineteenth centuries. During Coleridge's lifetime there were rumblings about Euclid's inaccuracies. As the decades passed, debates concerning these matters gained momentum so that eventually British geometers were catching up with and joining their European counterparts. A number of these mathematicians began carefully considering both the form and the arrangement of Euclid's propositions so that they could be presented in a more perfectly logical sequence. In particular, Euclid's fifth proposition concerning the validity of parallel lines disturbed them. This and other concerns created a group of "rivals" who questioned, though never fully discounted, parts of Euclid's system.

After giving an overview of these various challenges, this final chapter discusses their possible effect on Coleridge's use of the geometric idiom. Recognizing that Coleridge was by no means actively involved in the various arguments and technical discussions brewing among mathematicians on the Continent and eventually in Britain, the chapter suggests that Coleridge, who was persistently responsive to Continental thought and was conversant with philosophical treatises about the nature of geometry, was probably peripherally aware of the debates concerning the validity of Euclid's ascendancy. With this in mind, the concluding section of the book explores Thomas Reid's section "Of the Geometry of Visibles" in his *An Inquiry into the Human Mind: On the Principles of Common Sense* (1764) and demonstrates how Coleridge in his notebook entries loosely approximates Reid's understanding that there is a need to consider an alternate geometry.

The chapter then remarks on Coleridge's sensitivity to the curvature of space and suggests that it peripherally recalls Carl Friedrich Gauss's development of a non-Euclidean geometry. Coincidentally both Gauss and Coleridge were in Göttingen around the same time and had climbed the Brocken in the Harz Mountains. Although there are significant differences between their accounts of their rambles among this landscape, Coleridge's descriptions and their attention to the curvature of those surroundings unsettle, as did Gauss's measurements, a Euclidean perspective. He, like Gauss, is alert to the curvature of the earth's surface. In the end, Coleridge, though still recognizing and paying homage to his mathematical training, finds that he must breach its limits and compellingly introduce a wild geometry that breaks out of the set forms associated with Euclid. In his own, yet enigmatic way, then, Coleridge modifies Euclid and unwittingly becomes yet another of his rivals. Though he does not participate in a mathematician's precise, numerical, and technical methods, he keeps company with those, such as Gauss, who at the same time as being beholden to the ancient geometry also recognize Euclid's shortcomings. In the end, both the traditional geometric figures and the wilder geometry worked for him. Each was Coleridge's companion.

CHAPTER I

# *Coleridge Walks*
## *The Measure of the Landscape*

> like a Leaf in Autumn: a wild activity, of thoughts, imaginations, feelings, and impulses of motion, rises up from within me – a sort of *bottom-wind*, that blows to no point of the compass, & comes from I know not whence, but agitates the whole of me; my whole Being is filled with waves, as it were, that roll & stumble, one this way, & one that way, like things that have no common master. I think, that my soul must have pre-existed in the body of a Chamois-chaser.
> (Excerpt from Coleridge, letter to Thomas Wedgwood, sent January 14, 1803, *CL* 2:916)

> The practice of surveying may be considered as consisting of four parts: 1. Measuring strait lines. 2. Finding the position of the strait lines with respect to each other. 3. Laying down or planning upon paper these positions and measures. 4. Obtaining the superficial measure of the land to be surveyed.
> (George Adams, *Geometrical and Graphical Essays*, 1791)[1]

In an 1803 letter to Thomas Wedgwood (quoted above), Coleridge, reflecting upon the "wild activity" and momentum attending a recent walking excursion among the Lakes, aptly conjectured that "my soul must have pre-existed in the body of a Chamois-chaser" (*CL* 2:916). There is a certain truth in his almost whimsical speculation about his "soul," for in his twenties and early thirties, Coleridge, as if replicating the Alpine hunter's daring wandering from height to height, scrambled through the hills, valleys, fells, and mountains of Britain. Before his health more completely broke down and personal as well as professional difficulties precipitated his move to Malta in 1804, he was undeniably the hardiest and most energetic of walkers who climbed over many a rock and often preferred the rough and tumble of the higher terrain to the

---

[1] George Adams, *Geometrical and Graphical Essays Containing a Description of the Mathematical Instruments Used in Geometry, Civil and Military Surveying Levelling and Perspective* (London: R. Hindmarsh, 1791), 194.

roads and paths in the lower regions.² Choosing to walk over uneven ground, break "through the straggling branches of a copse-wood" or run out "bare-headed to enjoy the commotion of the elements,"³ he, for a decade between 1794 and 1804, as if moved by a "*bottom-wind*," vigorously tramped from place to place, and filled his pocket notebooks with descriptions of the sights, sounds, textures, and colors of the terrain and prospects that emerged as he wended his way and ascended over rough ground – amazing feats in view of his intermittent physical distress: trouble with his bowels, boils, swollen limbs, inflamed eyes, and infected teeth.⁴

These excursions were vital not only to his sense of wellbeing but also to the development of his unique powers as an observer. They enhanced his sensibility to the shifting forms of a landscape and nurtured the growth of his spatial imagination. Furthermore, the excursions provided occasions to reflect upon and often replicate, through his line drawings accompanying his descriptions, the topography of his surroundings. The notebook entries dashed off while Coleridge was rambling through the countryside reveal a dynamic perspective frequently grounded in the tread of his steps. In a sense, Coleridge's walks often provided the "footing" of his thoughts. For this reason, before going on in subsequent chapters to explore his sensitivity to the concept of line and the geometric idiom in his understanding of landscape and eventually the influence of these elements in the writing of his poetry, I want first to consider the culture of walking in the late eighteenth and early nineteenth centuries as well as the character of Coleridge's actual walks, for these expeditions were, as I have stated, the literal groundwork of his spatial imagination. In particular, his almost compulsive walking and dynamic sense of movement between 1794 and 1804 significantly distanced his experience from fashionable aesthetic ways of seeing. His rigorous, physical immersion in the valleys and hills of Britain released him from the tyranny of

---

² William Ruddick writes that when Coleridge took his family to live at Greta Hall in July 1800, he "soon discovered that he preferred a higher terrain than the Wordsworths did." See "'As Much Diversity as the Heart That Trembles': Coleridge's Notes in the Lakeland Fells," in *Coleridge's Imagination: Essays in Memory of Peter Lauer*, ed. Richard Garvis, Lucy Newlyn, and Nicholas Roe (Cambridge: Cambridge University Press, 1985), 93.
³ William Hazlitt, "My First Acquaintance with Poets," in *The Complete Works of William Hazlitt in Twenty-One Volumes*, vol. 17 (London: J. M. Dent, 1930–34), 119, 120.
⁴ Even when he was suffering from various ailments, Coleridge displayed strength. On April 21, 1804, for instance, on his way to Malta, Coleridge wrote to Daniel Stuart about "scrambling about on the back of the Rock [of Gibraltar] among the Monkeys." He humorously boasted: "I am a match for them in climbing, but in Hops & flying Leaps they beat me" (*CL* 2:1133).

the eye so that both his sight and body – and particularly his feet – informed his understanding of a landscape.[5]

## Part One: Walking

### *A Culture of Walking*

Coleridge belonged to a time when walking was no uncommon enterprise. For many, it was obviously an everyday activity, especially for the working classes, whose repetitive, relentless trudging was survival – a necessary part of life if they were to eke out a living.[6] During the decade of his walking, Coleridge would have passed by the drovers who led their cattle from one town to another, the shepherds who daily scrambled up into the hills, under all conditions, and created footpaths out of their attendance to their flocks. He would have also been aware of the miners going to and from their toil as well as the endless slogging of the itinerate laborers and tradesmen. In October 1800, Dorothy Wordsworth interrupted a lyrical passage in her Grasmere journal to describe an encounter with one such individual:

> The Cockermouth traveller came with thread, hardware, mustard, etc. She is very healthy; has travelled over the mountains these thirty years. She does not mind the storms, if she can keep her goods dry. Her husband will not travel with an ass, because it is the tramper's badge; she would have one to relieve her from the weary load.[7]

And Coleridge would have been aware of those desperate people who, struggling "with fatigue and poverty and unknown ways!" (*The Grasmere Journal*, 249), suffered from the prejudices that frequently associated the walking poor with impropriety or possible criminal intent – for many they

---

[5] In volume 1 of *The True Intellectual System of the Universe* (London: Richard Priestley, 1820), Ralph Cudworth notes that Aristotle believes that "all sensitive souls must need be corporeal, because there is no walking without feet, nor seeing without eyes" (172–73).

[6] An instance of this necessary mode of walking occurred in July 1800 when Coleridge, rambling in the Lake District, met an old woman and asked her the way. She replied,

> Up the gap – a gay canny road – How far – Two mile & more? – Is there much to climb beyond the highest point we see? – as much again before you get on a level – Tis a gay canny climb – / You may get there in an hour – I'self could ga there in an hour who's eighty & over. She was eighty three – her son had 9 children those we saw were the 4 youngest – (*CN* 1:762; f. 8)

[7] Dorothy Wordsworth, *The Grasmere Journal*, in *Journals of Dorothy Wordsworth*, vol. 1, ed. E. de Selincourt (New York: The Macmillan Company, 1941), 65.

were to be avoided and not quite trusted.[8] Once more Dorothy noted the worrying presence of these traveling beggars who walked from village to village – sometimes barefooted – and pleaded for a penny or food. In her journal she recorded many a disturbing incident, such as the time when she and Wordsworth, while walking on the Rays, met a woman with two little girls,

> one in her arms, the other, about four years old, walking by her side, a pretty little thing, but half-starved. She had on a pair of slippers that had belonged to some gentleman's child, down at the heels, but it was not easy to keep them on, but, poor thing! young as she was, she walked carefully with them; alas, too young for such cares and such travels. (*The Grasmere Journal*, 143)[9]

For a few others, however, during the late eighteenth and early nineteenth centuries, walking long distances had scarcely anything to do with earning a

---

[8] Rosamond Bayne-Powell's *Travellers in Eighteenth-Century England* (London: John Murray, 1951), 30–33 gives more details about the walking of paupers. See also Celeste Langan's *Romantic Vagrancy: Wordsworth and the Simulation of Freedom* (Cambridge: Cambridge University Press, 1995), 13–30. Robin Jarvis also comments on the "mistrust, intolerance and discrimination that awaited pedestrian travelers in the 1780s and 1790s" in his *Romantic Writing and Pedestrian Travel* (Houndmills, Basingstoke: Palgrave, 1997), 27. An example of this mistrust of the poor is also registered in A. Rambler [Joseph Budworth], *A Fortnight's Ramble to the Lakes in Westmoreland, Lancashire, and Cumberland* (London: Hookham and Carpenter, 1792), in which the journalist is annoyed by vagrant children begging for money. He writes:

> We afterwards walked to the head of the lake [Derwentwater] to judge what we had in the future to expect; some children troubled us by asking us for money and uselessly running before us to open a gate; we gave one of the boys a penny, and because one half-penny was a bad one, he asked us to change it; this refinement of beggary in the young vagrant hindered us from afterwards countenancing them, and they ceased to trouble us. (66)

This distrust also finds expression in the Rev. Richard Warner's *A Walk through Wales in August 1797* (Bath: R. Crutwell, 1798) when he enters an inn at which are seated "a motley groupe [sic] of noisy Welsh rustics, who voraciously devoured the good things before them" (57). Occasionally, however, this suspicion could be reversed. For instance, when Warner and his friends after rambling and being caught in the rain entered an inn looking "wet, dirty, and tired," they found that their

> appearance and mode of travelling had excited suspicions no way favourable to our honesty, for scarcely had we seated ourselves by the fire, when a maid, entering the room, proceeded to a corner-cupboard, and slyly conveying into her apron three or four silver spoons, and a small silver cup, which had hitherto formed the splendid ornaments of the parlour, removed them from a situation in which our host and his wife evidently conceived it was dangerous to allow the *family plate* to remain. (206–07)

[9] In a recent issue of *Romanticism* (27.1, 2021) dedicated to "Romantic Walking," several articles reconsider walking's complex cultural and literary history. Kerri Andrews and Tim Fulford bring together a number of essays, among which is one that considers walking as "a mode of informing oneself about the condition of the poor and the social injustices they suffered" ("Introduction"). See, for instance, Gabriel Cervantes and Dahlia Porter's essay, "Walking with John Howard: Itinerary and Romantic Reform" (4–15).

living or poverty but rather was the occasion for a popular, competitive sport in which a person, for a wager, would walk many miles in successive days, such as the time a Mr. Podger covered 400 miles in eight consecutive days and earned £200 on a bet that he might not complete what he had set out to do. Walter Thom in his 1813 *Pedestrianism: Or an Account of the Performances of Celebrated Pedestrians during the Last and Present Century* published tables containing the names of these notable pedestrians, the distances they covered, and the time each of them required as well as the year of "performance." He recorded, for instance, that in 1762, John Hodges walked a distance of 100 miles in twenty-three hours and fifteen minutes and that in 1773, Foster Powell walked from London to York and back again in six days – a feat that Coleridge was aware of, for in a letter to Robert Southey, written while on his walking tour of Wales, he laughingly quipped that two fellow university students who passed him by in a post chaise on their so-called pedestrian tour were no rivals for a Powell.[10] In 1778, John Batty managed 700 miles in thirteen days and nineteen hours. The most celebrated of these competitive pedestrians was Captain Robert Barclay Allardice, who in 1809 walked 1,000 miles in twelve days and eight hours for a wager of 1,000 guineas. The pictured figure of "Captain Barclay in his walking dress" opposite the title page of Thom's book cuts quite a figure. Although the shoes are not convincing (they seem more like slippers), the muscles on his legs look well developed.

Like many others, Thom asserted that this long-distance tramping was a means of preserving the health and morality of a people. Although "performance" and competition were definitely not components of Coleridge's tramps (though in his letters he occasionally bragged about how many miles he had walked in several days),[11] he did participate in that culture's

---

[10] "On the Road we met the Cantabs of my College – these rival *pedestrians*, perfect *Powells*, were vigorously pursuing their tour – in a *post chaise*! We laughed famously" (*CL* 1:89). Apparently Foster Powell was well celebrated, for he also gained Walter Thom's notice in 1773 for walking 396 miles in six days, in 1787 for walking 100 miles in twenty-five hours and fifty minutes, in 1788 for managing 100 miles in twenty-two hours, in 1790 for covering 395 miles in five days and eighteen minutes, and in 1792 for managing to cover 399 miles in five days and fifteen hours. See Walter Thom, *Pedestrianism: Or an Account of the Performances of Celebrated Pedestrians during the Last and Present Century* (Aberdeen: D. Chalmers and Co., 1813), 94–95.

[11] In a letter to Thomas Poole, for instance, Coleridge, as did the competitors, counted the hours and minutes a walk had taken him. He bragged: "However, I am somewhat better – and so far from weak now that I walked yesterday, tho' suffering grievously from asthma in consequence of the Drizzle, Fog, & Stifling Air, the 19 miles from Grasmere to Kendal in four hours & 35 minutes, & was not in the least fatigued" (*CL* 2:1035). Foster Powell, a lawyer by profession, was a minor celebrity for his amazing walks. For a discussion of this athletic walking. See Jarvis, *Romantic Writing and Pedestrian Travel*, 2–5.

conviction that walking encouraged and maintained one's sense of wellbeing. After returning from his 1803 excursion in Scotland, for instance, he explained to Sir George and Lady Beaumont that he had "walked 263 miles in 8 days, in the hope of forcing the Disease [gout and stomach problems] into the extremities" (*CL* 2:993). Indeed, throughout his rambling years Coleridge often turned to his lengthy walking excursions in attempts to restore some feeling of equanimity and health, to find relief from quarrels at home, and even to try and wean himself from his opium addiction – "to keep the Fiend at arm's Length" (*CL* 2:993) – a burden that had its beginnings in medication given during his schooldays to treat various ailments and, more specifically, to remedy what then was diagnosed as a neuralgic attack or rheumatic fever.[12] Unfortunately, as the years passed his dependency grew, so by the time Coleridge was living in

---

[12] There is always an interest in Coleridge's addiction to opium. Indeed, after his death, there was an autopsy performed (the report is printed in E. L. Griggs's edition of Coleridge's letters) whether or not he had anything like "rheumatic fever," which was supposedly the occasion for his first taking the drug. Throughout his correspondence, there are references to his subsequent practice of taking laudanum and his dependency on it. For instance, Walter Jackson Bate in *Coleridge* (Cambridge, MA: Harvard University Press, 1969) notes that a letter written by Coleridge while a student at Jesus College to his brother George contains the first reference to opium (laudanum), which, as Bate rightly reminds readers, "was prescribed very commonly at the time" (11). Of course, Coleridge's addiction did not come at once. The dependency grew as he used opium to help himself get through bouts of dysentery, distressing times, and various aches and pains as well as rheumatic symptoms and gout, but the substance, especially during periods of withdrawal, caused physical problems, such as profuse sweats at night, constipation, nightmares, and sleeplessness. Eventually James Gillman, a friend and physician who lived in Highgate, took Coleridge in and attempted to regulate his use of the drug. Even though addiction was not fully understood during much of Coleridge's lifetime, he felt guilty for using it and periodically tried to wean himself away from it. In a January 9, 1803 letter to Thomas Wedgwood, written in Keswick, Coleridge, for example, confessed,

> my right eye was blood-shot, & the Lid swoln –. That morning however I walked home – & before I reached Keswick, my eye was quite well – but I felt unwell all over ... I took no opium or laudanum /; but at 8 o/clock, unable to bear the stomach uneasiness & the bowel threatenings, & the aching of my Limbs, I took two large Tea spoonfuls of Ether in a wine glass of Camphorated Gum water, and a Third tea spoonful at 10 o/clock – I received compleat relief. (*CL* 2:915)

Earlier letters show that Coleridge had previously taken opium both for medicinal purposes and to relieve the strain of agitated spirits. It seems evident that his habitual use of drugs did not begin until his illness of 1800 (see E. L. Griggs, "Samuel Taylor Coleridge and Opium," *Huntington Library Quarterly* 17.4 [August 1954]: 357–78). A later letter to John Thelwall (November 26, 1803) reveals just how agonizing his dependency was:

> My Health is in a most distressful State; my Bowel & Stomach attacks frequent & alarming ... If this Letter reach you in time, you will oblige me by going to the best Druggist in Kendal for me, & purchasing an Ounce of crude opium, & 9 ounces of Laudanum, the Latter put in a stout bottle & so packed up as that it may travel a few hundred miles with safety. (*CL* 2:1019)

the Lake District, he was more and more enslaved. Desperately wanting to sort himself out, Coleridge is thought sometimes to have deliberately left his laudanum behind by not packing it in his knapsack. For instance, Carol Kyros Walker observes that, while on the 1803 tour with the Wordsworths in Scotland, Coleridge "appears to have taken a smaller amount of morphine with him, possibly to use the journey as an opportunity to wean himself from this drug."[13] There were, however, exceptions. For instance, during his 1802 tour in the fells, he carried a small amount of Kendal Black Drop (extra-strength laudanum) with him. He externally applied the laudanum to his joints, and possibly also took it internally to relieve what he thought were symptoms of gout.

In addition to the tramping of the working classes and these sporting performances, another prevalent mode of pedestrian activity during the period was, of course, the recreational walking undertaken by members of the professional and commercial classes who, beginning in the 1740s, traveled to Wales, the Lake District, and eventually Scotland to explore the beauties and varieties of the British landscape – a vogue thoroughly researched by Peter Bicknell and Robert Woof (*The Discovery of the Lake District 1750–1810*), by Malcolm Andrews (*The Search for the Picturesque*), and by John K. Walton and Jason Wood in their collection of essays *The Making of a Cultural Landscape*.[14]

When Coleridge was rambling through the countryside, he was, more or less, joining the company of men and women of the middling classes: clerics, doctors, lawyers, public schoolmasters, artists, university graduates,

---

[13] Carol Kyros Walker, *Breaking Away: Coleridge in Scotland* (New Haven, CT: Yale University Press, 2002), 7. This resolution had its difficulties, for in a September 10, 1803 letter to Southey from Edinburgh (on his way back to Keswick), Coleridge talked about the pains of sleep as a result of abandoning "all opiates, except Ether be one" (*CL* 2:982).

[14] Peter Bicknell and Robert Woof, *The Discovery of the Lake District 1750–1810* (Grasmere and Wordsworth Museum, 1982); Malcolm Andrews, *The Search for the Picturesque: Landscape Aesthetics and Tourism in Britain, 1760–1800* (Aldershot: Scolar Press, 1990); John K. Walton and Jason Wood, *The Making of a Cultural Landscape: The English Lake District as Tourist Destination, 1750–2010* (New York: Routledge, 2016). The history of the road is an interesting subject. Before the coming of the railroad and its extension into the Lake District in the mid-nineteenth century, travelers depended upon roads, of which there were many kinds. Roads began to be turnpiked in the Lake District in the 1750s and 1760s, and the road from Keswick to Penrith in 1762. Ordnance surveys did not reach Cumberland until the 1860s. Contemporary maps show enclosed roads, open roads, roads open on one side and enclosed on the other, tracks, some maintained by the parish and others by landlords, and military roads, as well as cart tracks. By the end of the nineteenth century, mass tourism eventually arrived, made possible by the extension of a railway network, first to Windermere (1847) and then to Coniston (1859) and Keswick (1865). Jarvis in *Romantic Writing and Pedestrian Travel* is quick to point out that in spite of the uncomfortable conditions of travel in the late eighteenth century, pedestrian expeditions were "a practice of rapidly growing popularity among the professional, educated classes" (12).

who had the means and the time to devote two weeks or so to take a pedestrian tour, more often than not supplemented by coach, carriage, or pony and assisted either by a servant (if one were wealthy) or by a hired guide.[15] As commentators point out, no longer was it as possible for the well-to-do or educated classes to embark on the Grand Tour, for the revolutionary wars in France as well as the Napoleonic Wars made such a rite of passage dangerous, if not impossible. Instead of taking such risks, these individuals, with some prompting, turned their attention to the landscape of Britain, to areas that were said to be just as alluring as the Alps yet even more diverse. Thomas West, in his popular *A Guide to the Lakes* (1778), for instance, patriotically proclaimed that visitors to the Lakes would enjoy the equivalent of the Alps, and that they would experience a variety of scenery not found elsewhere within such a small geographic area:

> Particularly, the taste for one branch of a noble art (cherished under the protection of the greatest of kings, and best of men), in which the genius of *Britain* rivals that of ancient *Greece* and modern *Rome*, induces many to visit the lakes of *Cumberland*, *Westmorland*, and *Lancashire*; there to contemplate, in Alpine scenery, finished in nature's highest tints, the pastoral and rural landscape, exhibited in all stiles, the soft, the rude, the romantic, and sublime, and of which perhaps like instances can nowhere be found assembled in so small a trait of country.[16]

Similarly, A. Rambler (Joseph Budworth) in his "Preface" to his widely read *A Fortnight's Ramble to the Lakes* (1792) declared: "We have no reason to depreciate other countries in commending our own; but Nature has sported such variety AT HOME, no views can exceed them in that delightful miniature which the eye takes in without being either glutted by expanse, or DISGUSTED by deformity" (xix).

The result was that when Coleridge and his friend Joseph Hucks set out on a pedestrian tour of Wales during the long vacation from Cambridge in 1794, they were certainly not the first. Wales was already a well-worn tourist route. Many a rambler would have been familiar with Thomas

---

[15] Dorothy Wordsworth in June 1800 noticed ladies "evidently Tourists" casting "an eye of interest upon our little garden and cottage." See *The Grasmere Journal*, 46. And in Scotland, she speaks of "A party of tourists whom we had met in the pleasure-grounds drove from the door [of the inn] while we were waiting for dinner; I guess they were fresh from England, for they had stuffed the pockets of their carriage with bundles of hether [sic] roots, and all, just as if Scotland grew no hether but on the banks of the Clyde." See *Recollections of a Tour Made in Scotland (1802)*, in *Journals of Dorothy Wordsworth*, 1:225.

[16] Thomas West, *A Guide to the Lakes in Cumberland, Westmorland and Lancashire*, 3rd ed. (London: B. Law and Kendal: William Pennington, 1784), 1–2.

Pennant's popular *Tour of Wales* (1778) based upon his three excursions to the area from 1773 to 1776; they might also later have read through other accounts, such as *A Walk through Wales in August 1797* (1798) and *A Second Walk through Wales, in August and September 1798* written by the Rev. Richard Warner of Bath.[17] The Lake District, of course, was to become even more popular. Consequently, in 1795, when first walking with Wordsworth in the Lakes, Coleridge would have been tromping through a landscape that was already considered to be a highly desirable destination.[18] During his early twenties, William Wilberforce, for example, in his 1799 diary, written while on his journey to the Lake District from Cambridge, often expressed his sense of the Lake District's superiority. He writes about "the Vale of Keswick" looking "beautiful beyond description" as well as about the "enchanting Views," "the grandest diversity of light and shade," the "wonderful" appearance of a waterfall, and the region's "new & unparallel'd Beauties."[19]

### *Coleridge Walks*

Even though Coleridge was part of a culture that encouraged holiday walking and that was, as Andreas Mayer has recently pointed out, keen to distinguish itself from the aristocracy's mode of travel,[20] his participation revealed a person who was willing to take more physical risks than a majority of others who walked for recreational purposes. For instance, in an October 1800 letter to Humphry Davy, Coleridge describes descending a mountain "by the side of a Torrent" and crawling "on all fours" with "one finger almost broken" (*CL* 1:638). A review of Coleridge's pedestrian excursions between 1794 and 1804 exposes just how extraordinarily vigorous, demanding, and numerous his were – at times, he really did resemble a chamois-chaser. The following summary of his rambling is exhausting but necessary if one is, later in the chapter, to comprehend Coleridge's idiosyncratic relationship to the landscape of his walks. It is

---

[17] Joseph Hucks himself also contributed to the literature by publishing his *A Pedestrian Tour through North Wales, in a Series of Letters*, ed. Alan R. Jones (Tydeman, Cardiff: University of Wales Press, 1979 [1795]), based on letters he had supposedly sent to a friend while on the tour with Coleridge.
[18] Thomas Pennant, for instance, had previously made his tour of the Lakes in 1772.
[19] William Wilberforce, *Journey to the Lake District from Cambridge 1799*, ed. C. E. Wrangham (Stocksfield: Oriel Press, 1983), 49–53.
[20] For a discussion of this impulse to distance oneself from aristocratic modes of movement, see the first chapter of Andreas Mayer's *The Science of Walking: Investigating Locomotion in the Long Nineteenth Century*, trans. Tilman Skowroneck and Robin Blanton (Chicago: University of Chicago Press, 2020).

also prefatory to reaching a better sense of his spatial orientation that was often distinct from his contemporaries'.

The first of Coleridge's extended walking tours began on June 15, 1794 when, aged twenty-two, as I have already mentioned, he and Hucks left Cambridge for Wales. After a three-week stop in Oxford (where Coleridge met Robert Southey), the two spent over a month hiking five hundred miles from the Wye Valley and up into the rural villages, ways, and mountains of North Wales. Coleridge's physical energy, at times, exhausted Hucks.[21] A sketch-map from Hucks's book recounting the tour offers some sense of their route. The map traces the bending line of their route from Bristol up to Devil's Bridge and west to the coast, which they followed from Aberystwyth up into Anglesey and across to Holywell and then back down a long way to Gloucester. A few years later, in May 1799, when visiting Germany, Coleridge walked for a week (sometimes thirty-five miles a day) in the Harz Mountains and climbed the Brocken; in November of that year and back in England, Coleridge, guided by Wordsworth, himself a most accomplished walker, crossed the Pennines and for nineteen days explored the Lake District on foot.[22] This expedition so impressed him that the entries in his notebook are full of wonder. He writes of the sun hanging over Ullswater: "The Sun, it being just past noon, hangs over the Lake – clouded so that any but a weak eye might gaze on it – the clouds being in part bright white, part dusky Rain-clouds, with islets of blue Sky – How the scene changes – What tongues of Light shoot out from the Banks!" (*CN* 1:549; f. 25). At another point in the entry he speaks of gaining the road that "runs close by the Lake," where he sees

> the bare knobby Cliff opposite, & the Shadow of it so soft in the water – and now I have gained the upper end of the first Reach, & look down to the other end, (towards Pooley) comprehending a long majestic Parallelogram but when I stand so as to take in part of the 2nd Reach the whole appears a

---

[21] Walking tours were already becoming popular among university men. For instance, four years earlier, from July to October 1790, Wordsworth and Robert Jones had walked and traveled from London through France to Switzerland and the Alps and back; William Frend had taken a pedestrian tour through France, and William Bowles had toured in Wales and Germany.

[22] In *Wordsworth and Coleridge: Tour of the Lake District 1799* (Fleetwood, Lancashire: David Walker, 1997), Dave and Kerry Walker attempt to clarify the itinerary and places where they spent the night:

> Wed. 30/10/1799 Temple Sowerby (Kings Arms); Th. 31/10/1799 Bampton; Fr. 1/11 Kentmere (probably); Sat 2/11 Hawkshead; Sun 3/11 –7/11 Grasmere (Robert Newton's Inn); Fr 8/11 – 9/11 Keswick (possibly Windy B.?); Sun 10/11 Ouse Bridge (Ouse Bridge Inn); Mon 11/11 Buttermere (Fish Inn); Ennerdale (possibly); Wed 13/11 Wasdale Head (Burnthwaste Farm), perhaps including also Tues 12/11; Thurs 14/11 Rosthwaite; Fri 15/11 Threlkeld; Sat 16/11 Patterdale (Patterdale "Hotel"); Sun 17/11 Pooley Bridge (Eusmere, almost certainly). (xi)

semicircle enfolding in its two arms the convex semicircle of the bare knobby crag – but I turn my Back to the Lake / & what a Cliff! (*CN* 1:549; f. 24)

Once residing in Grasmere and later settled in Keswick in 1800, Coleridge, following his own impulses, frequently left home alone to take ridge walks, survey the silent shores of the lakes and the mountains, and break through "the straggling branches of a copsewood" (Hazlitt, "My First Acquaintance with Poets," 119). For instance, from August 1 until August 9, 1802, he walked for one hundred rigorous miles through the Western Fells – an excursion that so enthralled him that he wished "for Health & Strength that I might wander about for a Month together, in the stormiest month of the year, among these Places, so lonely & savage & full of sounds!" (*CL* 2:844)[23] – and in January 1803 he took off over the Kirkstone Pass, a steep three-mile ascent, and on to Grasmere in the teeth of a ferocious storm.[24] In his letter to Thomas Wedgwood, Coleridge excitedly reported:

> Before I was half up Kirkstone, the storm had wetted me thro' and thro' . . . I am no novice in mountain-mischiefs; but such a storm as this was I never witnessed, combining the intensity of the Cold with the violence of the wind & rain. The rain-drops were pelted, or rather *slung*, against my face, by the Gusts, just like splinters of Flint; & felt, as if every drop *cut* my flesh. My hands were all shriveled up, like a Washerwoman's, & so benumbed, that I was obliged to carry my stick under my arm. O it was a wild business! Such hurry-skurry of Clouds, such volleys of sound! (*CL* 2:914)

[23] In a letter to Robert Southey, Coleridge summarizes his strenuous route:

> On Sunday August 1, after morning church I left Greta Hall, crossed the fields to Portinscale, went thro' Newlands, where 'Great Robinson looks down upon Maiden's Bower,' and drank Tea at Buttermere – crossed the mountains to Ennerdale, & slept at a farm House a little below the foot of the Lake / Spent the greater part of the next Day mountaineering, & went in the evening thro' Egremont to St Bees & slept there – returned next day to Egremont & slept there – went by the Sea Coast as far as Gosforth, then turned off, & went up Wasdale, & slept at T. Tyson's at the head of the vale / Thursday morning crossed the mountains, & ascended Sca'fell, which is more than a 100 yards higher than either Helvellin or Skiddaw / spent the whole day among clouds, & one of them a frightening thunder-cloud – slipt down into Eskdale, & there slept – & spent good part of the next day – proceeded that evening to Devock Lake, & slept at Ulpha Kirk / on Saturday passed thro' the Donnerdale Mountains to Broughton Vale, Torvor Vale, Torvor Vale, & in upon Coniston / Sunday surveyed the Lake etc. of Coniston, & proceeded to Bratha, and slept at Lloyd's House / this Morning walked from Bratha to Grasmere, & from Grasmere to Greta Hall. (*CL* 2:846)

[24] A few people have followed the routes of Coleridge's longer walks. For instance, Alan Hankinson reconstructed Coleridge's 1802 nine-day journey across the Western Fells in the Lake District. See Alan Hankinson, *Coleridge Walks the Fells: A Lakeland Journey Retraced* (Cumbria: Ellenbank Press, 1991). And when Kathleen Coburn was editing Coleridge's notebooks, she called upon the expertise of a fell walker, Mr. Denwood of Cockermouth, in order better to understand the routes of Coleridge's walks referred to in his entries.

From August to September of that year Coleridge also joined William and Dorothy Wordsworth in Scotland on a holiday in which they alternately rode in a jaunting car (a hired horse and cart from which one could easily dismount) and walked, often visiting waterfalls away from the roads.[25] After the beginning of a cold, wet, and quarrelsome third week – both Wordsworth and Coleridge were not in the best of moods, especially the latter (who was suffering from withdrawal symptoms) – a complaining Coleridge, wishing he had never seen them, broke loose of his companions in Arrochar and found his way home alone, an eight-day pedestrian journey of 263 miles that took him south through the Grampian Highlands after he reached the northern end of the Great Glen Road.[26] His account of this separation is notably understated: "Tuesday, Aug. 30, 1803 – am to make my own way alone to Edinburgh – <O Esteesee! That thou hadst from thy 22nd year indeed *made they own way & alone!*>" (*CN* 1:1471; f. 30).

In addition to these recreational excursions, walking was simply a part of Coleridge's everyday existence, so in his twenties, for example, while preaching in Unitarian chapels, he would tramp from his home in Nether Stowey, Somersetshire, to the congregation in Bridgwater (a journey of eight miles) or to the gathering in Taunton (twelve miles).[27] Moreover, during that period, he thought nothing of striding forty-one miles to Bristol to see Mrs. Barbauld or forty miles to see Wordsworth, who was at that time living in Dorset. And frequently, either alone or rambling with Southey, he would climb and wander through the Quantock Hills or the nearby combes.[28]

---

[25] Before departing on this excursion, Coleridge wrote to Wordsworth concerning his reservations about using a jaunting car: "I begin to find that a Horse & Jaunting Car is *an anxiety* – & almost to wish that we had adopted our first thought, & *walked*" (*CL* 2:957–58). In another letter, Coleridge explains that when riding in a jaunting car, "Your feet are not above a foot – scarcely so much – from the ground / so that you may get off & on while the Horse is moving without the least Danger" (*CL* 2:975).

[26] For a study of Coleridge's six-week tour of Scotland, see Carol Kyros Walker's *Breaking Away*. See also Dorothy Wordsworth's *Recollections of a Tour Made in Scotland*. Coleridge's letters and notebooks also describe this tour. In a September 1803 letter to Robert Southey, for instance, Coleridge from Perth describes his journey after he departed from the Wordsworths: "I have been on a wild Journey ... I have walked 263 miles in eight Days – so I must have strength somewhere / but my spirits are dreadful, owing entirely to the Horrors of every night – I truly dread to sleep ... I have abandoned all opiates except Ether be one ..." (*CL* 2:982).

[27] Before he was awarded a lifetime annuity of £150 per year, in 1798, by Thomas and Josiah Wedgwood, philanthropists and dissenters who wanted to support intellectual movements of the time, Coleridge was required to make his living as a Unitarian minister.

[28] For a recent article on Southey's walking, see Jonathan Gonzalez, "'Peripateticating among the mountains': Robert Southey and the Aesthetics of Pedestrian Motion," *Romanticism* 27.1 (2021): 75–87.

Later, when Coleridge resided at Greta Hall (Keswick), in addition to his daily rambles, he habitually strode across the fells, by day and by night, to visit William and Dorothy in Grasmere – a practice to a lesser degree shared by the Wordsworths, who occasionally, taking a more modest route (but not by our standards!), walked thirteen miles from Grasmere over Dunmail Raise and past Thirlmere to spend a few hours at Coleridge's home.[29] On one notable occasion, in August 1800, Coleridge made the first recorded walk (by someone other than a local) from Keswick to Grasmere along the tops of Calfhow Pike, Great Dod, Stylarrow Dod, Raise, and Helvellyn – an amazing feat. Even though often physically distressed, suffering from swollen eyes, "atonic Gout," blistered feet, cut fingers, and various symptoms attending his opium habit, he nevertheless, as a younger man, had speed and stamina. He could, as Kathleen Coburn recognizes, outwalk them all. Furthermore, he was not afraid of blustery weather. Rather, he relished the thrill of being on the edge of danger. An August 25, 1802 letter to Sara Hutchinson describing a brisk walk in the driving rain to a waterfall eight miles from Keswick catches this species of excitement:

> I had a glorious Walk ... climbed up by the Waterfall as near as I could, to the very top of the Fell – but it was so craggy – the Crags covered with spongy soaky Moss, and when bare so jagged as to wound one's hand fearfully – and the Gusts came so very sudden & strong, that the going up was slow, & difficult & earnest – & the coming down, not only all that, but likewise extremely dangerous. However, I have always found this *stretched & anxious* state of mind favorable to depth of pleasurable Impression, in the resting Places *& lownding* Coves. (*CL* 2:853)

Indeed, so integral was rambling to Coleridge's earlier life that when visitors, like William Hazlitt, came to see him, they frequently walked and talked together. In 1798, for instance, Hazlitt eagerly trekked on "untried feet" to Nether Stowey from London. Once he had arrived, he, John Chester (a native of Nether Stowey), and Coleridge set out on a thirty-three-mile "long march" to Lynton and the Valley of Rocks, an expedition which Coleridge and Wordsworth had done the previous year. Recalling the occasion, Hazlitt affectionately reported that his own feet kept time to the echo of Coleridge's tongue while Chester trotted by the

---

[29] Wordsworth, for whom walking was central to his life and work, generally preferred to stick to the less rugged pathways. The Wordsworths were strong walkers, but not walkers who reached for the heights. See Ruddick's essay "'As Much Diversity as the Heart That Trembles.'" Molly Lefebure mentions that "The majority of the walks recorded in Dorothy's *Journals* were made on then empty roads, or on shepherds' paths such as the one up Easedale, relatively close to home" ("First of the Fellwalkers," *Cumberland Heritage* [London: Victor Gollancz, 1970], 134).

poet's side so as not to miss a single word.[30] Southey and Coleridge also often walked for many miles together. In the 1790s, for example, they left Bristol on a pedestrian tour through Somerset and climbed the Mendip Hills; then, in 1803, after Coleridge's return from his aborted tour of Scotland, the two embarked on a modest hiking excursion.[31]

## Part Two: "every man [is] his own path-maker"

During the time Coleridge was actively walking, a plethora of travelogues and guidebooks promoted, above all, the advantages of visiting the Lake District, a region which, as I have pointed out, was rapidly becoming the most fashionable destination – the closest thing to the Alps in England.[32]

---

[30] Hazlitt reported that Chester "kept on a sort of trot by the side of Coleridge like a running footman by a state coach, the he might not lose a syllable or sound that fell from Coleridge's lips." See "My First Acquaintance with Poets," 119.

[31] In a note accompanying entry 1519 in *CN*, vol. 1, Kathleen Coburn outlines the 1803 pedestrian journey:

> The itinerary from Keswick over Saddleback and Bowscale Fell took them [Coleridge and Southey] down to the road at Mosedale Tarn, then to Hesket Newmarket, then to Caldbech for the night ... Then, instead of going as far as Cockermouth, they turned back on the other side of Skiddaw Forest passing Overwater and on to Keswick. In entry 1520 (f. 14), Coleridge adds that "On our return from Caldbeck it seemed to threaten rain, one shower came, Southey was weary and already homesick / so we turned off at the 5th milestone."

[32] So popular a destination had the Lake District become in the late eighteenth century that it predictably attracted the scathing pen of the satirists such as James Plumptre, whose *The Lakers* (London: W. Clarke, 1798), a comic opera (not performed during his lifetime), mocked not only visitors who came to the Lakes to collect botanical specimens but also the "pedestrians" who frequented the region for "health and improvement!" (38). Plumptre, while a Fellow of Clare College, Cambridge, had taken three long walking tours throughout the region in 1796–97 and 1799, so in Scene III of *The Lakers*, an aria satirizing two such pedestrians was no mere fantasy:

> First Ped.
> *In viewing Nature's varied scenes,*
>    *Sweet is the pleasure they impart,*
> *For Reason scarce has better means*
>    *To soften and improve the heart.*
>
> Second Ped.
> *From exercise what spirits flow!*
>    *Sweet is the meal that Hunger finds,*
> *And sweet the slumbers that we know,*
>    *The calm repose of tranquil minds.*
>
> Both
> *Then let us range the vallies still,*
>    *And o'er the mountain's summit wind,*
> *Trace with delight the gurgling rill,*
>    *And still preserve the tranquil mind.*
>
>                   (38)

Indeed, the region was to become so popular that by the late 1700s there were entertainments, such as regattas, mock sea battles on Derwentwater, cannon shots (so a person could listen to the echo off the crags), and by the 1870s even a refreshment hut on the path to the summit of Skiddaw[33] – an "improvement" that more than a century before would have been unthinkable, for then a majority of visitors as well as most inhabitants, except for the shepherds, would have skirted or avoided its heights.[34] These publications offered advice about the best season in which to visit the Lakes. For instance, West's *A Guide to the Lakes* claimed that the optimum time was from the first of June to the end of August. And Jonathan Otley's, acknowledging the various classes of tourists who frequented the Lakes in the early 1800s, suggested that "Pedestrians will feel the month of May an agreeable season, and they will then find more room at the inns. Towards the end of June many professional gentlemen are at liberty, and students at the Universities often find it advantageous to spend three months among the lakes, thus blending instruction with healthy recreation."[35]

Besides commenting on the splendid scenery, guides to the region included observations about the state of the roads, advice about routes, lists of towns and villages, mileages between destinations, reflections about the oppression of poverty, descriptions of industrial areas, accounts of fleas in the beds as well as other discomforts of travel, and narratives about the inhabitants. For instance, the account of "A. Rambler" (Budworth) devoted space to recounting the tales of an aged matron, a barber, and a village dancing master – a reminder of the degree to which walking and

---

[33] Paul Readman, *Storied Ground: Landscape and the Shaping of English National Identity* (Cambridge: Cambridge University Press, 2018), 93.
[34] A partial listing of these publications gives some sense of the vogue's popularity: Joseph Sullivan's *A Tour through Parts of England, Scotland, and Wales in 1778* (1785); Arthur Young's *A Six Month's tour through the North of England* (1771), Ann Radcliffe's *A Journey Made in the Summer of 1794 through Holland and the Western Frontier of Germany, with Return Down the Rhine: To Which are Added, Observations during a Tour to the Lakes of Lancashire, Westmoreland, and Cumberland* (1795), William Wilberforce's *Journey to the Lake District from Cambridge* (1799), John Housman's *A Descriptive Tour and Guide to the Lakes, Caves, Mountains, and Other Natural Curiosities in Cumberland, Westmorland, Lancashire, and a Part of the West Riding of Yorkshire* (1800), Richard Joseph Mawman's *An Excursion to the Highlands of Scotland and the English Lakes* (1805), William Green's *The Tourist's New Guide Containing a Description of the Lakes, Mountains, and Scenery in Cumberland, Westmorland, and Lancashire, with Some Account of Their Bordering Towns and Villages*(1819), Theodore Fielding and J. Walton's *A Picturesque Tour of the English Lakes* (1821), and Jonathan Otley's 1823 *A Concise Description of the English Lakes*, which included information for tourists, such as expedition planners, large-scale maps, and details of means of transport and accommodation.
[35] Jonathan Otley, *A Concise Description of the English Lakes and Adjacent Mountains with General Directions to Tourists*, 5th ed. (Keswick: published by the author, 1834), 89.

narrative are integral to the travelogue and were companions in Dorothy Wordsworth's journals, but not always in Coleridge's, which were almost entirely devoted to descriptions of the landscape – though there are occasional exceptions.

Throughout the decade of Coleridge's walks, West's 1778 guide, with its incorporation of Thomas Gray's account of his 1769 tour in the Lake District, was, as is commonly known, the most widely read by these tourists. This guide reinforced the picturesque tradition advanced by such proponents of pictorial taste as William Gilpin in his *Observations, Relative Chiefly to Picturesque Beauty* (1772), and, of course, Gray. Written to facilitate a visitor's pleasure, as well as to "relieve the traveler from the burthen of dull and tedious information on the road, or at the inn, that frequently embarrasses, and often misguides" (2), West's publication instructed tourists and "the lovers of landscape Studies" ("Preface") – those already tutored by the vistas of a Claude Lorrain, Nicolas Poussin, or Salvator Rosa painting – how and where to locate the most impressive scenery. As has been frequently acknowledged, West verbally mapped preferred routes (given the condition of roads) to reach select and numbered "stations" where a person could advantageously stand and observe astonishing panoramic views of the lakes, mountains, and dells.[36] A passage from West's guide illustrates this orientation:

> STATION III. A third station on this side, will be found by keeping along the line of the shore, till Stable-hills be on the right, and Wallow-crag directly over you on the left; then, without the gate, on the edge of the common, observe two huge fragments of ferruginous coloured rock, pitched into the side of the mountain by their descent. (88)

Coaching tourists or the artists in where to place their gaze, West, for instance, directed that one particular station "is found by observing where you have a hanging rock over the road, on the east, and an ash-tree on the

---

[36] Some of West's "stations" are now almost difficult to locate, though there are current efforts to identify and mark where these might have been. See www.geocaching.com for directions to the stations around Coniston Water. The website mentions that at Station 1 a person barely needs to get out of the car to find it. The instructions add, however, that "unfortunately the trees have matured at Stations 1 and 2 to obscure the views."

It should be pointed out that in *Romantic Marks and Measures: Wordsworth's Poetry in Fields of Print* (Philadelphia: University of Pennsylvania Press, 2016), Julia S. Carlson, who explores Wordsworth's poetic response to contemporary cartographers' efforts to inscribe the nation's terrain onto two-dimensional maps, describes the industry of supplying portable or pocket maps to tourists visiting the Lake District, particularly in the last quarter of the eighteenth century. For a discussion of this development and the maps rendered by Peter Crossthwaite see 38–53.

west side of the road" (47), and yet another – "a most awful scene of mountains heaped upon mountains, in every variety of horrid shape" – by ascending "a steep hill, surrounded with wood" (53). Eager for his readers to view a scenic prospect in the most dramatic way, West also instructed that to reach another station a person must "mount the hill without turning your head, (if I was your guide I would conduct you behind a small hill, that you might come at once upon the view), till you almost gain the top, which you will be struck with astonishment at the prospect spread at your feet" (69). Dedicated to enhancing the pictorial experience, West also encouraged the use of telescopes and the tinted Claude glass or mirror to allow the viewer to frame and take in a large prospect at one sweep. He suggested that the mirror is of "greatest use in sunshine, and the person using it ought always to turn his back to the object he views" and that "the dark glass answers well in sunshine; but on cloudy and gloomy day, the silver foil answers better" (12–13). Indeed, following West's lead, at one of the stations on Lake Windermere which looked out toward the eastern slopes of Claife Heights, a small building was constructed in the 1790s with a bay window of variously colored glass so that a tourist could better imagine how the lake appeared in the four seasons, at midnight, and in a thunderstorm.

In what ways Coleridge conformed to or shared the orientation of these visitors coached by the likes of Gilpin, Gray, or West has already been addressed by such people as Harold Baker, Patricia Ball, Robin Jarvis, Raimondo Modiano, and William Ruddick.[37] The question, however, is worth briefly re-engaging, for the topic casts additional light on how Coleridge's walking influenced his idiosyncratic representations of landscape.

As critics have suggested, when Coleridge set out on his rambles during the decade of 1794–1804, he did not entirely escape the enthusiasm for the picturesque, nor did he always separate himself from the modes of seeing encouraged by the popular guidebooks mentioned above. Although he found fault with Gilpin and West for their tendency, for example, to exaggerate the ragged wildness of a mountain or a cataract, he did occasionally subscribe to the fashion of utilizing the Claude glass (he even tried on a pair of tinted glasses to enhance the view) and, more frequently, of

---

[37] For instance, Ruddick in "'As Much Diversity as the Heart That Trembles'" observes that when walking with Wordsworth before he moved to Keswick, Coleridge was influenced by his friend's aesthetic sense that "had been powerfully affected by the publications of late eighteenth-century picturesque-topographical writers" (90).

seeking the panoramic prospect or the grand view.[38] Like so many of his contemporaries, he intermittently reached for places that might present him with the "means to command a view" (*CN* 1:1205; f. 2) and that, like a painting or a print, a reflected image, or a framed mirror, proffered a "oneness of the view" (*CN* 1:1207; f. 3).[39] Coleridge's notebooks occasionally register his sheer joy, even ecstasy, in attaining a point from which a panorama bursts upon him. In November 1799, he exclaimed: "What a scene! Where I stand, on the shore is a triangular Bay, taking in the whole of the water view" (*CN* 1:551; f. 22), and in August 1800, elated when he reached the very top of Gill, he cried out, "(O Joy for me!) ... the whole Vale / Ulswater like a pond in the midst of it, & then just a turn of my Head and lo! Bassenthwaite in the shape of a Wedge – & Derwentwater (the higher third of it) a Dusky yellowy richness, indented & tongued, & with a rim of *brightness* along all its tongued & indented Shores –" (*CN* 1:798; f. 32).

In the picturesque tradition that located the delicate touches of a Claude at Coniston, the noble scenes of Poussin at Windermere, and the stupendous romantic ideas of Rosa at Derwentwater, Coleridge occasionally appreciated a vista that brought him into living contact with the pictorial effects of paintings, such as those rendered by the all-too-familiar artists named above as well as the plentiful engravings, aquatints, pencil sketches, oils, and watercolors of the Lake District rendered by such competent artists as George Beaumont, Joseph Farrington, or Joseph Wilkinson, whose *Select Views in Cumberland and Westmorland and Lancashire* appeared in 1810. For instance, on one 1802 ramble, Coleridge exclaimed: "I never beheld a more glorious view of its kind – I turn & look behind me / what a wonderful group of mountains – what a scene for Salvator

---

[38] In June 1803, for instance, Coleridge records using "colored Glasses":

> ½ of a mile from John Stanley's toward Grasmere ... put the colored Glasses to my eyes as a pair of Spectacles, the red to the left, the yellow Glass to the right eye – saw only thro' the yellow – closed my right eye with my finger, without in the least altering the position of the left eye – & then I instantly saw thro' the red Glass. The right eye manifestly the stronger, tho what is curious, & to be explained by the greater Light of the yellow Glass, when I altered the Glasses, namely the yellow to the left eye, the red to the right then I saw the Landscape as thro' the yellow – perhaps a very little reddish, while the clouds & skies were now as thro' the red. /. These experiments must be tried over again & varied – (*CN* 1:1412; f. 28)

[39] Josie Dixon remarks, "Coleridge was fascinated by the effects of landscape reflected in water and frequently turned to this image in his Notebooks when straining for a cohesive vision and a unifying intuition to govern his perception." See Dixon, "The Notebooks," in *The Cambridge Companion to Coleridge*, ed. Lucy Newlyn (Cambridge: Cambridge University Press, 2002), 80–81.

Rosa / and before the glorious Sea with the opposite high shores & mountains / not a single minute object to break the oneness of the view, save those two green fields of Buttermere" (*CN* 1:1207; f. 3). And later in August 1803, he knew a scene "instantly" from a "recollection of Mr Wilkinson's Drawing" (*CN* 1:1468; f. 3).[40]

Coleridge, as an avid rambler, however, did not fully subscribe to the practices and tenets of the so-called picturesque tourists, especially those whom he once caught reading Gilpin "while passing by the very places instead of looking at the place" (*CN* 1:760; f. 6). As a vigorous walker, he, obviously, did not identify with the class of visitor who took shorter rambles and piled into a carriage or chaise that carried a person over a prearranged route from one vista to another.[41] (Perhaps the closest he came to that was the 1803 tour of Scotland taken with the Wordsworths when they traveled together from place to place in an open cart.) Nor did he keep company with those like Wilberforce, who, describing his 1799 journey to the Lake District from Cambridge, in the mode of West's guide, offered detailed instructions concerning the most advantageous routes and where to stand for the best views. As someone living among the Lakeland fells, Coleridge was not particularly captivated by what the guidebooks said he should do or by telling others what to do, though occasionally he did slip into the rhetorical "you" as if offering advice to readers about where to place themselves in order to view the landscape.[42] And as part of a culture that tended to believe that moving one's body through one's surroundings allowed one to absorb and better understand the world around one, Coleridge chose to walk and follow his own pace.[43]

---

[40] See *Select Views in Cumberland, Westmorland and Lancashire* (London: R. Acherman, 1810) by Rev. Joseph Wilkinson. For a study of the impulse to equate a prospect with a painting see Russell Noyes, *Wordsworth and the Art of Landscape* (New York: Haskell House Publishers, 1973) and Timothy Fulford, "Virtual Topography: Poets, Painters, Publishers and the Reproduction of Landscape in the Early Nineteenth Century," *Romanticism and Victorianism on the Net* (May 2010): 57–58.

[41] Aware of this failing or tendency among tourists, some travel writers suggested that people should at least glance out of the vehicle's window or even take a backward glance to catch a prospect while the vehicle made its way – and by no means sleep: A. [Adam] Walker in *Remarks Made in a Tour from London to the Lakes of Westmoreland and Cumberland ... to Which is Annexed ... an Excursion to Paris* (London: G. Nicol and C. Dilly, 1792) pleads, "But do not sleep in it [the coach]; alight on every eminence, and every eminence will afford you an interesting prospect; nay, if you look on through the window you will see Woods, Rocks, Cliffs, Mountains vanishing or rising into view" (91).

[42] One such moment occurs in his 1802 fell walk: "nearly at the bottom of the Hill, you may stand so as to command 5 of them [falls]" (*CN* 1:1218; f. 18).

[43] In *The Science of Walking*, Mayer writes: "Moving one's body becomes a central condition for humans to understand and absorb the world around them" (12).

Because of his tendency to wander and not follow prescribed itineraries, Coleridge, I suggest, was especially not to be found among the picturesque tourists who religiously followed the mapped routes in the guidebooks. Rather, he was what the cultural anthropologist Timothy Ingold calls a "wayfarer" who is continually on the move and "pauses here and there ... always somewhere ... on the way to somewhere else."[44] Believing that "every man [is] his own path-maker" (*CN* 1:1207; f. 4) and often lost in meandering thought, he drifted like a fog, here and there, and stalked pathless craggy hills (*CN* 1:551, 691).[45] Stepping away from what had not been plotted, he sometimes left the road and "clambered among woods almost to the top of the Fells" (*CN* 1:1471; f. 16).[46] Going off route and leaving behind the shepherds' tracks, he also occasionally lost his place and speculated, "what is the name of that high round hill, which I have left?" (*CN* 1:798; f. 27). On his August 1802 fell walk, he queried, "It must have been here that I lost my way, for I now went on till I found myself coming down upon Ulpha again, about a mile about the House & Kirk which I had just quitted" (*CN* 1:1225; f. 27). And in a letter written in the same month to Sara Hutchinson, he declared: "When I find it convenient to descend from a mountain, I am too confident & too indolent to look round about & wind about 'till I find a track or other symptom of safety; but I wander on, & where it is first *possible* to descend, there I go –" (*CL* 2:841).

As a person who threaded his way through a landscape, rather than concentrate first on one numbered "station" and then on another, he enjoyed a perspective that neither anticipated nor solely focused upon a final destination but, rather, was committed to what was to be seen during the ongoing course of his rambles. As Jarvis observes, Coleridge inhabited "a continual present-tense of pure phenomenality."[47] He preferred to sanction what Dixon recognizes as the "raw immediacy" of what lay before him and to heed "the wayward and incidental."[48]

---

[44] Timothy Ingold, *Lines: A Brief History* (London: Routledge, 2009), 89.
[45] Other examples of this tendency to wander or drift can be found in his notebooks. For instance, in August 1802, Coleridge noted: "what thoughts I wandered about with" (*CN* 1:1214; f. 14); and in September 1803, he wrote: "About two miles from the Glen of Fingal, Glen-falloch – how altered its character altogether – I had been lost in reverie – and on awaking found myself with low Hilly Ridges to my Left, for the road itself was now very high indeed" (*CN* 1:1477; f. 39).
[46] Joseph Budworth, who published under the pseudonym of A. Rambler, was one of the few among Coleridge's contemporaries who also left the road and explored the fells, which was unusual for his time.
[47] Jarvis, *Romantic Writing and Pedestrian Travel*, 135.   [48] Dixon, "The Notebooks," 76, 78.

## Part Three: A Landscape in Motion

For this reason, I propose that the static and silent cartographic representation of a landscape was not as necessary to Coleridge's finding his way or locating himself as it might have been for others who followed the guides. Unlike Wordsworth, whose point of view, according to Julia S. Carlson, was sometimes influenced by cartographic practices of the period, Coleridge was not strongly attracted to a genre that invites a retrospective view and that colonizes space by formalizing borders and eradicating the individual journey: as Michael De Certeau observes, the map eliminates all trace of the practice that produced it.[49] Nor was Coleridge eager to engage a mode of seeing in which "there are no variations of light or shade, no clouds, no shadows or reflections. The wind does not blow, neither disturbing the trees nor whipping water into waves."[50] And how true. As the quotations in this chapter from his notebooks and letters have already made abundantly clear, Coleridge traced his whereabouts by heeding the shifting, sequential hues of light, the fluctuating movements of trees, clouds, and water, and the shadows of a tree's leaves "playing on its silver Bark" (*CN* 1:1449; f. 4). For him, a landscape was a continuous process; therefore, a map that rendered a region immobile, omnipresent, or removed from time failed to honor his particular experience of a scene. For Coleridge, the pleasure of a landscape was in "its *running*, its *motion*, its assimilation to action" (*CN* 2:2402; f. 129). As a result, hardly a still moment rests among his descriptions of a natural setting.[51]

Because of Coleridge's sensitivity to a landscape's kinetic character, it is, perhaps, slightly surprising to come across a December 1804 entry remarking on a "wet track," left by a fly "that has been rescued from drowning" (*CN* 2:2338), an image that momentarily suggests to him the course of a river marked on a map. This cartographic allusion seems out of character for Coleridge, who was not particularly drawn to the solid, stationary, timeless lines of maps when he was actually walking through a landscape.

---

[49] Michael De Certeau, *The Practice of Everyday Life*, trans. Steven F. Rendall (Berkeley: University of California Press, 1984), 97.
[50] Timothy Ingold, *The Perception of the Environment: Essays on Livelihood, Dwelling and Skills* (London: Routledge, 2000), 242.
[51] Many critics have remarked on Coleridge's sensitivity to movement in a landscape. See Dixon, "The Notebooks," 75–79. Dixon draws attention to the "changing aspects of the landscape" and "the fleeting natural phenomena" in the notebooks (79). See also Ruddick's "'As Much Diversity as the Heart That Trembles,'" which mentions Coleridge's "moving panorama" (91). Moreover, Jarvis in *Romantic Writing and Pedestrian Travel* comments that "The reader is never allowed to forget the nuances of motion and perspective" in Coleridge's descriptions (136).

Admittedly, he occasionally consulted maps, such as the time in the summer of 1802 when he opened William Hutchinson's *History and Antiquities of Cumberland* (1776) and copied it into his notebook so that he might consider his forthcoming route (see *CN* 1:1206). The sketched map roughly replicates his possible itinerary, scribbles in the names of places, approximates the course of the "sea," diagrams certain landmarks such as an "abbey," and crosses out areas that he perhaps incorrectly noted or deemed irrelevant. And on that same walking tour he paused along the way to sketch a tentative map of his view of the "Lake-part of Wastdale" and the "Sca Fell Ridge" (*CN* 1:1213; f. 11). This "map" is somewhat confusing, for Coleridge seems, according to Coburn's note to the text, to have transposed what is on the left and placed it on the right. However, once underway, Coleridge was no longer a resident of the cartographic sphere but more often an inhabitant of shifting perspectives and a denizen of areas that did not stand still. I suggest that for Coleridge, a map was merely a preface to going but not a preface to seeing. His experience is a reminder that the world is not anything we look at but a process that we are part of. For this reason, it is interesting to note that when Coleridge planned a route by consulting Hutchinson's map, the resulting 1803 entry, verbally charting his proposed journey with Southey, lacks the verve of his more active descriptions. Stifled by the paradigm and permanency of the cartographic image, the passage describing the actual journey leans toward a dull and ordinary prose. The prose carries no senses of a setting's "assimilation into action" (*CN* 2:2402; f.129): "The Glenderamachen flows from S. Tarn, receives four becks from Bowscale Fell, winds round Souther Fell, crosses the road, & runs on the other side of Souther Fell ... & so on till it meets the Penrith Road, where it receives a Beck from near Dothwaite Head, just under Great Dod" (*CN* 1:1518; f. 10).

What a relief it is to return to the more vivid prose once Coleridge actually gets underway, walks past, and glories in the Great River "stretching strait in an oblique line" (*CN* 1:1624; f. 78). The landscape comes to life again and rejoins the passage of time.

### *Extended Motion*

Absorbed by what falls into and out of sight between the point of departure and arrival, Coleridge, during his walks, attended more to the unfolding scenery than to a map, and, I propose, was continuously conscious of being in the midst of a scene and, therefore, always somewhere. Rather, than centering his thoughts exclusively upon some named destination and leaving blank the intermediary spaces (as one does in a map between named places), he located himself "between the woody Hill / & a stone wall with trees growing over it & seeing nothing else" (*CN* 1:537; f. 39); he walked "thro' a Lane ~~with~~ of green Hazel Trees, with Hay-fields & Hay-makers" (*CN* 1:1213; f. 10), and he climbed "<under & between> low crags" (*CN* 1:1225; f. 27). One consequence was Coleridge's sensitivity to what he termed the "interspaces" within a landscape – to what can be seen in the midst of something else: he walked over a "bridge of Rocks in whose Interstices the Foam still lay of the yester night's Torrent" (*CN* 1:454; f. 61); he observed the "thinner mist" that fills up the "interspaces" between "long dividuous flakes" gliding in a moving mist" (*CN* 1:808; f. 13); and he delighted in the image of "a stream of white Cows, gleaming behind the Trees, in the Interspaces" (*CN* 1:1589; f. 56), as well as the sight of a moon that "fills the interspaces, just touching the Cloud above & below" (*CN* 1:1627; f. 19). In Scotland he delighted in a "remarkable naked rock" that rests at the top of an "interspace" (*CN* 1:1487; f. 45), and in the green and yellow coloring filling the "Interspace" of a "Mountain Bank" (*CN* 1:1495; f. 67).

Complementing his inclination to set himself apart from the cartographic imagination, he also rebuffed the formal, stilted style of the set pictorial views that, in addition to the maps, illustrated the guidebooks and were visible in many of the paintings and prints rendered in the late eighteenth century. On my study wall hangs a pen and ink color wash of *Travellers in a Landscape* by Thomas Barker of Bath (1769–1847; see Figure 1). Two figures rest quietly in the center of the painting's foreground, which opens up to a panoramic view of a rural scene. The two ramblers are momentarily stationary, and so too are the valleys and hills below or beyond; a border of bushes and woods on either side arrest any idea of fluidity. Only the softness of the artist's touch, perhaps, introduces some trace or memory of movement.

The image bears a resemblance to Farrington's view of "Lowdore" (c. 1780) which appears as an engraving in West's guide. One immediately notices that print's unrelenting immobility: the frozen figures in the boat, the unruffled lake, the stolid mountain and hills framed by motionless trees bordering the shore, the stationary waterfall, and the solid blocks of buildings. These details stultify the drawing; they silence as well as hold the landscape still.[52]

---

[52] This image can be seen opposite p. 1 of Thomas West's *A Guide to the Lakes in Cumberland, Westmorland, and Lancashire*, 8th ed. (Kendal: William Pennington, 1802).

Figure 1   Thomas Barker of Bath, *Travellers in a Landscape*. Privately owned.

If one reads through West's descriptions of his stations, more or less the same orientation is legible, for even though West writes of rivers running into the lake and sporadically elicits active verbs and phrases, such as "the lake spreads itself into a noble expanse" (*A Guide to the Lakes*, 51), he contains and controls these kinesthetic moments by exercising the conventions of a picturesque vocabulary, such as the word "noble," and by remarking on what cultivation surrounds the lake or what occupies the margins of the lake. Clichés, borders, enclosures, and the very frame of the prospect hold wildness in check.

For Coleridge, on the other hand, nature's pictures are all in motion; they are organic. Hardly a still moment rests among them. As commentators have recognized, his notebook entries written between 1794 and 1805 quicken with abundant examples of his sensitivity to what is stirring or boldly advancing within a landscape: roads tremble (*CN* 1:335), the moon thrusts "thro' a thin slip of white Cloud" (*CN* 1:455); ferns shake in the wind (*CN* 1:785), rivers pour down, and waterfalls convulsively twitch in fits and starts (*CN* 1:1426). And, as if a living body, the moon pulsates with the chemistry of life:

## Part Three: A Landscape in Motion 35

> the Moon is more than a half moon / it sank to a rude – then to a crescent, its bow stiffly & imperfect & still keeping this shape, thinned & thinned & thinned, till *once* it became a star, at its vanishing – but immediately after sent up a *throb* of Light in its former Shape & dimension – & so for several Seconds it throbbed & heaved, a soft Boiling up or restlessness of a Fluid. (*CN* 1:1614; f. 72)[53]

If it were not for the fact that Coleridge often recorded his responses to the landscape in notebooks that he carried in his pocket, one would not have such a vivid sense of his sensitivity to the organic nature of his surroundings. These notebooks allowed him to pioneer a style of describing a landscape that captured the motion of his own pace and of his surroundings in a distinctly raw and vividly immediate manner. Setting off on his rambles, Coleridge, along with a walking stick and a change of shirt, regularly carried with him a small notebook and lead pencils (sometimes a pen and ink horn) so that he could record what was directly unfolding before him. During his wanderings, Coleridge habitually took out his notebook and rapidly, at the very moment of perception, scribbled entries replete with dashes, slanting lines, and swift phrases that replicate the movement within a scene as well as his spontaneous reaction to what he was observing.[54] In these entries, a scene's kinetic elements stray or thrust past the limits of vision. Coleridge removes grammatical barriers so that a gust, a breeze, or some other natural gesture journeys beyond the final phrase. Breathless, he describes the appearance of a mountain lake so that its spray, whipped by the wind dashing across its surface, extends beyond an entry's images and touches the reader. This immediacy and vitality are even more apparent in the original manuscripts that are not reined in by the demands of the printed page, which regularizes the uneven hand. In these manuscript pages, words, lines, and sketches slide, slant, twist, and overlap in a manner outlawed by the mandate of the printed copy. Messy and worn by weather and use, the manuscript notebooks, in contrast to the published set, exhibit a living, intimate document that has not yet succumbed to the mechanized control of print or the posture

---

[53] The image recalls Coleridge's approving delight when in October 1800 he noticed his six-week-old son Derwent attending to the bending of the trees "in the strong wind" (*CN* 1:835).
[54] For examples of Coleridge pausing in the midst of his walk to write in his notebook, see *CN* 1:1223 (f. 23), where he writes: "It seems that I have gone 2 miles round about & ought to have crossed over at Dalegarth Hall … sate & wrote this at near the top of Easterfield Common"; and in entry *CN* 1:1449 (f .4) he declares: "As I write this, I turn my head, & close by me I see a Birch, so placed as among a number of Trees it alone is in full sunshine."

of retrospect. Furthermore, in the original version, the handwritten words and line drawings extend and often seem to charge from one margin to the other, at times almost threatening to fall off a page's edge. Motion, consequently, is far more explicitly alive in the original than in the edited notebooks; exiled are the stultifying passive constructions that, for example, interrupt the flow of water or occasionally blunt the prose of West's guide, in which West instructs the reader to look to the south where "a sweet bay *is formed* [italics mine] between the horns of two peninsulas" (*A Guide to the Lakes*, 48).

In Coleridge's experience, motion rarely ceases, distances, or abstracts itself into seeming stillness. For him, movement is basic and continuously present – necessary – I believe, if sight, color, and sound are to come into being. Images reveal themselves in time so that water ruffled by a breeze makes visible a stationary shadow of a tree (*CN* 1:1589) and "the swelling unequal noise of mountain Water from the streams in the Ravines" (*CN* 1:1469; f. 24) alerts him to the water's presence. One cannot exist without the other. In this respect, it is interesting to note that when Coleridge was in Germany, he refined his command of the language by creating lists of words under various headings. One of the categories was "Sight and Motion"; another, "Sound and Motion." A selection follows: "Gewahr warden – to perceive," "Hervorstürzen – to rush out," "kriechen – to creep into," "Wandern – wander or travel," "Wandeln to walk" (*CN* 1:354).

I suggest that what is particularly remarkable about Coleridge's sensitivity to motion within a landscape is not just his oft-appreciated consciousness of its activity but, more significantly, his sense that its movements travel beyond the line of sight or the edge of words (or even language or the very words themselves). Because he has little inclination to reduce or contain its force throughout his descriptions in his notebooks, a scene's kinetic elements stray or thrust, as I have already suggested, past the limits of vision and blow off the margins of a page. He removes grammatical barriers so that a gust, a breeze, or some other natural gesture journeys beyond the final phrase. Breathless, Coleridge describes the appearance of a mountain lake so that its spray, whipped by the wind dashing across its surface, extends beyond the entry's images and continues to ruffle the viewer or reader. Like an enjambment in a poem, the phrases rapidly follow each other as if rushing into each other. The slanting dashes capture not only the immediacy but also the exuding force of the scene so that the blasts of wind and the mist from the waves persist after the full entry's conclusion. No frame is imposed here:

Grysdale Tarn, rolling towards its outlet like a sea / the Gust on the broad Beck snatching up Water made the smooth & level water as full of small breakers, & white waves, as the rough & steep part / The Spray fell upon me, *lownded* in the Rock, like rain / The Sun setting behind the Hill behind me made a rainbow in the Spray across the Beck (20 yards from the Tairn) every time a Gust came. (*CN* 1:1204; f. 29, f. 28)

Thinking of Berkeley in 1804, Coleridge observed, it is not possible for "Motion to exist without extension" (*CN* 1:1842; f. 69).[55] As if heeding this principle and refusing to close what should not be contained but, rather, should proceed with all its organic force and energy, Coleridge inevitably abandoned the full stop or period. Moreover, in his notebook entries describing a landscape, dotted lines and horizontal dashes within and at the end of each entry keep the margins open and what they depict continuously on the move. The experience continues:

travelling along the ridge I came to the other side of those precipices and down below me on my left – no – no! no words can convey any idea of this prodigious wildness / that precipice fine on this side was but its ridge, sharp as a <jagged> knife, level so long, and then ascending as boldly – what a frightful bulgy precipice I stand on and to my right how the Crag which corresponds to the other, how it plunges down, like a waterfall, reaches a level steepness, and again plunges! – (*CN* 1:798; f. 40)

Coleridge's extraordinarily vibrant metaphors contribute to this sustained dynamic force. For instance, he protracted the sweeping motion of shadows of clouds over the corn and woods by associating their movement with "the motion of the Air in Sails" (*CN* 1:1458), and he extended the continuous motion of "Starlings in vast Flight" by comparing their advancing course not only to mists of smoke but also to "a body unindued with voluntary Power" (*CN* 1:1589; f. 56). Similarly, when he observed a "A whole Flight of small Birds" flinging "themselves down in a gale of wind into Borrodale [*sic*] like a *shoot* of Stones – each Bird seemed to dart onward by projection, & to descend by its own lifelessness and weight. –" (*CN* 1:1610; f. 71), he continued to release the image's drive and energy via the metaphors' vehicle that propels and hurls its tenor beyond the boundary of the particular moment.

---

[55] In a January 1804 entry Coleridge observed: "Not that it is possible for Colour or Motion to exist without extension; but only that the Mind can frame to itself by *Abstraction* the idea of Colour exclusive of extension, and of motion exclusive of both Colour and extension" (*CN* 1:1842; f. 69).

## Part Four: Feet and the Measure of the Landscape

### *A Physical Presence*

Just as Coleridge was sensitive to the movement of the landscape itself, he was also acutely alert to his own passage within it – to the motions and sensations of his body as he rambled along a pathway, ascended a hill, or walked among what Wordsworth referred to as "untrodden ways." Consequently, Coleridge's understanding of a landscape was not exclusively based upon what his eyes monitored but also upon how his body, during his rambles, responded to, communicated with, and even identified with its surroundings.[56] Though, as I have already pointed out, frequently attending to the mandate of the picturesque tradition by privileging the course of his eye ("The Firs looked divine & carried down the Eye divinely back to some Firs in Brother's Wood" [*CN* 1:1812; f. 56]) as well as focusing on "what was before my eyes while it was before my eyes" (*CN* 1:1572), he never completely fell prey to the "tyranny" of sight that gave precedence to the scrutiny and range of the eye.[57] Like many Continental thinkers, he understood that "the natural use of movement in the lower limbs" is necessarily tied to an awareness of the objects all around us."[58]

In Coleridge's experience, the detached eye was not the only organ that registered what lay before him; his limbs, his head, his skin, and his lungs did so too. Jarvis's point that Coleridge renounced the conventions of the picturesque gaze by calling attention to his fatigue or to the many aches and pains attending his walking, as well as to the discomforts associated with heat and bad weather is well taken. One, for instance, cannot forget

---

[56] In "Poets in a Transnatural Landscape: Coleridge, Nature, Poetry," *Romanticism* 27.1 (2021): 46–62, Gregory Leadbetter shows a sensitivity toward Coleridge's physical reaction to a landscape and remarks on how "The rhythm of [Coleridge's] physical body, continuously [responds] to the living environment within which it travels by its own power." Throughout this essay, Leadbetter often returns to the interplay between "the perceiving body and that which it perceives" (48, 49).

[57] It should also be pointed out that Coleridge was interested in the phenomenon of seeing. In November 1803, for instance, worried about his eyes, he wrote:

> I for the first time in my Life felt my eyes near-sighted, & tho' I had 2 Candles near me, reading in my bed, I was obliged to magnify the Letters by bringing the Book close to my Eye – I then put out the Candles, & closed my eyes – & instantly there appeared a spectrum, of a Pheasant's Tail, that altered thro' various degradations into round wrinkly shapes, as of <Horse> Excrement, or baked Apples ... (*CN* 1:1681; f. 88)

[58] Mayer, *The Science of Walking*, 48.

*Part Four: Feet and the Measure of the Landscape* 39

his "Perspiration: A Travelling Eclogue" (sent in a 1794 letter to Southey after a long walk), his periodic allusions to stretching his muscles, his throbbing headaches, swollen toes, nor his intimate complaint to Thomas Wedgwood of uneasy pains in his "Groin & right Testicle" (*CL* 2:914) after a demanding outing over the fells.[59] At times, one can almost hear Coleridge gasp and register his physical discomfort.[60] For instance, in a letter to Sara Hutchinson, written in August 1802, Coleridge not only told her what he saw during his walk on the fells but also complained of being overheated and of the bodily irritation attending an ensuing heat rash. The body is as much at play as the eye:

> I began to descend / when I felt an odd sensation across my whole Breast – not pain nor itching – & putting my hand on it I found it all bumpy – and on looking saw the whole of my Breast from my Neck [to my Navel] [inked out in MS] – & exactly all that my Kamell-hair Breast-shield covers, filled with great red heat-bumps, so thick that no hair could lie between them ... a startling proof to me of the violent exertions which I had made. (*CL* 2:843)

Several weeks later in another letter to Sara, he described ascending a waterfall "to the very top of the Fell" and finding the surface so craggy and "jagged as to wound one's hand fearfully" (*CL* 2:853). Because of this orientation, he occasionally metaphorically assimilated the body into the landscape and saw, for instance, "the whole Breast-work of the Hills" (*CN* 1:1266; f. 34), the "Knees & Elbows" in the bend of a larch (*CN* 1:1460; f. 14), a promontory resembling "a stretched out Arm" (*CN* 1:1471; f. 27), and the "Toes of mountains" (*CN* 1:1499; f. 75).[61]

---

[59] The poem "Perspiration. A Travelling Eclogue" reads:

> The dust flies smothering, as on clatt'ring wheel
> Loath'd Aristocracy careers along;
> The distant track quick vibrates to the eye,
> And white and dazzling undulates with heat.
> Where scorching to the unwary traveller's touch,
> The stone fence flings its narrow slip of shade;
> Or, where the worn sides of the chalky road
> Yield their scant excavations (sultry grots !),
> Emblem of languid patience, we behold
> The fleecy files faint-ruminating lie.
> (*CP* 1:56)

[60] Jarvis observes that Coleridge "vividly displaces the intermittent strains of pictorial detachment in his landscape descriptions by referring to the most intimate oral contact with rugged mountain terrain: 'I applied my mouth ever and anon to the side of the Rocks and sucked in draughts of Water cold as Ice, and clear as infant Diamonds in their embryo Dew!'" (*Romantic Writing and Pedestrian Travel*, 129).

[61] Coleridge often regarded the surrounding terrain as an organic body. He spoke of the "breast" and "ribs" of a mountain, the "veins" of a field, and the "elbow" of a road. One striking example of the

This identification of the body in the landscape, however, was not simply a matter of anthropomorphizing what he saw but an expression of his sense that his own body was actually a part of, even an extension of, the natural world. The result is that Coleridge spoke of gazing at the landscape that reflected his shadow (*CN* 1:1216) and sensing while passing a group of mountains that their forms are "seizing my body" (*CN* 1:523). In a January 14, 1803 letter to Wedgwood, quoted at the head of this chapter, his understanding of this connection is more fully addressed. In the letter, he describes the ways in which his body internalizes the movement of the outer world; his body and surroundings intermingle to unite and become one physical entity:

> In simple earnest, I never find myself alone within the embracement of rocks & hills, a traveller up an alpine road, but my spirit course, drives, and eddies, like a Leaf in Autumn: a wild activity, of thoughts, imaginations, feelings, and impulse of motion, rises up from within me – a sort of *bottom-wind*, that blows to no point of the compass, & comes from I know not whence, but agitates the whole of me; my whole Being is filled with waves, as it were, that roll & stumble, one this way, & one that way, & one that way, like things that have no common master. I think, that my soul must have pre-existed in the body of a Chamois-chaser. (*CL* 2:916)

How different this orientation is from the pose of distance that the guidebooks encouraged their readers to maintain when directing them to stand, physically detached, in a certain spot and gaze across or down upon a selected view.

### *The Pace and Tread of His Feet*

What has been overlooked by critics who speak of Coleridge's sensitivity to his physical presence in a landscape is Coleridge's particular attention to his feet – a practice that was integral to his understanding of a landscape and an important component in his spatial exploration of his surroundings. In this respect, it is amusing to recall a charm, passed down since the founding of Christ's Hospital School, which Coleridge remembered

---

way in which Coleridge experienced this correspondence between the landscape and the body is in a January 1804 entry in which he compared the movement of tadpoles in a pool to the progressing sensation of the nerve endings throughout his physical frame: "On returning we prolonged our walk on to Rydale, saw two quite perpendicular black Rocks ... & under this glided in pulses the innumerable Tad Poles – like one's nervous Creepings down one's limbs, back & thighs" (*CN* 1:1812; f. 57).

repeating as a young student. The rhyme perhaps foretells his desire to protect and keep his feet alert:

> Foot! foot! foot! is fast asleep
> Thumb! thumb! thumb! in spittle we sleep:
> Crosses three we make to ease us,
> Two for thieves and one for Christ Jesus![62]

During his walking days, Coleridge partially perceived his surroundings through the pace and tread of his feet. As a result, on his rambles, he not only occasionally complained of his feet being swollen ("my left Foot Swoln / plunged it in very hot [water]" [*CN* 1:1568; f. 52] or their hurting (because of the stones along a pathway [*CN* 1:1489]) or the "hard Fold" in his boot that had bruised "the cross of my foot" (*CL* 2:893–94) but also registered his consciousness of their "trespass" over the ground, especially when, in the Lakes, he was accosted by Sir Fleming's servant who reproved him "for having passed before the front of the House – / = by our Trespass of Feet" (*CN* 1:514; f. 47). As a consequence, throughout his early notebooks Coleridge was mindful of his feet when crossing a landscape. In August 1803, for instance, he noted that he entered "Scotland on foot," and recorded that he strode across a heath and walked at a brisk pace (*CN* 1:1477, 1482). He was also occasionally aware of the marks left by other feet, such as the day he noticed sheep tracks inclosing an irregular oval area (*CN* 1:1783).

With the alertness of an intruder, Coleridge paid attention to the telling feel of what lay underneath the tread of his soles. In this respect, I am sympathetic to Ingold's claim that "it is surely through our feet, in contact with the ground that we are most fundamentally and continually 'in touch' with our surroundings."[63] Indeed, in a letter to Sara Hutchinson, he admitted as much when he observed that a lake he comes across "is wholly hidden 'till your very Feet touch it" (*CL* 2:838). An opening line of an early poem, "On Bala Hill" (1794), also registers this reality when the tedious paces of the speaker's feet ("With many a weary step at length I gain / Thy summit") prefaces the second verse in which "the eye" beholds an "extended Vale."

It was in his notebooks and letters, however, that Coleridge most frequently and explicitly acknowledged his trespass. He wrote about the

---

[62] *Christ's Hospital Recollections of Lamb, Coleridge, and Leigh Hunt*, ed. R. Brimley Johnson (London: George Allen, 1890), 99.
[63] Timothy Ingold, *Being Alive: Essays in Movement, Knowledge and Description* (London: Routledge, 2011), 65.

tactile sensations of tramping over marshy ground, through "splashy & boggy" soil (*CN* 1:412; f. 26), over jagged rocks, trudging and toiling knee-deep through the snow, positioning his steps among the perilous slipperiness of peat-moss on a hill of stones, the dangers of descending over "spongy soaky Moss" (*CL* 2:853), or "walking over hollow ground, with the fountain Streams of the Esk rumbling & gurgling under my feet" (*CN* 1:1218; f. 17). And he remarked on the ease of rambling on even ground up "the steep breast" of a mountain (*CN* 1:1782; f. 51) as well the alarming jolt he experienced when he dropped down from a ledge onto his feet: "I put my hand on the Ledge, & dropped down ... & the jolt of the Fall on my Feet, put my Limbs in a *Tremble*" (*CL* 2:841). Such sensitivity to the presence and feel of what lies beneath the soles of his feet contributed to his attention to the texture of the landscape's surface: to the smoothness of rocks, the roughness of a river, the furrowed and wrinkled torrents of a waterfall, and the surface of hills, as well as the "raggednesses" of distant mountains at the end of Bassenthwaite (*CN* 1:1689; f. 27) and the "deep, rich dark Mould" tenaciously clinging to some rocks (*CN* 1:926; f. 25).

### *Coleridge the Surveyor*

Significantly, Coleridge did not just register the feel of the land with his feet, but also measured the terrain with them. They and their paces were as much a part of his spatial understanding as were his eyes. He was, for instance, alert to the fact that by stepping "two paces" he had lost the view of the glorious sunlight (*CN* 1:551; f. 21). In this respect, his topographical entries in his notebooks often take their cue from the act of surveying, an art with which he would have been familiar because of the current projects to measure land in the building of roads, enclosing estates, and conducting the early ordnance surveys.[64] Perhaps more to the point, Coleridge's mathematical training at both Christ's Hospital School and Jesus College would have also introduced him to the manner in which an area of land is measured. If one looks at the copybooks diligently executed by late eighteenth- and early nineteenth-century schoolboys when learning geometry, one soon understands that exercises in surveying land followed instruction

---

[64] There are a number of helpful critical responses to Coleridge that address his interest in topography. See, for instance, J. Hillis Miller, *Topographies* (Stanford, CA: Stanford University Press, 1995) and Fulford, "Virtual Topography," 27–28. None, however, addresses Coleridge's interest in and use of surveying. For an informed history of surveying see Rachel Hewitt, *Map of a Nation: A Biography of the Ordnance Survey* (London: Granta, 2011).

## Part Four: Feet and the Measure of the Landscape  43

concerning the principles of Euclidian geometry.⁶⁵ For instance, J. Stubb's 1753 copybook (Item S9) opens with Euclid's definitions of a point and a line and then, like many others in the John Hersee Collection, housed in the archives of the University of Leicester Library, proceeds to work out the measurements of a particular area.⁶⁶ In the archives at Christ's Hospital School, there is also a copy of an 1802 mathematical exercise book of Charles Shea.⁶⁷ One sees the same principle at work, for Shea first writes out Euclid's definitions and then proceeds to survey a body of water.

Often modeling his understanding of a landscape in the spirit of these surveying exercises, Coleridge approximated the orientation of a surveyor by measuring and counting his paces over a portion of ground (with his feet and the depth of his walking stick rather than with a chain and a pole) by estimating the height of an incline, observing its angles, noting its contents, and recording his findings in a field-book (Coleridge's notebooks) in which, as was the practice, he adopted his own symbols and marks.⁶⁸ For example, as if implementing the shorthand of the surveyor he describes a monument ∠ of Tyll Eulenspiegel in Germany by inserting the mathematical symbol for a "half-angle " (*CN* 1:395; f. 35).⁶⁹

---

⁶⁵ One example of a book designed for school children is A. [Abraham] Crocker, *The Elements of Land Surveying for the Use of Schools and Students* (London: Richard Phillips, 1806). The book opens with rehearsals of Euclid's definitions. It was, of course, common knowledge that the art of surveying requires an understanding of geometry. Coleridge's mathematical education will be thoroughly discussed in Chapter 3 of this book.

⁶⁶ The John Hersee Collection at the University of Leicester is dedicated to mathematical notebooks made by students in the eighteenth and early nineteenth centuries. See Chapter 5 n. 14. J. Stubb's 1753 copybook can be seen in the John Hersee Collection, Item S99.

⁶⁷ See Charles Shea's "The Elements of Navigation Perform'd by Charles Shea Educated in the Royal Mathematical School Christ's Hospital, 1802" in the archives of Christ's Hospital School.

⁶⁸ In his *Treatise on Land-Surveying, in Seven Parts*, 5th ed. (London: Whittaker, Treacher, and Co., 1829), Thomas Dix explains that "the Surveying-Chain contains one hundred links, and is twenty-two yards, or four poles, in length ... The offset-staff is ten links long, divided into links. In Land-Surveying, the dimensions are taken in links, with a chain 100 links long, and the areas are found in square lines" (72). Dix explains the surveying methods of the late eighteenth and early nineteenth centuries. George Adams in his 1791 *Geometrical and Graphical Essays* discusses the paces a surveyor must learn to make:

> Distances of a certain extent may be measured by the time employed in pacing them; to do this, a person must accustom himself to pace a given extent in a given time, as 600 paces is five minutes, or 120 in one minute; being perfect in this exercise, let it be required to know how many paces it is from one place to another which took up in pacing 1 hour and ¼ or 75 minutes. (438)

⁶⁹ For other examples of this kind of practice see *CN* 1:1457, 1466, 1482. Interestingly, in William Enfield's *The History of Philosophy* (London: J. F. Dove, 1891) first published in 1791 and carefully read by Coleridge, there is a reference to Pythagoras, who

Like the geometric caterpillar he once described in his book on logic, Coleridge periodically becomes the surveyor who walks out to create a line with which to measure and plot the earth. Examples of Coleridge's tendency to follow this mode are multiple. The notebooks written from 1794 through 1804 are replete with such as the following from October 1798 when he was describing an area he was visiting in Germany:

> Left Bank – wood recommences or rather the village of Buchholtz, a *neighbourhood* of houses with Trees round each house – making all together a wood – of rather more than a Furlong, perhaps two furl. – Left Bank recedes – and as far as I can see is naked or only with hedge-trees, & both banks cease to be beautiful – to the end of the lake, which Is (they say) ten miles in length & 2 ½ in breadth. (*CN* 1:360; f. 45)

This tendency continues so that in August 1800, while in the Lake District, Coleridge observed:

> The fields on the other side so green till you reach the Caldew – I counted 21 fields in this hamlet in its broadest one long field is its breadth, about 4 ½ acres in length is that field whose length forms the breadth of the vale – from the foot of Carrock to the Caldew – the last & small house with 2 trees is only a wintering House for Hogs ... I now wound along up to the Tarn – the water runs nearly from East to West in something of this form A. A. A. A. (*CN* 1:797; f. 22)

Throughout the period when Coleridge was actively rambling, there are many more examples of this orientation. On a walk in Germany in May 1799, for instance, he recorded coming to "an exquisitely beautiful Rotund of Greenery, 170 strides in diameter –" (*CN* 1:411; f. 23), and earlier he surveyed a monument itself "3 yards high & one broad" (*CN* 1:395; f. 36). During one of his walks in August 1800, Coleridge calculated that a tarn's shore "rises up into a round low Hill of gradual ascent, not about 80 strides, for I measure it" (*CN* 1:797; f. 22). In Scotland, he took note of a large single rock, "25 strides in length" and "60 strides round" (*CN* 1:1475; f. 34), and stopped to examine the wild "Burial Ground of Stratherick, 40 strides long, 35 broad" (*CN* 1:1495; f. 66). Later, in 1804, he described, in an inserted poem, an Alder tree's projecting

> inferred the stature of Hercules from the length of the Olympus Course, which measured six hundred of his feet. Observing how much shorter a course six hundred times the length of the foot of an ordinary-sized man was then the Olympic court, he inferred by the law of proportion, the length of Hercules's foot, where the usual proportion of the length of the foot to the height of a man enabled him to determine the problem. (1:307)

branches by calculating that the shortest of them is "twice 6 of a tall man's Strides" (*CN* 1:1837).

Notably, Coleridge also employed the measure of his feet to estimate the dimensions of Wedgwood's shooting cottage which he visited in December, 1802. Coleridge calculated its length and width by counting the shoe lengths of its various rooms and recorded the results in his notebook:

> 4 ½ strides from the window to the Stairs Door – 4 strides across from the fire place. – 16 Shoes – by 14 ... Room within that which looks into the Garden, 16 Shoes by 12 ... The (Floored) Passage with a door into the field – & stairs – 13 shoes – utmost breadth from Door to field Door 12 – / The Stone Passage – 18 Shoes by 3 ½ ... Floored passage 10 shoes. (*CN* 1:1288; f. 42)

This habit of mind was to follow him when he left England for Malta. On his way, in October 1804, Coleridge surveyed an old Roman Forum in Naples: "the standing Column, occupies from the <beginning of the> square of the 1st part to the end of the Sq. of the Third 8 strides only – from the end of the Square, in which the 3rd Base stands, to the end of the 5th is 12 strides"; later that day, when exploring a cavern, he recorded that "the part admitting standing was 13 Strides by 8 / a sort of window-like opening above the entrance" (*CN* 2:2202; f. 53, f. 55). Once in Malta, he remarked on being in a room "of 4 Strides by 4, but that the seats & railed Covering ... of the Stairs take up the greatest part & make this breadth only one Slip of a stride's length" (*CN* 2:2268; f. 108).[70]

## *Coleridge's Boots*

This attentiveness to the tread and measure of his feet reflected, and perhaps occasioned, his periodic preoccupation with the construction and quality of his shoes and his walking boots – not entirely surprising for a person who trekked so rigorously. And perhaps not necessarily surprising if one believes Coleridge's anecdote that at the age of thirteen, when a student at Christ's Hospital School, he had attempted to apprentice himself to a local shoemaker who had befriended him on his leave

---

[70] It needs to be noted here that Coleridge's impulse to measure his surroundings by counting the number of feet or strides while he moved through a landscape has something in common with the ways in which he composed, measured, or counted the stresses in the lines of his poetry that, like his footprints, chronicled the imprint of his walking while journeying through a landscape. This vital connection will be discussed and exemplified in Chapter 4.

days. In a May 27, 1830 issue of *Table-Talk*, Coleridge recalls the harsh treatment he received after approaching James Boyer, the headmaster, with a request to learn and practice the craft – a plea that met with a strongly unfavorable response, for Boyer was intent upon training Coleridge to be among the elite "Grecians" and win a place at the University of Cambridge:

> I had *one* just flogging. When I was about thirteen, I went to a shoemaker and begged him to take me as his apprentice. He, being an honest man, immediately brought me to Bowyer [*sic*], who got in a great rage, knocked me down, and even pushed Crispin [the shoemaker] out of the room. Bowyer asked me why I had made myself such a fool? To which I answered, that I had a great desire to be a shoemaker, and that I hated the thought of being a clergyman.
> "Why so?" said he. "Because to tell you the truth, sir" said I, "I am an infidel!" For this, without much ado, Bowyer flogged me. (*Christ's Hospital Recollections*, 98)[71]

Coleridge was scrupulous about his footwear.[72] For example, in November 1802, during a period when he was almost obsessively rambling in the fells, he made meticulous and demanding notes in his notebooks about how his boots should be made – a request that reflects considerable thought and knowledge about the matter and divulges just how attached Coleridge was to their design and the necessity of wearing a well-made boot:

> N.B. Have two Lasts made exactly the shape of my natural foot – the Boots to have a sole less on the hollow of the foot – Mutton suet 1. Hog's Lard 2. Venice Turpentine ½ – all mixed & melted – always put on warm, Shoe or boot being held to the fire, while it is being rubbed in – The middle sole of the Boot covered with Cobbler's wax – or still better, steeped thoroughly in the above Composition / the Leather of the Boot should be stout Horse

---

[71] Richard Holmes in his biography of Coleridge writes:

> Another, more hare-brained, ambition at the age of fifteen was a scheme to apprentice himself to a local shoemaker, largely because the man and his wife had been so kind to him during the lonely 'leave-days.' Perhaps this was a serious attempt to escape from Christ's Hospital early (apprenticeships were, after all, allowed by the statutes), and to flee back into a less demanding, domestic existence. At all events the kindly shoemaker, a Mr. Crispin, was sent packing by [James] Boyer [the headmaster] after a ferocious interview – Crispin might have sustained an action in law against him for assault – and Coleridge was flogged again to remind him of his privileged status as a future Grecian.

See Holmes, *Coleridge: Early Visions* (New York: Viking, 1990), 29–30.

[72] Coleridge's scrupulousness is perhaps shared by Robert Southey, who was often his walking companion. Evidence of just how carefully Southey looked after his shoes can be found today in the Keswick Museum, which displays a pair of Southey's beautifully crafted and preserved shoes.

leather – if none to be had, Cow-leather / a piece of oil Silk 6 inches above the Heel, 2 inches wide with a back strap to the Boots. (*CN* 1:1273; f. 39)

Half a year later, in February 1803, he once more fastidiously revealed his precise knowledge of a well-crafted shoe:

> Shoes, soles at least ½ inch thick, the upper leather 3 quarter galocked. Nails of Tempered Steel must be provided, the points screws, their heads near ½ an inch diameter, must be cut into the form of a square pyramid, wch will have 2 points in consequence of the notch cut into each for the Screw-driver to fix them into the Shoes. 12 of these nails must be put into each sole, 7 round the forepart, & 5 round the fore-part, & 5 round the Heel as near the edge of the Sole, as possible without endangering the bursting of the Leather. The interval between these nails ought to be filled up with common large-headed nails, so close that their heads might touch each other. (*CN* 1:1358; f. 52)

Without good boots or shoes Coleridge was lost, so after parting from the Wordsworths on their quarrelsome tour of Scotland, in August 1803 and deciding to walk back to Keswick alone (as I have already mentioned, a pedestrian journey of 263 miles that took eight days), Coleridge was shattered when he accidentally ruined his shoes by holding them too close to a fire while attempting to dry them out. Desperate to acquire a new pair and eager to carry on until he could reach a town where there was a shoemaker, he continued to walk and climb mountains in the damaged footwear – a circumstance that injured his heel and blistered his toes. As one knows, getting ready-made shoes was not then an expeditious task. Recall that Dorothy Wordsworth in her Grasmere journal speaks of making shoes. Coleridge did not have sufficient funds with which to pay for a new pair, so in a September 1, 1803 letter to his wife, he bemoaned his fate and urgently pressed Sara to send him money:

> I am unfortunately shoeless – there is no Town where I can get a pair, & I have no money to spare to buy them – so I expect to enter Perth Barefooted – I burnt my shoes in drying them at the Boatman's Hovel on Loch Ketterin / and I have by this means hurt my heel – likewise my left Leg is a little inflamed /& the Rheumatism in the right of my head afflicts me sorely when I begin to grow warm in my bed, chiefly, my right eye, ear, cheek, & the three Teeth / but nevertheless, I am enjoying myself having Nature with Solitude & liberty; the liberty natural & solitary, the solitude natural & free! – But you must contrive somehow or other to borrow 10 £ – or if that cannot be, 5 £, for me, – & send it without delay, directed to me at [the Pos]t Office, Perth. (*CL* 2:979)

Indeed, a day later a desperate Coleridge wrote to Sara again, once more urging her to send money:

> I had determined to buy a pair of Shoes whatever befell me, in the way of money distresses; but there are none in the Town ready made – so I shall be obliged to go as far as Inverness with these – perhaps to Perth / & I speak in the simplest earnest when I say, that I expect I shall be forced to throw them away before I get to Inverness, & to walk barefoot – My bad great Toe, on my left Foot is a sore Annoyance to me. – I am bepuzzled about this money. This Letter will not reach you, I fear, till Wednesday Night – However, you must at all events send me the money (I can & will Make 5 £ do) Mr. Coleridge, to be left at the Post Office, Perth, N. Britain. (*CL* 2:981)

A few days later, writing from Perth, he was to report to his wife:

> At Fort Augustus I got a pair of Shoes – the day before I had walked 36 miles, 20 the worst in conception, & up a Mountain – so that in point of effort it could not be less than 46 miles / the shoes were all to pieces / and three of my Toes were skinless, & I had a very promising Hole in my Heel. – Since the new Shoes I have walked on briskly – from 30 to 35 miles a day, day after day – & three days I lived wholly on Oat cake, Barley Bannock, Butter, & the poorest of all poor Skim-milk Cheeses – & still I had horrors at night! – I mention all this to shew you, that I have strength somewhere ... (*CL* 2:985)

Because of this attentiveness to his footwear, it is no wonder that Coleridge periodically commented on how others were shod. During his 1798 trip to Germany, for instance, he was impressed by the sight of a shepherd "walking up & down with his dog, with iron-solid boots" (*CN* 1:355; f. 45), and later in Scotland, he was disturbed, even disgusted, when he caught sight of people going barefooted – a reflection perhaps of his own testy mood at this moment of the Scottish tour with the Wordsworths:

> Say what you will "the naked feet" is disgusting more so in Scotland than in Germany, from the *tawdry* or *squalid* appearance of the bare-footed // In Germany there is a uniform Dress in the Class that go bare-footed & they always have their Shoes in their Hands or on their Heads / In Scotland Cabin Gowns, white Petticoat, all tawdry fine, & naked Legs, & naked Splaid-feet, & gouty ancles. (*CN* 1:1437; f. 8)

As part of this vigilance, Coleridge sometimes imagined the shape of the boot in the landscape. On one occasion he watched a moon setting behind a mountain ridge and saw "its various segments presented as it slowly sunk – first, the foot of a Boot, all but the Heel – then a little pyramid $\Delta$"

(*CN* 1:983; f. 32). And on his August 1802 descent from Scafell, he sought out a rock, known as the "four-foot Stone" (a geological phenomenon), on which were clearly imprinted what appeared to be the footprints of animals and a child. Notably, and perhaps predictably, when he recorded this sighting, Coleridge measured the size of each foot. He recorded the occasion both in his notebook and in an August 6, 1802 letter to Sara Hutchinson. The following quotation is taken from the August letter and once more reveals his impulse to measure and survey:

> The Stone is in it's whole breadth just 36 inches. (I measured it exactly [with his walking Stick]) but the part that contains the marks is raised above the other part, & is just 20 ½ Inches. The length of the Stone is 32 ½ Inches. The first foot-mark is an Ox's foot – nothing can be conceived more exact – this is 5 ½ Inches wide – the second is a Boy's Shoe in the Snow, 9 ½ Inches in length / this too is the very Thing itself, the Heel, the bend of the Foot, etc. – the third is the Foot-step to the very Life of a Mastiff Dog – and The fourth is *Derwent's very own first little Shoe*, 4 Inches in length … (*CL* 2:845)[73]

All this attention to his own boots as well as to others' footwear and imprints of shoes in the landscape emphasizes the fact that Coleridge substantiated his perception and understanding of a landscape with not just his eyes but also the tread and feel of his feet. I am reminded of a detail from *Old Ways* when Robert Macfarlane recalls Richard Long's walk of thirty-three miles a day for thirty-three days, from the Lizard in Cornwall to Dunnel Head in northern Scotland. On this ambitious excursion, Long wrote a letter and signed it off "with a red-ink stamp that shows an outline of two feet with eyes embedded in their soles, gazing out at the looker."[74] In a way, this stamp could also have been Coleridge's, for he too experienced a landscape with both his eyes and his feet – feet that touched the very ground he trod and, sometimes in the manner of a surveyor, also measured what he saw. As his sensitivity to the motion in a landscape reveals, his was a dynamic perspective that was distinctly rooted in the pace, the feel, and the marks of his footsteps. For this reason, during his walking years, Coleridge's notebook descriptions of landscape are alive, immediate, and not detached – qualities that his habit of jotting down an entry in his notebook while rambling made more possible. The entries live in the organic present and replicate not only the movement of his body but also a landscape in endless motion.

---

[73] Another account can be found in his notebooks. See *CN* 1:1220; f. 20.
[74] Robert Macfarlane, *Old Ways: A Journey on Foot* (New York: Penguin Books, 2013), 29.

## Conclusion

As this introductory chapter demonstrates, Coleridge was a vigorous rambler and scrambler. His wandering in the hills, mountains, fells, and valleys of his surroundings did not only effect his sense of well-being but also developed his unique powers as an observer. His extensive and rigorous walking between 1794 and 1804 significantly distanced his experience from fashionable aesthetic ways of looking at a landscape and allowed him to honor his impulse to survey what was before his eyes as well as to recognize the feel of his physical presence within his surroundings. Notably, Coleridge sensed that he was part of the organic pulse that brings a place to life. Moreover, as we have seen, his rambling contributed to his spatial understanding by enhancing his consciousness of a scene's fluctuating shapes. As a consequence, the resulting rapid notebook entries feature vivid verbs, expanding metaphors, and idiosyncratic punctuation that capture the sequential immediacy and energy of each step and turn.

For Coleridge, however, words were not always what represented the shifting topography of his surroundings. In his letters and particularly in his notebooks, he also periodically, as we shall see, summoned diagrams to help him record the shape or bearing of what he passed through. The next chapter, "Lines of Motion," will explore not only Coleridge's acute awareness of lines in a landscape but also his use of two-dimensional line drawings in his notebooks and correspondence to record what unfurled before him. These diagrams were an important, if not fundamental, part of his landscape vocabulary and eventually, as we shall see in the third chapter, linked to his indebtedness to and use of the geometric idiom, a mode of thought and representation that offered him yet another means of portraying the scenery and phenomena he passed by when he trod the ground of his walking. Eventually, in the fourth chapter, I shall explore how all these experiences and perspectives helped shape the topography of his nature poetry.

CHAPTER 2

## *Lines of Motion*

1. A Point is that which hath no part
2. A line is a longitude without latitude
3. The ends, or limits, of a line are points
4. A right line is that which lies equally betwixt it's points
5. A Superficies is that which hath only longitude and latitude
6. The extremes, or limits, of a superficies are lines
7. A plain superficies is that which lies equally betwixt lines
    (*Euclide's Elements: The Whole Fifteen Books*, ed. Isaac Barrow, 1722)[1]

A Point is the beginning of magnitude, and the bound of a line, and may be conceived to be infinitely small, though we may represent it by a small speck or dot with a pen thus (.) . . . A Line is generated or produced by the motion of a point . . .
    (B. Talbot, *The Compleat Art of Land-Measuring*, 1784)[2]

A Hill exactly like Grysdale Pike & Bason, two round Hills, the nearest delved with Fast Torrents, in a line with each other – & just beyond the furthest & roundest the mountain wall runs across & locks me in . . . I can sometimes look down upon from the edge of the Terrace-like Road. The variety of outline, Lines parallel, & crossing, of Mountain, Hill, Hillock, & Rift in each outline – a wall of 13 strides built up against the tremendous precipice. It is one of the loveliest Rifts I have ever seen, the sides chasmy.
    (*CN* 1:1497; ff. 3–4)

All Snow – the Hollow under Grysdale Pike thro' dingy deep vapour! In Borrodale on the mountains behind the Castle beheaded by a straight Line of black Cloud; on all below that line a yellow brilliance on white Snow – & black Barenesses interpatch'd.
    (*CN* 1:1667)

---

[1] Isaac Barrow, ed., *Euclide's Elements: The Whole Fifteen Books Compendiously Demonstrated: with Archimedes' Theorems of the Sphere and Cylinder Investigated by the Method of Indivisibles* (London: J. Redmayne, 1772), 4.
[2] B. Talbot, *The Compleat Art of Land-Measuring or, a Guide to Practical Surveying* (London: T. and W. Lowndes, 1784), 2–3.

One result of Coleridge's extensive walking and his inclination to survey all that he beheld was his exceptional attention to the tangible lines that run through and lend character to a landscape. During the period of his rambling excursions, Coleridge habitually, verbally and visually, traced their presence in the areas through which he walked. This orientation goes to the very core of his understanding and deserves attention, for his practice of recording their passage not only helps isolate what made his portrayals of natural settings in his notebooks distinctive but also prefaces his appreciation of the geometric idiom's presence in a landscape, a subject that follows this chapter.

### "The endless endless lines of motion"[3]

Like the spider who "lives along the line,"[4] Coleridge, during his decade of walking, traveled, as he observed, "along with the Lines of a mountain" (*CN* 2:2347; f. 118). Understanding that lines are the "first and simplest manifestable forms in nature" (*CC* 13:73), he might have agreed with a recent anthropologist's suggestion that people inhabit a world consisting not of things but of lines.[5] Such markers are everywhere and form the web and knots of life. As a walker, he would have concurred with Tim Ingold's observation that the wayfarer, as he moves along, inhabits a world that is composed of a network of tracks. To sustain himself he must always be on the lookout for them. As a consequence of this conviction, Coleridge's notebook entries and letters written during the period of his walking heed the larger outlines of mountains or precipices, as well as those "bold," "firm," "straight," "wild," and "fantastic" lines visible within a scene's smaller details. He found satisfaction, for instance, in seeing the moss running down a wall "like a serpent in its firm lines" (*CN* 1:510; f. 51), "the Unbroken Line of the steep Crag" (*CN* 1:541; f. 34), the long Bracken dangling like "unkempt red brown Hair" (*CN* 1:1160; f. 35), and the "wild outline of the *black* masses of mountain" (*CL* 2:917), as well as the threads of ivy reflected in a pool (*CN* 2:2810; f. 88). Occasionally, dependent upon this diagrammatic perspective, he even transformed a human figure into the lineal mode, such as the time he witnessed an old woman spreading out her arms so she could catch the warmth from a fire: "The old Woman ... could not get warmth in her, so came in & spread

---

[3] A phrase from *CN* 1:1495; f. 66.
[4] Alexander Pope, *Essay on Man*, ed. Henry Morley (London: Cassell & Company, 1891), epistle II, section vii.
[5] Ingold, *Lines: A Brief History*, 5.

her poor arms out to the sticks flaming under the Teakettles in the Inn Kitchen" (*CN* 1:1169; f. 27). The lines generated by her arms and the fire's burning sticks compose the portrait of the moment.

As a result of this orientation, Coleridge, while scrambling up and down the fells, repeatedly focused upon the various fissures, threads, roads, paths, ridges, streaks, and stripes that moved across and cut through a landscape. Entries from his notebooks reflect this perspective. For instance, when rambling in Germany in May 1799, he caught the topography of his surroundings by calling attention to their defining lines. In the following passage, he remarks on the road, rivers, and paths as well as the trees, walls, and the contour of the nearby hills to delineate and trace his progress through a particular scene:

> Here the path divides, a road thro' a fir wood running one way, & the river losing itself immediately in another deep grove of Fir, the other – a huge Steep Angle of Rock forming this division – We left the River unwillingly – & journeyed into the deep woods where the pillars of Rock seemed to live among the black Fir Trees ... till we came to the Foot of a Hill up which the Road winded with scattered Firs by the side...We saw the plain with rocks on the right hand, an immense wall, & on the left & curving round & forming the front view surges of woody Hills, beeches – & the Town & Castle of Blankenburg at our feet. – Castle – on the right a hill of most noble outline ... (*CN* 1:415; f. 27)

Sometimes Coleridge's awareness of these defining lines helped him not only capture the composition of his surroundings but also establish his bearings.[6] Like the spider he observed in October 1803, spinning a thread to reach a lower point and then re-ascending to spin another, he found stability in a multiple moving web of lines.[7] As a result, rambling through an unfamiliar part of Scotland, he established his route by noting and tracking the various courses produced by torrents of water, wall-like hills, rims, outlines, and ridges that

---

[6] In the previous chapter, I see a correspondence between Coleridge's activity and that of a surveyor tramping over and walking through the land.

[7] Often when Coleridge paused during his rambles, he noted the lines in a prospect that helped him orient himself. For instance, in August 1802, he remarked: Second Resting Place, two thirds up the Fell – a part of Wastdale Lake on my right, then the back of the Screes, with Burmoor Tairn, and the two Moorfells, on its other side, Screes & Irton Fells run in a ridge down to the level Plain seaward on one side of the Tairn – Moor Fells, I know not their names, on the other side / Mitterdale lies between, & is full in sight – / On the other side of these Fells Eskdale, partly in sight – on the other side of Eskdale, from the Sea upward, Black Comb, Stones <Head> Fell, Corney Fell & others unknown to me at present – / Close on the screes & on the same line with the Moor Fells a ridge called Mulcaster Fell. (*CN* 1:1215)

came into view. These allowed him to plot the land and gain his point of reference. For example, near Dumbarton, in a surveying mode, he oriented himself by charting the islands in a lake near Mount Inchdevannoch:

> The last Island, which I see (there are four running across the Lake in one line) – the second & third small & fish shape ... the first & fourth, very large – you look over the first to Dumbarton Rock, and the fourth vaults in those plunging Lines ⌢, & connects itself with the mountain, whose Tongue of Land almost meets it, of the same bounding, plunging, vaulting Line of Descent. (*CN* 1:1462; f. 17)[8]

Earlier, while walking in the Lake District, he had similarly situated himself within the landscape around Eskdale by concentrating on the contours created by the River Esk and those formed by the ridge of a hill:

> The Esk runs down the left hand of the ridge (as you go down) – both vales are in their course of very unequal breadths, often little more than the River Channel in the one, and as much space as would serve for the bed of a good river in the other/ – Now then the Hill-ridge intermits and the vale becomes one ... (*CN* 1:1222; f. 22)

And there were many other occasions when he positioned himself by remarking on a landscape's leading lines and gazing at ridges "which one might stride across, some running straight on, some curving into arcs of circles, & forming Basons & hollows" (*CN* 1:1477; f. 39) or watching how these intercepted or interrupted one another to create a "jagged saw-toothed outline" (*CN* 1:1227; f. 39).

Predictably, however, he was especially drawn to those lines that registered his keen sensitivity to the fluctuating, shifting nature of his surroundings discussed in the previous chapter. Therefore, while trudging through the stirring, advancing scenery of his rambles, Coleridge

---

[8] Another example of this practice during his tour of Scotland occurs in entry *CN* 1:1497 (f. 3). The entry reads:

> A Hill exactly like Grysdale Pike and Bason, two round Hills, the nearest delved with Fast Torrents, in a line with each other – & just beyond the furthest & roundest the mountain wall runs across & locks me in ... Under the wall-like Hill, purple & pebbly about two miles below the Bank a wood & a blue Lake in a bason, the rim of various outline, & the inside variously brown with cultivation ... Then a laborious Ascent of 3 miles, & on the top of the mountain a Tairn, with a ridge of Hill to the right, far over the ridge a high [hill] – / black, of various Outline, not unlike Skiddaw.

repeatedly paid attention to what he termed "lines of motion" (*CN* 1:1489; f. 59) and to such details as the paths of rivers, the plunging outlines of cliffs, and the "serpenting" lines of roads (*CN* 1:1213; f. 11). His early notebook entries describing the terrain of his walking move forward with multiple references to those streaks and tracks that are slanting, bending, running, bounding, stretching, vaulting, and projecting – all participles that extend the activity's momentum and reflect, as well, his own rambling progress through a scene that was forever evolving. Reveling in the primal force of a landscape's being, he persisted throughout his walking years in noting, for example, the sight of ridges darting and dipping, the lines of a mountain "pushing toward" a "Bridge Bank" (*CN* 1:1489; f. 57), and a Scottish moorland displaying "a dipping leaping, tipsy outline," behind which loom "29 great lines of motion or direction" (*CN* 1:1489; f. 58). Later in Malta, he remarked on the "plunging Descents" of the cliffs bordering the country's coast (*CN* 2:2028), and when studying a Washington Allston landscape he was thrilled to see a "noble Tree with its graceful Lines of motion" exhaling "up into the sky" (*CN* 2:2831; f. 95).[9]

As if transcribing this awareness into the landscape of his notebooks, Coleridge fills their leaves with various lines and diagrams.[10] As a result, he periodically slices the page with angular streaks that cut across a sequence of the words. For instance, pages from his manuscript notebooks in the British Library and in the Special Collections of Victoria University Library contain deliberate and firm diagonal lines that censor an entry he has written in Latin or Greek (languages to which he sometimes reverted when wanting to keep his thoughts more private). Other leaves include sketches of sloping outlines of hills, cliffs, and waterfalls that cut across what he is verbally describing. Occasionally, these diagrams take up the entire space of the page; they record the organic and living contours of what is being described or considered. At times in the manuscript notebooks, he also separates entries with hastily drawn and often uneven lines

---

[9] In these entries as well as in innumerable others, exiled are the stultifying passive constructions that, for example, occasionally blunt the prose of Thomas West's 1780 *A Guide to the Lakes* in which West instructs the reader to look to the south where "a sweet bay *is formed* [italics mine] between the horns of two peninsulas" (48).

[10] It is helpful to be reminded that Coleridge was not the only Romantic writer to fill his notebooks with visual marks and images. In her "Introduction: Text and Figure" in *Shelley's Visual Imagination* (Cambridge: Cambridge University Press, 2011), 13–16, Nancy Moore Goslee describes the images sketched by Shelley in his notebooks containing drafts of his poems. These, however, are not geometric, nor are they explicitly topographical. They function as figurative and allegorical prompts in Shelley's creative process.

that stretch across the page in order to indicate a break or the beginning of a new notion or observation. Incidentally, the published notebooks do not include these – an editorial decision that unintentionally detracts from Coleridge's lineal sensibility.

It is interesting to note that when Coleridge wrote his entries, he dashed them off following imaginary lines in his notebooks' blank pages. In November 1799, as if registering his desire not to be restricted by the regularity of printed lines and wanting to replicate the freer linear movement of what he was observing, he wrote himself a directive: "Rule your paper lightly with black Lead, write in the Lines – & then rub them out" (*CN* 1:588). Such a practice permitted the looser action of the hand and its observing gestures. If one looks at any page from his manuscript notebooks, one immediately notices the scrawl that, although carrying a faint memory of the ruled line, carelessly stretches from margin to margin and indulges in the less restricted liberties of a moving pencil or pen. As a result, the handwriting frequently alters its course or shape; according to Coleridge's mood, the words slope, bend, and smudge.[11] Moreover, the varying spaces between lines also catch the tenor or character of the moment. All these features offer a sense of immediacy. They allow one to be present with Coleridge at the very moment of his observation.

Because Coleridge was particularly alert to the lines of motion in a landscape, throughout his early notebook entries (and occasionally in his letters) he intermittently dashed off diagrammatic sketches that replicated and traced their evolution. Emerging from the landscape's temporal dynamic, these functioned, as he later admitted, as emblems of time and motion.[12] In a sense, Coleridge with the point of his pencil went out for a walk and drew schematic diagrams that were as active, scruffy, and uneven

---

[11] One is reminded of Tim Ingold's observation that "we fail to recognize the extent to which the very act of writing, at least until it was ousted by typography, lay in the drawing of lines." See *Lines: A Brief History*, 128.

[12] In November 1804 Coleridge wrote the following entry into his notebook. This entry captures Coleridge's sense of landscape as an emblem of motion:

> the Prototyped in Nature is indeed loveliness – there there [*sic*] are no <or all> straight lines, that comprehend having the soul of curves whose from activity & positive rapid energy; give the semblance of straightness – or if it indeed appear whether it seem curve or *straight*, here *is* motion, motion in its most significant form, it is motion in that form, which has been chosen to express motion in general, hieroglyphical from preeminence, & made to mean *all* by being there the most / therefore <tho' it appear all straight, yet there's> no need here of any curve, whose effect is that of embleming motion, & counteracting actual solidity by that emblem / here it is vice versa. (*CN* 2:2343; f. 117)

as the terrain he trod.¹³ With a flourishing gesture of his pencil or pen, he provided visual equivalents to his verbal descriptions of his surroundings. One such occasion was when he followed a description of a mountain ridge in the Highlands:

> – the Mountain ridges so backlike, odd & void of connection or harmonizing Principle. The mountains in perhaps 8 main lines, all pushing toward the Bridge Bank but each so savage, & broken, 4 ridges, the next 7 or 8, semicircle Basons or Coves ⌒⌒⌒⌒⌒ O it is indeed a High Bridge. What can Shappho's Leap have been beyond this? – The building of the Bridge mixes so indistinguishably with the schistous slanting Strata, that form the Banks of the River. (*CN* 1:1489; f. 58)

A few critics have commented on these linear images, but have, I believe, sometimes erroneously proposed that they are either merely surplus appendages or expressions of frustration when words seemed no longer to suffice, such as the time Coleridge, attempting to describe the profile of a mountain, complained of his "miserable Scribble" and proceeded to draw the outline of its peak.¹⁴ I suggest, however, that rather than being some desperate postscript, these hastily rendered drawings and diagrams resolutely blended and worked with Coleridge's written text to represent the lines of motion that come into view and define a landscape's character. As Coleridge once wrote, "Without Drawing I feel myself but half invested with Language" (*CN* 1:1554). Consequently, they are neither extraneous nor some afterthought but, instead, fundamental to his comprehension and representation of what he sees and experiences.

Honoring the character of Coleridge's entries as much as possible, Kathleen Coburn in her meticulously thorough edition of the notebooks includes most of Coleridge's original line drawings.¹⁵ A sampling from the published text follows. In the first volume, for instance, are entries in which he literally traces with his pencil the semicircular lines running up a

---

¹³ Very rarely did Coleridge do drawings in which he replicated shadows and the surfaces of Helm Crag. An example of when he did is *CN* 1:1419, 1420 (f. 26). I think these are the only ones.

¹⁴ Several commentators have looked at these sketches and thought of them as being addenda to the text – an "overflow" – rather than being integral to an entry's meaning. See Dixon, "The Notebooks," 79. Edmund Blunden, for instance, in "Coleridge's Notebooks," *A Review of English Literature* 7.1 (January 1966): 25–30 writes: "The Notebooks carry certain pictorial helps by Coleridge, one or two of them not inartistic, but in general it does not look as if he spent much time or paid much attention in the old-established Drawing School at Christ's Hospital" (29).

¹⁵ Unfortunately, Earl Leslie Griggs's edition of the letters chose not to include most of the line drawings. And sometimes, the original notebooks also contain a sketch that is left out in the published notebooks, such as the line drawing of the ruined sheepfold in *CN* 1:1207. This can be seen in British Library, Add. MS 47497.

wooded bank in Ratzeburgh (*CN* 1:360; f. 45) ⁓⁓/; he tracks the line of a bending bow-like path in the Lake District (*CN* 1:798; f. 33) ⌣, the curving lines of a river falling into Ravenglass Bay (*CN* 1:1205; f. 1)         , and the path of two becks tumbling over stones and eventually joining to create one track of water (*CN* 1:1214; f. 13])         . Later in this first volume, the lead of his pencil traces the course of waterfalls cascading over rocks (*CN* 1:1449; f. 6)         , the curving route of an alder tree bough (*CN* 1:1489; f. 54)         , and the "savage," broken lines of a mountain pushing toward a ridge (*CN* 1:1469; f. 23)         .[16]

---

[16] These examples are taken from entries in the first volume of Coleridge's notebooks that cover the period of his rambling. See, for instance, October 1798 in Ratzeburgh: "The woods on the left bank run up into semicircles & Triangles leaving green banks for the water – ⁓⁓ so the woods run for a mile from Rat"(*CN* 1:360; f. 45); August 1800 (Lake District): "my path bends like a bow ⌣, and again another Bow toward Helvellin / & besides these two bows ⌣⌣ " (*CN* 1:798; f. 33); June–July 1802: " The River now curves, like an *S* – rudely made by a tremulous Hand, as far [as] Drigg, then runs *straight* south into Ravenglass Bay – at King Camp in the middle of the *S* it is joined by the Irt – the Mite . . . comes out of Burnmoor Tairn, between Sca Fell & the Screes, & unfed . . . it runs straight West, & falls into the Bay" (*CN* 1:1205); and in September 1803 a reference to the curves of Ben Nevis that "runs slant" and is "curving round 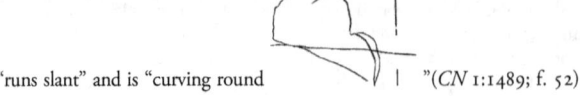 "(*CN* 1:1489; f. 52).

Although these published images proffer some sense of these diagrams' demeanor, they do not fully capture the spontaneity or fluidity of the originals in the manuscript notebooks. Just as Coleridge's handwriting, with its slanting lines, pauses, flourishes, and irregularities, displays the tone of a moment, the original pencil drawings with their less regularized and uneven profiles better expose his excitement as well as the kinetic character of what he is describing. A line drawing illustrating the contour of a coastal cliff that Coleridge saw on his way to Malta in Notebook K. 52 (housed in the Victoria University Library) displays the hurry with which Coleridge turned to the page so that he could quickly capture the landscape's defining lines. More convincingly than the static, evenly printed version of this sketch, this manuscript drawing reveals the speed of his attempt, the varying pressure of the pencil applied to the uneven fabric of the page, and the markings of his multiple efforts to make as accurate a representation as possible during the fleeting moments in which the cliff is visible. Executed by the naked hand and its erratic touch, these penciled lines palpably reflect the impulse of the moment as well as a human presence. The same is true for other line drawings in these manuscript notebooks. Some are tentative; some wobble; others are rubbed out and show Coleridge's mind at work, and yet others run across pages turned or swiveled to create a larger space so as to catch the momentum of a line's motion. And still others, as if honoring the urgency of the moment, overlay his account of another time and unintentionally blend the past and the present.[17]

Yet to be disciplined by the demands of the printed page and not as yet sacrificed to the mechanized control of print which can obviate time and sensation, these manuscript diagrams more readily connect word with deed and more directly become gestures of Coleridge's consciousness and emotional response – an element important to Coleridge, who after reading and taking notes on Christian Garve's *On the Beauty of Mountainous Regions* remarked that "The View of an Extensive Plain, all cultivated, from a high mountain would be merely an amusing object – a curiosity – a map – <a model> – were it not for the imposingness of the situation from

---

[17] One example of this over-layering can be found in British Library, Add. MS 47497, in which Coleridge sketches a map over his account of leaving a Lakeland inn and gazing at Irton Fell:

> Irton Fell, with a deep perpendicular Ravin, with a curious fretted Pillar, of crosier-shaped, standing up in it / but you can look at another but the Screes, which are directly before you, on the right Hand / to the left a rough coppy head Hill, covered with Hazels / the Lake is wholly hidden, & to a stranger the Burst would be very striking / for you come upon it without the least warning / O what a Lake / I am sitting at the foot almost ... (*CN* 1:1213; f. 10)

which we view it – the feelings, possibly worked on by the air etc" (*CN* 1:1675; f. 61).

In her edition of the notebooks, Coburn occasionally attaches textual notes about the position and size of these original sketches so as to compensate for the differences between the printed and manuscript texts. These explanations are helpful, but if one is fully to catch the tenor of the moment as well as the disposition of what Coleridge is describing, one must actually look at the original line drawings. Only by scrutinizing the manuscript notebooks can one more thoroughly appreciate that sometimes in her published text these sketches are wrongly set off in their own spaces and incorrectly left standing alone.[18] For example, in entry *CN* 1:1213 (f. 10) a line drawing illustrating the shape of slanting "Screes" is sequestered in the midst of the printed page, but actually, in the manuscript folio, extends right down through several lines of writing. Traveling downward and appropriately crossing the word "streaking," the drawing more directly catches the rush and force of the image. Interweaving with his scribbled words the original penciled lines offer a more complete and vivid portrait of their subject. In other entries, the hand-drawn diagram shifts from one margin to another, such as the series of lines representing "8 heaps of moss" in Notebook 5½ (British Library, Add. MS 47502). The printed version pushes this diagram from the middle of the journal page to the right-hand margin of the published page.[19]

In particular, seeing these sketches in the context of the manuscript page makes one realize the extent to which Coleridge interlaced his words and images. Reminding one that the hand that writes does not cease to draw, Coleridge's manuscript diagrams often interact with, traverse the path of, or emerge from his handwritten words – sometimes because of a lack of space, sometimes accidentally, and sometimes consciously. Indeed, in the original notebooks, a majority of the manuscript drawings appreciably intermingle with the script so that occasionally Coleridge's handwritten words cluster around a sketch as if impersonating or supporting its distinctive linear shape. For example, in British Library, Add. MS 47502, a diagram of a boulder in a stream is connected to and emerges

---

[18] A close comparison of these manuscripts and their published version occasionally reveals that diagrams are even occasionally overlooked. For instance, a line drawing of a ruined sheepfold in British Library, Add. MS 47497 is not included in the edited notebooks.

[19] In addition to the shifting of a diagram's position on the page, the published notebooks occasionally upset the proportion of Coleridge's sketch on the page. For instance, in British Library, Add. MS 47497, one of Coleridge's diagrams takes up a far larger portion of the page than it does in the published entry.

from the word "huge" that prefaces it; however, in the published entry not only is the diagram of the stone "misquoted" but it is also separated from its qualifying adjective so that one is left with a less powerful sense of the phenomenon of the water rushing and striking this obstruction.[20]

Throughout his early notebooks Coleridge's diagrams and his handwriting often intersect. Look, for instance, at the published diagram in entry *CN* 1:1519 (f. 12):

> Ivy & outhouse, thro' Threlkeld, up Saddleback, over Blenkarthur having the Horse road a great deal to our Right, to Saddleback Tarn/I had quite forgotten the fearfully sublime Precipice & striding Edge on its farther or Northern ⟍⎯ Side, and the colours of this little Tarn, ~~purple~~ blood-crimson, and then Sea

and compare its solitary placement on the printed page with its position in the original notebook (British Library, Add. MS 47513), where the image and the handwriting are not set apart, but rather are executed so that they penetrate each other. Moreover, in the manuscript notebooks, line drawings occasionally mingle with letters and purposefully function as extensions of the surrounding words. A taped-in passage following the manuscript entry 1471 of British Library, Add. MS 47504, for instance, shows that Coleridge has extended the final letters of the last words of the second and third lines so that they drift off into fugitive streaks that neither form subsequent words nor conclude Coleridge's movement of thought: "Heart breathing / for such a⎯⎯ / Being ⎯⌒⎯." These lines glide and wander on as if he were rambling through the landscape of his mind. Moreover, penciled diagrams representing a vibrant contour of a hill or a body of water periodically move directly out of or are attached to the last letter of the word that precedes it. In this way, words turn into line drawings, such as the time when Coleridge, in a manuscript entry, mentions a river and spells it out as if he were depicting its course. In British Library, Add. MS 47497, a long curving line follows the final letter "r" as if replicating what it names. Note, however, that, in the published notebook entry (*CN* 1:1211; f. 8), the sketch of the river's path is absent and the word "River" left alone to exhibit its conventional, regularized form. And consider entry *CN* 1:1210, in which Coleridge writes about the presence of the rapid motion of

---

[20] If one compares the published image of this boulder with Coleridge's diagram in British Library, Add. MS 47502, one will notice that the left side of the original drawing is not reproduced.

clouds. In the handwritten entry, he spreads out the word "presence" as if following with both his eye and pencil the path of the clouds' movement (see British Library, Add. MS 47497). A long undulating line follows the final "e" and dips down into the line below. In this respect, his manuscript entries periodically exhibit a hieroglyphic character and integrate letter and image so that, for instance, the letter "g" in the word "Cragg" (*CN* 1:793; f. 18) crooks in a way that resembles both the word's meaning and its appearance (see British Library, Add. MS 47502). A most striking example is in entry *CN* 1:494 (f. 58), where the images and numbers blend to represent the defining contours of a village. In the entry, Coleridge offers a key to the diagram: "1. A Gentleman's House sweetly buried – Major Trotter's – 2. low Cottages – 3. The Bridge. 4. The grey flat-roofed church peeping between two Tress – 5 – A little neat parsonage house – 6. Meadow – 7. Gentleman's House with an avenue of Trees."

## Line and the Translation of George Beaumont's Landscapes

Perhaps the most concentrated or obvious example of this distinctive use of word and image appears in Coleridge's descriptions of Sir George Beaumont's paintings and sketches. A cluster of notebook entries entirely dedicated to describing Beaumont's picturesque oils and sketches definitively demonstrates not only how indispensable the concept of line was to Coleridge's comprehension and portrayal of a landscape but also how necessary was the interweaving of words and images. Coleridge was eager to create what Morton D. Paley refers to as "pictographs" so as to capture and memorize the scene before his eyes. An account of the circumstances for this exercise follows.[21]

While in his early thirties, Coleridge stayed at least twice with Beaumont and his wife. Significantly, during both visits he spent considerable time studying and taking notes on his host's landscapes with the intention of composing poems about them. One visit was in March 1803 and another in February 1804.[22] The occasion for the first of these was when Coleridge left his family in Keswick and was considering sailing

---

[21] Morton D. Paley, *Samuel Taylor Coleridge and the Fine Arts* (Oxford: Oxford University Press, 2008), 20.
[22] Paley, *Samuel Taylor Coleridge and the Fine Arts*, 18. Sir George Beaumont (1753–1827) was a patron of the arts (who supported both Coleridge and Wordsworth), a collector, and an accomplished amateur landscape painter. He often traveled to the Lake District to paint. As a result, many of his works are now housed in the Wordsworth Museum, Grasmere. Eventually he helped found the National Gallery. He and Lady Beaumont had houses in Essex, London, Leicestershire, and the Lake District. For a discussion of this episode, see Paley, *Samuel Taylor Coleridge and the Fine Arts*, 18–23.

either to Madeira or Malta. As he often did, he sought help and support from others and so contacted the Beaumonts, who invited him to visit.[23] Motivated by not only a lifelong need to be looked after but also a genuine interest in George Beaumont's paintings and sketches, Coleridge accepted, so on September 22, 1803 he posted a letter in which he promised eventually to compose poems based upon his friend's pictures: "If you should really like them, I will go on & make a Volume" (*CL* 2:995). As a result, when he arrived at the Beaumonts' home, Coleridge set to work making elaborate notes on twenty-one of Beaumont's pictures bound together in a "Blue Book" – a collection that was probably later disbound and its drawings scattered.[24] He, however, mislaid his observations and, as with many of his projects, failed to complete what he had planned.[25]

But the project itself was not forgotten. Later, in January 1804, claiming not to have abandoned his desire to "translate" Beaumont's pictures into verse, Coleridge wrote once more to Beaumont and stated that he was still "persuaded of the excellence of the Idea." He pledged that as soon as he was "settled," he would "dedicate a certain portion of my Time to the realizing about 20 [poems] – which I calculate, will be a small Volume, of 13 of which I have already the *leading Idea*." In this letter, after admitting to having lost his previous notes and merely retaining "a floating & general recollection of all, but an accurate & detailed Imagery only of three," he proposed to begin the project again and pay the Beaumonts another visit "if it should be perfectly convenient to you" (*CL* 2:1055).

Once more the generous Beaumonts obliged, so in early February 1804 Coleridge traveled to their Essex home.[26] The results of this short stay before he finally sailed for Malta are thirty-one detailed entries in *CN* 2:1899 (ff. 90–97) dedicated to transcribing, both verbally and visually, a number of his host's sketches – a task he seems, as Paley suggests, to have become absorbed in for its own sake. Which pictures they were is

---

[23] Coleridge decided to go to Malta to regain some sense of equilibrium. He lived in Malta from April 1804 until 1806, when he returned to England. While there he was Acting Public Secretary of Malta under the Civil Commissioner, Alexander Ball.

[24] As so often in Coleridge's writings, the means became the end. Coleridge's notes on Beaumont's pictures occupy a place midway between *aides-memoires* and *ekphrasis*, taking the latter term in its straightforward sense of "the verbal representation of visual representation" (Paley, *Samuel Taylor Coleridge and the Fine Arts*, 19).

[25] Those familiar with Coleridge's life realize that it was full of schemes or projects that were never completed. This is one example of many that possibly resulted from the chaos of his life – his quarrels with his wife, his addiction, and his moving from place to place.

[26] On February 8, 1804 Coleridge wrote to Wordsworth: "I arrived at Dunmow on Tuesday, & shall stay till Tuesday Morning ... I was not received here with mere kindness – I was welcomed *almost* as you welcomed me when first I visited you at Racedown ... Indeed, indeed, they *are* kind & good people" (*CL* 2:1060).

Figure 2   Sir George Beaumont (1753–1827), *Keswick*, 3 July 1798. Pencil and ink wash. The Wordsworth Museum, GRMDC, B377.15. By permission of the Wordsworth Trust.

unknown (except for one) but an ink, watercolor, and gouache sketch from the collection of Beaumont's work in the Wordsworth Museum, Grasmere, gives some sense of their style (see Figure 2).[27]

Coleridge's subsequent diligent and systematic commentary in his notebooks makes it abundantly clear that the leading principle he used to think about translating Beaumont's pictures into poems was line. Consequently, as was his habit while walking through and describing a live, natural landscape, Coleridge, when writing his aides-memoires of Beaumont's paintings, noted the significant contours or edges that trace the motion of a scene and connect one point to another.[28] As a result, in these entries Coleridge does not just verbally catch, for instance, the

---

[27] Exactly which of Beaumont's pictures Coleridge selected is difficult to determine. In her textual notes to the relevant notebook entries, Kathleen Coburn attempts to identify exactly which pictures Coleridge was looking at but repeatedly remarks that she either cannot identify their subject matter or is left to speculate, for instance, that a particular piece is "reminiscent of Peel Castle on the Isle of Man" (*CN* Notes 2:1899.3). See also Paley, *Samuel Taylor Coleridge and the Fine Arts*, 17.

[28] Kathleen Coburn remarks that "In addition to Coleridge's interest in line and colour and composition in general, one notes his kinetic responses – a desire to cross bridges, pass under arches, as in No 29 – and his sentimental and narrative inferences as in Nos 7, 18, and 29" (*CN* Notes 2:1899).

line of a shadow "running out of the Picture," the curving and ascending lines of rising mountains, the "sweep-line of Trees," the course of a river, or the contour of a steep precipice but also illustrates such details by sketching diagrams that follow their trails. See, for example, these drawings from *CN* 2:1899 (f. 91). He also worked out a lineal notational system so that he could navigate the pictures. Paley explains: "**A** would mean the right hand of the picture, **B** the left. A vertical sign like a capital **I** would denote the sideline of the picture frame, while the same horizontally would mean parallel to the lower frame, or with the addition of a small crossbar in the middle parallel to the upper frame."[29] An example of this system in action is entry *CN* 2:1819 (f. 91) describing one of the paintings:

> 5. A fine Rubens-like ~~Gentleman's~~ noble man's Seat with a Cottage (or farm-house) clustered close to A**I**.—all under a mountain rising with two compleat curve lines 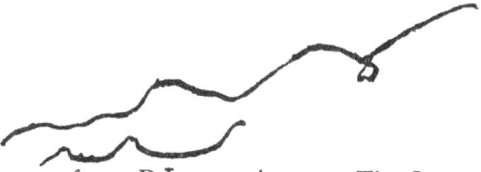 from B.**I**. to A⊢⊣. The Seat on a Hill, smooth **I** in the Front—another Hillock ~~B.**I**.~~ at B**I**. Trees on it, and a man under their Shade—all the middle from B **I** to A **I** a sweep-line of Trees, & the Mansion rising up above them, with Trees climbing up the ~~Hill~~ Mountain behind it.
> **I** Sheep & two figures on the smooth Hill in front.

*f91ᵛ*

Moreover, as was his tendency, Coleridge followed his impulse to survey so would register and follow the course of a river or the outline of a mountain. In his notes on Beaumont's paintings, he concentrated on such details as "A river with well wooded banks thro' a plain with a mountain of the most beautiful outline, – filling the whole background,"

---

[29] Paley, *Samuel Taylor Coleridge and the Fine Arts*, 19.

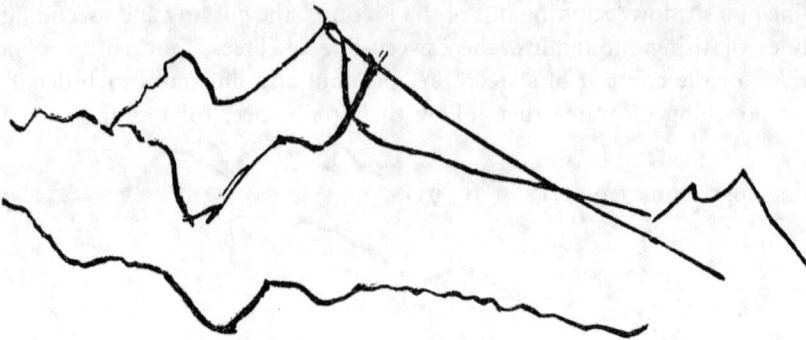

(*CN* 2:1899; f. 93) and would periodically calculate the distances between one point and another. He sometimes recorded such measurements in a manner that recalls the figure of a surveyor with his chain and field notebook:

> Trees, detached rocks, a Cottage with Chimney & *column* of smoke / but the rest of the whole Picture a river in a Woodland Scene – with a very long bridge, railed on the inner side all the way along; not at all on the outer side / but the Half <(not quite 3 ¼) > nearest the House is supported on two Arches / the other Half extending from AI. Four Inches a thick Plank supported by two <parallel> Stakes in the middle ... (*CN* 2:1899; f. 94)

If Coleridge had completed his project and actually translated these notes into verses, it would have been interesting to see how he might have transformed the drawn into the poetic line.[30]

A few years later, in 1806, Coleridge was to attempt another "translation" – yet another uncompleted project. This time it was a scheme to write a poem based on Washington Allston's *Diana and Her Nymphs in the Chase* (Rome, 1805).[31] To prepare for this, Coleridge, in his notebook, once more verbally and visually attended to the various lines that organize the painting's content. He recorded the "Line of the Edge" that is broken by a patch of *"Bushage,"* the trodden Ferns which "almost hide a small Cleft or Fissure in the rock," a noble tree's "graceful Lines of Motion," as well as the boundary lines of the picture's frame. And, as he had also done

---

[30] It is good to be reminded of Wordsworth's "Elegiac Stanzas Suggested by a Picture of Peele Castle in a Storm, Painted by Sir George Beaumont." For a full discussion of Coleridge's sensitivity to line when composing his own poetry, see Chapter 4 of this book.

[31] Washington Allston was an American painter who went to England in 1801 and was admitted to the Royal Academy School. He and Coleridge became friends. In 1814, Allston painted a portrait of Coleridge that hangs in the Dove Cottage Museum.

when analyzing Beaumont's landscapes, he included line drawings that trace its features – this time the contours of a large stone ⌢ and a snowy mountain ⌒⋀ (*CN* 2:2831; ff. 95–96). It is interesting to note that in the midst of describing this painting, Coleridge writes as if he were actually immersed or rambling through its landscape. For example, attending to a large boulder in the Allston painting, he remarks, "I must climb over it to get the prospect of the far valley, hidden by the Stone & the Rock" (*CN* 2:2831; f. 96).[32] Memories of his walking return and elicit the movement and sensations of a living landscape. This commentary is yet another reminder of his sensitivity to his own body's kinetic relationship to its surroundings, discussed in the previous chapter.

### The Context

When focusing on these lines to capture the composition of a landscape, either in a painting or when observing a scene, Coleridge was obviously recalling a topographical tradition that took note of and marked the fixed contours of a mountain, the set path of a river, and the various boundaries that separate a body of water from land – a practice, of course, fully visible in the body and margins of maps as well as in the various published guides to the Lakes in which, for instance, Thomas West directed his readers to follow "the line of shore from Coniston-hall to the upper end of the lake" so that they could see Coniston Lake spread "itself into a noble expanse of transparent water" (*A Guide to the Lakes*, 51). This convention prompted other writers such as William Gilpin to suggest that when gazing at a mountain, visitors to the Lakes should first attend to "it's line" before noting "the *objects*, which adorn it's surface – it's *tints* – and it's *light* and *shade*."[33] And the practice occasioned John Housman's tendency to alert his readers to such topographical markers as a road's "winding lines" or

---

[32] In *Samuel Taylor Coleridge and the Fine* Arts, Paley also comments on this characteristic: "one special aspect of Coleridge's ekphrasis should be mentioned, his introducing his reader and himself *into* the scene" (23).

[33] William Gilpin, *Observations, Relative Chiefly to Picturesque Beauty 1786* (Poole: Woodstock Books, 1996), 82–83. In *Topographies*, J. Hillis Miller emphasizes the instinct to show how lines in maps influence a work of art. He comments:

"the line" of a lake's shore.³⁴ Given this orientation, it is not surprising that William Hutchinson, depending on their presence, lamented the loss of a landscape's lines as a result of a fog or a cloud.³⁵

Coleridge was also probably prompted by definitions of the picturesque, which often dwelt on the concept of line and, therefore, drew attention to the preferred irregularity, roughness, and variety of a landscape's lines. Gilpin, for example, insisted that the picturesque nature of a distant mountain depended, in a great measure, not only on "the line it traces along the sky" (*Observations*, 82–83) but also upon the variety of its contour. Uvedale Price too, when describing the intricate ways of "hollow lanes and bye roads" in *On the Picturesque* (1796), spoke of the broken, irregular line as a necessary condition of this aesthetic:

> the banks [are] sometimes broken and abrupt; sometimes smooth, and gently but not uniformly sloping; now wildly over-hung with thickets of trees and bushes; now loosely skirted with wood; no regular verge of grass, no cut edges, no distinct lines of separation; all is mixed and blended together, and the border of the road itself, shaped by the mere tread of passengers and animals, is as unconstrained as the footsteps that formed it; even the tracks of the wheels (for no circumstance is indifferent) contribute to the picturesque effect of the whole; the lines they describe are full of variety; they just mark the way among trees and bushes . . . .³⁶

> paths are discursive fissures setting boundaries, dividing this side from that side. Paths give the world edges and measures. They also join this place to this place. They establish a place where opposition between earth in its self-enclosures and world in its openness can be brought out, in an intimacy of proximity and distance. The paths are also clefts. The paths in a given terrain form a rudimentary design. They make a legible pattern like the features of a face or the preliminary sketch for a building or a painting . . . Any work of art as such, poem, painting, song, statue, or temple, is only an extension of the work of art made when roads are laid out. (14–15)

³⁴ John Housman, *A Descriptive Tour, and Guide to the Lakes, Caves, Mountains, and Other Natural Curiosities in Cumberland, Westmorland, Lancashire, and a Part of the West Riding of Yorkshire* (Carlisle: F. Jollie, 1800), 79, 120.

³⁵ William Hutchinson, *An Excursion to the Lakes in Westmoreland and Cumberland; with a Tour through Part of the Northern Counties, in the Years 1773 and 1774* (London: J. Wilkie, 1776), 148. On several occasions in this work, Hutchinson remarks on the lines in a landscape. For instance, when bemoaning the fact that the antiquities in Ambleside are "almost defaced," he gazes at the traces of one site that forms "an oblong square with obtuse angles" and follows its "lines now distinguishable" that are "one hundred and thirty paces in length and one hundred in breadth" (184).

³⁶ Uvedale Price, *On the Picturesque* (Ottley: Woodstock Books, 2000 [1796]), 29–30.

Although Coleridge's consideration of a landscape's contours and composition certainly must have partially taken its cue from the perspective of the topographical observer – especially from Price's lively passage quoted above – his interest in a scene's lines is far more indebted to his desire to trace the force of their motion in a landscape rather than a map-like rendition of a region's contours. As I have already suggested, Coleridge was not just interested in plotting a landscape but was more intent on replicating its emerging organic vitality – a different view altogether. His animated, shifting portraits of mountains in his notebooks, therefore, obviously have little affinity with the set, systematized graphs of mountains drawn by Gilpin in his *Observations, Relative Chiefly to Picturesque Beauty* (1772) to illustrate which of their outlines was either "the truest source of beauty" or "disagreeable" and "disgusting."[37]

To exemplify this point, one figure in Gilpin's text displays the various settled shapes of a mountain: one with "Round swelling lines without any break," another with a contour of "easy lines," and yet another with "Parallel lines." Each graph embraces a stolid, everlasting form and expels the fluctuations of weather, time, and place. They are stultified abstractions that override the organic conditions of light, shadow, movement, or change; they carry no tactile memory of a mountain's sensual exterior, its irregular ground, and its hidden crevices.

Coleridge's lineal perspective, however, was not solely indebted to a contemporary topographical mode or commentary on the picturesque. It seems also to have been participating in a more comprehensive orientation shared, as well as modified, by generations of writers and painters, who either preceded or followed Coleridge and who relied on traveling, linear rhythms to replicate the energy and form of what they were representing. During Coleridge's lifetime, for instance, there is the example of Laurence Sterne's linear diagrams in *The Life and Opinions of Tristram Shandy*,

---

[37] Analytically William Gilpin lists and draws examples of those lines that are "the truest source of beauty" to those that are "disagreeable" and "disgusting." See Gilpin, *Observations*, 83. For instance, he proclaims:

> Mountains *in composition* are considered as *single* objects, and follow the same rules. If they break into mathematical, or fantastic forms – if they join heavily together in lumpish shapes – if they fall into each other at right-angles – or if their lines run parallel – in all these cases, the combination will be more or less disgusting; and a converse of these will of course be agreeable. (*Observations*, 84)

In fairness, however, it should be pointed out that Gilpin preferred a composition showing a variety of lines, a concept that often is expressed in Coleridge's descriptions.

*Gentleman* (1761–67), especially those that track the evolutionary progress of the novel's narrative in volume 6, chapter 40 and that

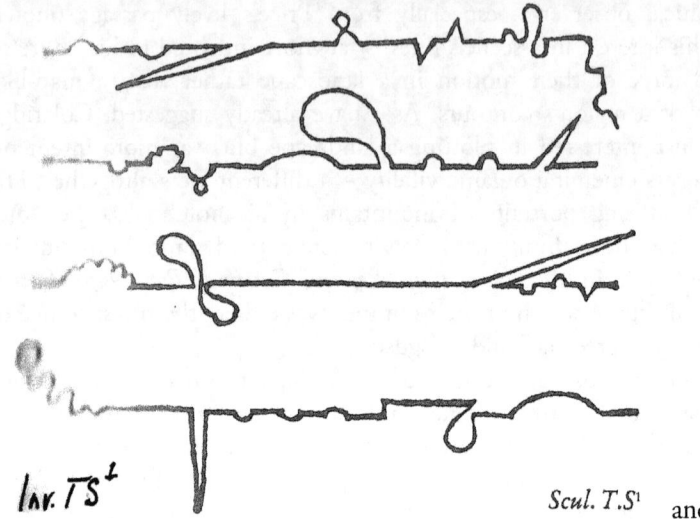

and that, later in the book (volume 9, chapter 4) trace the flourishing course of the corporal's walking stick as it wafts through the air. This diagram not only gives the reader a sense of the visual experience of watching the corporal but also reproduces the length of its motion in time. Sterne's lines are temporal gestures of movement. And there is the page in A. Walker's little-known *Remarks Made in a Tour from London to the Lakes of Westmoreland and Cumberland* (1792) in which the author, as if following Sterne's example, with his pen, replicates or inscribes the movement or what he refers to as the "progress" of the narrative journey depicted on a tapestry he sees in Paris. Walker explains: "The Story rises under the hand of the Artist as if it were by

Magic! – for the progress is by no means in a straight line, but goes on in this direction" (171):[38]

It is interesting to find this impulse in such a minor publication as Walker's account of his travels. The discovery of the line drawing in this publication suggests that more is going on than a cultural interest in cartography or topography. It advises that these writers were also probably beholden to the eighteenth-century practice of diagramming phenomena – an impulse that continues to find expression in subsequent decades. Take, for instance, Edward Lear's 1869 diary entry in which he comically diagrams Miss Alderson's "bad singing" that he had endured while listening to her perform "The Last Rose of Summer." Lear's lineal depiction of the event certainly allows the reader to sympathize with Lear and vividly illustrates his thought that "I had rather have had a tooth taken out" than have been obliged to listen (see Figure 3).[39] Lear captures the unpleasant trail and movement of the singer's vocal sounds as they meander through the air and grate upon the ear. Notice that the graphic lines, as they often did in Coleridge's notebooks, flow out of the words that precede them. They are the physical counterpart of what they describe.

To some extent, Sterne, Walker, and Lear – and so too Coleridge – are all inheritors of a diagrammatic culture that became popular after the publication of Denis Diderot and Jean le Rond d'Alembert's seventeen-volume *Encyclopédie* (1762–77).[40] With its 2,569 reductive, diagrammatic plates published separately in eleven of these volumes, this encyclopedia offered, at a glance, an immediate chance to grasp the whole of what was being described. These engraved images illuminated or clarified various entities and mechanical operations that otherwise were difficult to depict

---

[38] In *Lines: A Brief History*, Tim Ingold observes: "just as the weaver's shuttle moves back and forth as it lays down the weft, so the writer's pen moves up and down, leaving a trail of ink behind it. But this trail, the letter-line, is no more the same as the line of text than is the line on a tapestry the same as the lines of its constituent threads" (69–70).

[39] For this reference to Lear's reaction to Miss Alderson's recital, I am thankful for Sara Lodge's *Inventing Edward Lear* (Cambridge, MA: Harvard University Press, 2019), 26—27.

[40] Coleridge would have, of course, been familiar with this encyclopedia. He would also have been reading its predecessor compiled by Ephraim Chambers. Chambers's *Cyclopaedia: or, An Universal Dictionary of Arts and Sciences* (London: James & John Knopton, John Darby and others, 1729) went through a number of printings in the eighteenth century. Its 1753 supplement contained two folio volumes with twelve plates. One plate is devoted to exhibiting geometric diagrams: "Tables showing Trigonometry."

Figure 3  Edward Lear's diagram of Miss Alderson's singing "The Last Rose of Summer," October 1869.
From Edward Lear's diaries 1858–88, D23. Houghton Library, Harvard University, MS Eng 797.3 (15).

verbally.[41] Take, for instance, the plate illustrating the *patissier* (vol. 8). The top half shows a full view of the shop and the second half (the bottom half) depicts a clear and deliberate lineal representation of each cooking utensil from that venue.[42] These tools of the trade are outlined in a methodical, diagrammatic way so that they function to educate the viewer/reader as simply and straightforwardly as possible. And like so many of the other depictions, these plates show a sensitivity to line. One striking instance of this feature can be found in the medical sections of the *Encyclopédie*, where one can regard, for instance, a plate that displays a human form, stripped of its flesh and bones so as to reveal and follow the tangle and threads of nerves – a mesh of interweaving lines – that run through the body.

Although Coleridge was by no means literally copying Diderot, he must have been indebted to a cultural impulse to diagram one's surroundings. His line drawing of a village (*CN* 1:494) already reproduced in this chapter is a perfect example of the desire to depersonalize, flatten, and strip down what is a complex image or construction and would take many paragraphs verbally to describe into something manageable and immediately graspable.[43] Like the illustrations in the encyclopedia, his diagramming makes the knowledge handily visible as well as complements his desire to capture the defining lines of a place. However, notably, not all is similar, for Coleridge's sensitivity to the motion in a landscape made it impossible for him completely to follow Diderot's lead and construct line drawings that are fixed, still, and autonomous. As already discussed, Coleridge's

---

[41] For a thorough description and discussion concerning the nature of these plates, see Stephen Werner's *Blueprint: A Study of Diderot and the Encyclopédic Plates* (Birmingham, AL: Summa Publications, 1993).

[42] For a history of this culture see John Bender and Michael Marrinan. *The Culture of the Diagram* (Stanford, CA: Stanford University Press, 2010).

[43] In *Samuel Taylor Coleridge and the Fine Arts*, Paley remarks that Coleridge's "'kinetic' quality" goes back at least to Diderot (23).

diagrams are fluid and integrated into his verbal descriptions so that they become part of the rhythms of thought and speech. Unlike the illustrations in the *Encyclopédie*, Coleridge's do not stand alone surrounded by a white margin but, instead, intermingle with the verbal passages and register the motion of what precedes and follows them.

It is this keenness to let the diagrammatic lines record or disclose the movement of what he is representing that distinguishes Coleridge's line drawings. And it is this impulse that links what Coleridge was doing in the late eighteenth and early nineteenth centuries to such works as Henri Ottmann's *The Luxembourg Station in Brussels* (1903), a painting (on display in the Art Gallery of Ontario) which focuses almost entirely on the long, energetic bend of multiple railroad tracks (their abstracted lines take up over two thirds of the canvas) that actively trace the movement of the steam locomotives traveling out of and into the Luxembourg railway station. These diagrammatic lines are essentially the subject of this painting. They sweep, curve, and press forward to catch or portray for the viewer the very motion, power, speed, and direction of the locomotives that are barely visible to the eye. And one is tempted to recall Winifred Nicholson's twentieth-century paintings of Cumberland that capture the defining lines of a prospect as well as to recollect Richard Long's "A Line Made by Walking" (England, 1967), a photograph that displays a worn track registering the tread of Long's feet repeatedly walking to and fro along a section of the landscape that emerges from a group of trees and extends straight into a meadow. The resulting path reflects the Inuit belief that "*as soon as a person moves he becomes a line.*"[44] Moreover, it is a photograph that recalls a section of an August 1800 poem in which Wordsworth wistfully remembers a path his absent brother John had worn by restlessly pacing back and forth in a grove they haunted while attending school in Hawkshead ("When, to the Attractions of the Busy World," lines 43–66).[45]

But most notably and perhaps surprising to some, one cannot overlook the theoretical and structural importance of the active lines that trace movement in the making of Paul Klee's and Wassily Kandinsky's paintings, a focus that has its origins in ancient Greek mathematics – a discipline that we shall see in the next chapter heavily influenced Coleridge. The modernist and the Romantic share this tradition. Basing

---

[44] Ingold, *Lines: A Brief History*, 75.
[45] I am grateful to Heather Glen for directing my attention to Winifred Nicholson (1893–1981) and her paintings of Cumberland. See Jovan Nicholson, *Winifred Nicholson in Cumberland* (Kendal: Abbott Hall Art Gallery, 2016).

their respective theories on Euclidean geometry that grounds its spatial imagination on the idea of a line that travels or extends between two points,[46] Klee and Kandinsky when speaking about their compositions dwelt upon this basic structural, geometrical element to generate and construct their works of art. As if replicating Coleridge's perspective when describing a landscape, they too attended to the lines of force that emerge, stretch out between points, and give form to their paintings or sketches of a scene.[47] The following illustrations showing a point "in dynamic terms" from Paul Klee's *The Thinking Eye* and from his *Pedagogical Sketchbook*

display Klee's reliance upon those lines that evolve from the point of departure and move between or connect one location to another to create an image.[48] As Klee once remarked, the point sets itself in motion,

---

[46] "Geometry" means "Earth Measuring." Book I of Euclid's Geometry always begins, as does this chapter, with a list of geometrical definitions. The first is that "A point is that which hath no parts, or which hath no magnitude"; the second is that "A line is length without breadth," and the third is that "A straight line is that which lies evenly between its extreme points." See, for instance, Robert Simson, MD, *The Elements of Euclid: viz The First Six Books*, 16th ed. (London: F. Wingrave, 1814), 5. The edition of Euclid prepared for the students of the Royal Mathematical School at Christ's Hospital when Coleridge was there is James Hodgson's *A System of the Mathematics, Volume 1 Containing the Euclidian Geometry* (London: Thomas Page, William and Fisher Mount, 1723). In that edition, the definition of line reads: "A *Line* then hath only *Length*, and is bounded by *Points*." Paul Klee often remarks on his indebtedness to mathematics. In *The Thinking Eye* (London: Lund Humphries, 1961), he writes,

> Mathematics and physics proved a lever in the form of rules to be observed or contradicted. They compel us – a salutary necessity – to concern ourselves first with the function and not with the finished form. Algebraic, geometrical, and mechanical problems are steps in our education towards the essential, towards the functional as opposed to the impressional. We learn to see what flows beneath, we learn the prehistory of the visible. We learn to dig deep and to lay bare. To explain, to analyse. (69)

[47] In his *Biographia Literaria*, Coleridge remarks on this principle. He writes: The first and most simple construction in space is the point in motion, or the line. Whether the point is moved in one and the same direction, or whether its direction is continually changed, remains as yet undetermined. But if the direction of the point have been determined, it is either by a point without it, and then there arises the strait line which encloses no space; or the direction of the point is not determined by a point without it, and then it must flow back again on itself, that is, there arises a cyclical line ... (*CC* 7.1:249–50)

[48] Klee, *The Thinking Eye*, 105; Paul Klee, *Pedagogical Sketchbook*, trans. Sibyl Moholy-Nagy (New York: Praeger, 1972), 17.

"moves off," and a line comes into being – "It goes out for a walk" (*The Thinking Eye*, 24, 105).⁴⁹ So many of Klee's paintings follow this principle and evolve from his hand holding a painting tool and traveling or sometimes wandering from point to point.⁵⁰ One painting that comes to mind is his *Child Consecrated to Suffering* of 1915.⁵¹ In this haunting painting, the child's face emerges as a series of lines (clear, long, black strokes) that start at one point and end in another so as to create a portrait that almost appears to be a composite of triangles, ellipses, circles, and curves.⁵²

In a mode similar to Klee's, Kandinsky was just as alert to the principal importance of line and remarked on the twists and turns of an emerging line that "experiences many fates" on his canvasses. For instance, he often spoke of the ways in which a "line curves, refracts, presses forward, unexpectedly changes direction" (*Complete Writings on Art*, 1:426), as well as thickens and thins.⁵³

---

⁴⁹ For Klee's discussion on the nature of line, see his *Pedagogical Sketchbook*, 16–19, 30, 47–49. For Kandinsky's discussion of line see *Kandinsky: Complete Writings on Art*, vol. 1: *1901–1921* and vol.. 2: *1922–1943* (London: Faber and Faber, 1982), 1:424–27, 2:505–671.
⁵⁰ It is interesting to note that Klee wrote with his right hand but drew and painted with his left.
⁵¹ Paul Klee's *Child Consecrated to Suffering* is owned by the Albright-Knox Art Gallery in Buffalo, New York.
⁵² Interestingly, just as Coleridge had combined writing and line, Klee's paintings often fuse the two so that many of his paintings display a hieroglyphic character. In *Child Consecrated to Suffering*, for instance, the *W* is a verbal/visual pun that both suggests the knotted lines of a worried brow and recalls its sound *weh*, which in German means "suffering" or "sorrow." This punning continues throughout the portrait. The *W* multiplies and patterns the child's hair, enclosing the child in suffering. Klee combines word and image in other paintings, such as *A Leaf from the Town Records* (1928) and his *Vocal Fabric of the Singer Rosa Silber* (1922). For a discussion of Klee's work, see "Klee and the Fantasy of Synthesis" in Ann C. Colley's *The Search for Synthesis in Literature and Art: The Paradox of Space* (Athens: University of Georgia Press, 1990), 47–66.
⁵³ Kandinsky's line drawings that illustrate this point are to be found in Kandinsky's *Complete Writings on Art*, 2:605.

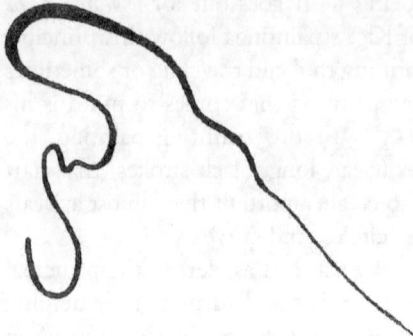

Kandinsky's remarks not only remind one of Klee's reflections on the changing character of lines as they move through and represent the forces composing a picture's subject matter but also recall Coleridge's own sensitivity to the changing and evolving character of these organic lines: for instance, when he remarks on a river that moves in "a strait Line to a curve" (*CN* 1:1450; f. 6), the stream that "widens from a foot to a yard & a half" (*CN* 1:753; f. 3), the "narrowing Line of Day-light" (*CN* 1:1823; f. 62), an "elliptical line" of a hill that "curves in a circle-segment" (*CN* 1:1225; f. 28), and the outlines of the setting sun on the water that narrow and almost become "points" (*CN* 1: 1405; f. 48).[54] These artists' inclination to apprehend and express the dynamic vitality of a space by means of lines that emerge and journey from one point to another is no different from Coleridge's.

## A Geometric Footing

In all these examples, there lurks the shadow of a geometric underpinning, a memory of geometric diagrams that utilize line to organize space and recall a mathematical set of relations. One recalls the fact that diagrams have a long history in mathematics,[55] and that Euclid's proofs are inherently diagrammatic.

When Sterne was drawing his lineal diagrams in *Tristram Shandy*, for instance, he participated in an ekphrastic device that translated a

---

[54] The entry reads: "Wednesday, June 29th, 1803. The Sun setting red over Wythop Fells, as I looked steadily at it, then glanced up above it, below on the water / [?over] that a number of black Orbs all as in a mirror – when the Sun dipped they followed the Shape, now ◯, now semicircles, now ⌒, and now almost to points –" (*CN* 1:1405; f. 48).

[55] For instance, ancient Babylonian clay tablets show diagrammatic proofs of mathematical problems, as do ancient Egyptian, Chinese, and Indian mathematical texts.

visual-mathematical paradigm into a narrative one, creating what Alex Solomon understands as an exchange between the conventions of novelistic narration and the geometric diagram.[56] And, as I have pointed out, Klee's and Kandinsky's concept of a line emerges from its geometric and mathematical footing. This groundwork is also very much at play in Coleridge's landscape descriptions. Influenced by his training in Euclidean geometry, Coleridge did not just call upon the tangible, visible lines discussed in this chapter but also utilized the abstracting lines attending the geometric figure – a phenomenon that is occasionally, but briefly, recognized when, for instance, Coburn speaks of Coleridge's desire to merge the individual into the abstract or when Dixon writes of Coleridge's "painterly tendency towards a distillation of fleeting natural phenomena into abstract, geometrical forms."[57] As we shall see, far more than his fellow poets and writers of descriptive prose, Coleridge, throughout the early notebooks, relied upon the geometric line. These and the geometric idiom in his renditions of landscape are the subject of the next chapter. This additional dimension is as significant and as integral to his descriptions as his consciousness of the visible lines of motion. And, as will emerge in Chapter 4, this geometric underpinning is also at play when in his composing of a number of his so-called nature poems.

---

[56] See Alex Solomon, "The Novel and the Bowling Green: Toby Shandy's Diagrammatic Realism," *Philological Quarterly* 95.2 (2016): 269–91 and Paley's observation: "This 'kinetic' quality, as Coburn's note aptly calls it, is not Coleridge's invention; entering the picture as an ekphrastic device goes back at least to Diderot, but it is notable how much Coleridge *enjoys* the fantasy" (*Samuel Taylor Coleridge and the Fine Arts*, 23).

[57] Dixon, "The Notebooks," 79.

CHAPTER 3

# A Geometric Frame of Mind

> Geometry ... supplies philosophy with the example of a primary intuition, from which every science that lays claim to *evidence* must take its commencement. The mathematician does not begin with a demonstrable proposition, but with an intuition, a practical idea.
>
> (CC 7.1:250)

### Geometridae

While studying at the University of Göttingen in 1799, Coleridge attended lectures delivered by Johann Friedrich Blumenbach, a physician and naturalist whose *A Manual of the Elements of Natural History* (first published in 1779–80) caught his especial notice. In this handbook, Blumenbach describes an order of caterpillars named *Geometridae* that, lacking the full complement of prolegs, must find their way by clasping a leaf or a twig with their front legs, then drawing up and clutching with their rear appendages, reach out for a new front attachment. In this mode the geometric caterpillar makes its way and gives the impression of calculating and outlining its journey in a manner similar to that of a surveyor or geometer who measures and diagrams the earth – this caterpillar even leaves a line of secretion behind to mark or diagram its route.[1]

This manner of moving through and evaluating a landscape would not have necessarily been alien to Coleridge, for, as I have already noted, like this species of caterpillar, Coleridge, when wending his way during his walking years (1798–1804), not only traced a landscape's lines, measured

---

[1] In volume 2 of William Kirby and William Spence's *An Introduction to Entomology: or Elements of the Natural History of Insects* (London: Longman, Hurst, Rees, Orme and Brown, 1817), there is the following passage: "Many caterpillars that feed upon the trees, particularly the geometers, have often occasion to descend from branch to branch ... Their name of geometer was given them, because they seem to measure the surface they pass over, as they walk, with a chain. If you place one upon your hand, you will find that they draw a thread as they go" (292).

its dimensions, and diagrammed its forms; he also, as we shall see in this chapter, elicited the geometric idiom to help him capture the shape of a scene's particulars. Even after he had last pulled on his walking boots in 1805 and was no longer hastily recording descriptions of what he saw while tramping through the countryside, his inclination to discover geometric constructions in what he beheld persisted. For example, in an 1821 fictitious didactic letter to a second-year undergraduate, Coleridge, perhaps thinking of Plotinus's directive, encouraged his "dear young friend" to "compare the process pursued by Nature, with that of the geometrician," and admitted that he, himself, seldom looked "at a fine prospect in mountain landscapes, or even a grand picture [as we saw in his treatment of Beaumont's paintings discussed in the previous chapter], without abstracting the lines." Tellingly, he added that he rather envied those who amused themselves "in the geometrical construction of leaves and flowers" (*CC* 11.1:940).

It was this orientation that also prompted Coleridge's admiration for William Kirby and William Spence's *An Introduction to Entomology* that described the shape of an earwig's wings as "the quadrant of a circle," portrayed a butterfly's body as a "zig-zag Line with vertical angles," and rendered the flight of moths as a formation of circles and equal triangles "placed end to end" (2:370). Moreover, for similar reasons, he appreciated R. A. F. de Réaumur's account of a river that flowed "in jointed and articulated triangles of silver light" (*CC* 13:74). Coleridge, it seems, was one of many for whom the pattern and form of geometrical figures facilitated the unlocking of the universe's structure[2] – though he was quick to point out that such an approach had its limitations, for geometry's reasoning did not fully engage the mind's thoughtful, imaginative faculty.

In spite of this qualification, however, Coleridge, to a greater extent than his literary companions, frequently unearthed the geometrical figures embedded in a landscape; he even occasionally spotted them within a person's gestures, such as the time he saw a widow marking the outlines of a circle with her hand while she talked (*CC* 6:209). As a result, his notebooks, composed during his walking years, are filled with scattered references to triangles, perpendiculars, ellipses, parallelograms, convex

---

[2] In *Wordsworth's Cambridge Education* (Cambridge: Cambridge University Press, 1957), Ben Ross Schneider, Jr. observes: "In those days it [geometry] was the key that unlocked the secrets of the universe, for by means of geometry alone, particularly Euclid's Book VI, 'so necessary to be known', [Sir Isaac] Newton had constructed his system of the world. Hence eighteenth-century philosophers believed that all natural phenomena could be explained by geometrical reasoning" (97).

semicircles, pyramids, angles, squares, inverted arches, ovals, and spheres, all of which helped him record the shapes of mountains, streams, rivers, clouds, bays, and flocks of birds he saw while trudging through the hills and byways of his many rambles. These recall "the grand outline & perpetual Forms" that he once perceived as "the guardians of Borrodale" (*CN* 1:1610; f. 71).

In particular, entries jotted down in the enthusiasm of the moment when walking alone abound with references to the geometric form. Perhaps one of the most graphic instances occurred, in October 1803, when Coleridge observed a murmuration of starlings "Borne along like smoke." Their collective flight shifts from one geometric figure to another:

> now it shaped itself into a circular area, inclined – now they formed a Square – now a Globe – now from complete Orb into an Ellipse – then oblongated into a Balloon with the Car suspended, now a concave Semicircle; still expanding, or contracting, thinning or condensing, now glimmering and shivering, now thickening, deepening, blackening! (*CN* 1:1589; f. 56)[3]

Throughout the notebooks, other examples catch the attention, among which are a "flat pink-colour'd stone painted over in jagged circles & strange parallelograms with the greenish black-spotted lichens" (*CN* 1:227; f. 36), the "broad low Hills" that "sink in a long gentle under curve of an Ellipse" (*CN* 1:1462; f. 16), and a mountain's wild "angular outline ... rising in triangles" and "sinking in inverting arches" (*CN* 1:1224; f. 24). Over the years, this sensitivity continued so that, for example, while walking in Scotland in 1803, he gazed at a cone-shaped mountain connected by a "semicircular Bason" to a "rude triangle-shaped Mountain, of equal Height" (*CN* 1:1487; f. 44), and months later, after his more ambitious walking days were over, a depressed Coleridge persisted by staring at "The Sea stretched out" before him and noticing that its surface was inscribed with "half gently ruffled ... curves and semicircles" (*CN* 2:2637; f. 90). Moreover, on his way back from Malta to England in October 1805, these geometric allusions re-emerged to guide his hastily

---

[3] This entry is a later version of what first appeared in his notebook on Wednesday, November 27, 1799:

> Starlings in vast flights drove along like smoke, mist, or any thing misty [without] volition – now a circular area inclined [in an] arc – now a globe – [now from a complete orb into an] elipse & oblong – [now] a balloon with the [car suspend] ed, now a concaved [sem]icircle & [still] it expands & condenses, some [moments] glimmering & shivering, dim & shadowy, now thickening, deepening, blackening! – (*CN* 1:582; f. 1)

written impression of a ruined tower perched on a mountain rock. The resulting notebook entry reveals an excitement both tempered and extended by a geometric frame of mind:

> O what a scene / Four ⋀'s / the first obtuse angled lying upon the 2nd larger, higher, & still more obtuse-angled / the 3rd & 4th abreast, with a high Tower like a Minaret between / the 3rd more acute-angled than the 1 & 2, even had its line been prolonged to the Top, but its Top is a very sharp-angled Sugar loaf / the 4th a gibbous Shape, struggling between a Triangle & semi circle / on these two the wild nest of House & Churches / the whole of the Surface from Top to Bottom grandly varied, & its forms so very distinct a feature. (*CN* 2:2690; f. 89)

As the preceding example demonstrates, this propensity to discover geometric figures in the landscape is made even more compelling by his intermittent habit of diagramming (a practice discussed in the previous chapter) as well as his commenting on the angles of the shapes that emerge before him. In August 1802, for instance, while rambling among the fells, he remarked on "a delightful ⋂ angle of sheltered Land" (*CN* 1:1209; f. 6), and while walking in the Lake District, he diagrammed the dripping water that fell from "a semiround stone" into a "tarn oval ⬭" (*CN* 1:784; f. 13). Furthermore, in August 1803, when touring in Scotland, he quickly sketched an outline of a road that "climbs on the side of the Hill a 100 yards leaving the stream on one's right beneath it in its green ellipse of grassiness – a cottage at the end of this ⌐ A a gravel end wall upstanding, in ruin, the other part inhabited, 7 trees, three of them blighted" (*CN* 1:1439; f. 9). Note that he marked this linear sketch with letters as in a geometric figure, a device he also used when writing to Samuel Purkis and outlining the view before Greta Hall in July 1800. The passage reads: "Close behind me at the foot of Skiddaw flows the Greta, I hear it's murmuring distinctly – then it curves round almost in a semicircle, & is now catching the purple Lights of the scattered Clouds above it directly before me – ⌇ A. A. A. Is the river & B. my House.— (*CL* 1:615).

Quite naturally the question arises: Why would Coleridge, who was so drawn to the moving, wild, shifting, tangible sensuous images discussed in the previous chapters, periodically turn to these geometric figures? Why would he evoke these stilted two-dimensional forms that exist outside time and space, have no breadth, no back or front, no sound, and no depth; why call to mind figures that cast no light and belong to a world without shadow? Furthermore, why, when describing a landscape, would Coleridge, who himself once criticized the "tyrannically strait parallelogram inclosures" of Egremont Castle's gardens (*CN* 1:1211; f. 7), rely on a practice thought by many to be "disgusting" or "deforming," such as the ornamental shaping of trees into cones, globes, and pyramids to create geometric landscapes? Indeed, why seemingly contradict those who believed that the "imagination revolts from the mathematical account of vision"? – a conviction that William Gilpin, in his 1791 *Remarks on Forest Scenery*, reiterated when he complained of the imposed geometric shapes that intrude upon and destroy the attraction of a wild, irregular setting:

> A copse is a plot of ground, portioned off for the purpose of nurturing wood. Of course, it must be fenced from cattle; and these fences, which are in themselves disgusting, generally form the copse into a square, a rhomboid or some other regular figure; so that we have not only a deformity; but a want also of a connecting tye between the wood and the plain. Instead of a softened, undulating line, we have a harsh fence.[4]

Given Coleridge's fascination with the uncultivated, irregular wild hills and rivers of his rambles, his propensity to honor and utilize the fixed geometric idiom is perhaps confusing. I suggest, however, that his attraction to the geometric figure is neither perplexing nor inconsistent. Like many in his generation, Coleridge was indeed immersed in an environment that nurtured a geometric frame of mind and believed in a mathematical ordering of an external universe. But, as we shall see in the concluding section of this chapter, this orientation did not negate Coleridge's sensitivity to the shifting fluidity and vitality of what he saw on his rambles.[5] From his perspective, neither the geometric nor the

---

[4] William Gilpin, *Remarks on Forest Scenery, and Other Woodland Views*, vol. 1 (London: R. Blamire, 1791), 230.

[5] Humphrey House in *Coleridge: The Clark Lectures 1951–52* (London: Rupert Hart-Davis, 1967) cautions his readers not to minimize the importance to Coleridge of the external world in which he lived. House fears that "we run the risk of diverting attention from some of his most characteristic strengths as a writer ... Even his critical idealism, whether expressed in poems or in his more technical philosophy, is grounded in a minute analysis of the phenomena of the sense" (14).

sensuous experience invalidated, smothered, precluded, or revolted against the other. Rather, both perspectives worked together to capture the vivid character of a scene.

## Part One: A Euclidean Culture

To begin answering the questions posed above, it is necessary first to review, in some detail, Coleridge's mathematical education both at Christ's Hospital School and at the University of Cambridge in order more fully to understand his attachment to a culture defined by a Euclidean sense of space. Without this backdrop, Coleridge's regard for the geometric form might otherwise seem all too causal and perfunctory – even accidental. But not so. Euclid's *Elements* was a standard and important part of the educational curriculum. As a young Coleridge was to find out, a thorough knowledge of Euclidean geometry was sacrosanct among his immediate intellectual and scientific communities during the late eighteenth and early nineteenth centuries; hence the emphasis upon it in his education. Non-Euclidean geometry, although making waves in Europe, had not yet fully reached English shores. Only a handful of British mathematicians, such as Thomas Reid in his 1764 *Inquiry into the Human Mind: On the Principles of Common Sense*, were beginning to challenge the Euclidean system of arranging and viewing space.[6]

### Christ's Hospital School (1782–1791)

Coleridge's awareness of the geometric idiom and its relevance to the physical structure of his surroundings, as well as to metaphysical thought, began with his training at Christ's Hospital School in London, a well-respected charitable educational institution initially founded in 1552 for the "poor and helpless".[7] At the age of nine, several months after his father's death in 1781 and with the support of the local curate, Coleridge was accepted at Christ's Hospital School.[8] Donning the yellow

---

[6] See Chapter 5 of this book for a full discussion of the challenges to Euclid and the coming of non-Euclidean geometry. The chapter also discusses Coleridge's perspective in terms of Thomas Reid's "Geometry of Visibles," a concept that often places Reid among the earliest of the non-Euclidean geometers in Britain.

[7] "Particulars of Christ's Hospital 1787," 1, MS, Christ's Hospital Museum Archives.

[8] The petitioner, Coleridge's mother, sent in his application on March 28, 1782. It is addressed to "the Right Honourable, Right Worshipful, and Worshipful Governor of Christ's Hospital, London" and reads: "That the Petitioner's Husband, the Revd. John Coleridge died in the month of October leaving her with a Family of three Children whom she finds it difficult to

stockings and long blue coat of its students, he initially attended the school's branch in Hertford, a town twenty miles from London (this branch also accommodated four houses for girls, the number of girls being between eighty and eighty-eight).[9] After six weeks, however, he was transferred to the main school for boys, "the great school in London" (*Christ's Hospital Recollections*, 88), where he arrived in September 1782 and remained until 1791, when he was nineteen years of age.[10]

Christ's Hospital was divided into several sections: a Reading School, a Grammar School, a Writing School, the Mathematical School (otherwise known as the Royal Mathematical School[11]), a Drawing School (designed for those who were being trained for a naval career), and a Singing School (the children were "taught Psalmody, and Anthems which they perform in Publick both at church and in the Hall": "Particulars of Christ's Hospital 1787," 50). Each trained its pupils to enter a profession.[12] Notably, however, a select few from among the students in the Grammar School were groomed so that they could receive exhibitions to attend the University of Cambridge or occasionally Oxford – "About 8 scholars are sent to the Universities in Seven years." Once at the university, this chosen scholar received an annual allowance of £50 for four years as well as money for apparel ("10£ for a suit of clothes"), books (£5), "Caution money," and "Settling Fees" ("Particulars of Christ's Hospital 1787," 8, 25).

---

maintain and educate without assistance." This and other particulars of Coleridge's time at Christ's Hospital School can be seen in Clifford Jones's *The Sea and the Sky: The History of the Royal Mathematical School of Christ's Hospital* (Horsham: Christ's Hospital, 2015), 190–92.

[9] In a report to the president of the school, the wardrobe keeper described the uniform (still, with modifications, worn this very day):

> The Boys have each a Coat, an Under-Coat, two [three pr (see Order Nov'r 1789)] pair of Breeches, four shirts, three pair of Stockings, four pair of Shoes, one Cap, one Girdle, and three Bands, in every Year; and each Boy has a Coat, an Under-Coat, a Shirt, a pair of Stockings, a Cap, a Girdle, and a Band on his Admission: the Parents or Friends being required to provide each child with Breeches, a Shirt, a pair of Shoes, a pair of Stockings and a Band, at his coming. ("Particulars of Christ's Hospital 1787," 13)

[10] When Coleridge was admitted, there were 700 boys, "of whom I [Coleridge] think nearly one-third were the sons of clergymen." See *Christ's Hospital Recollections*, 88.

[11] The Royal Mathematical School was perhaps the most elite part of Christ's Hospital. Founded in 1673 by King Charles II, this part of Christ's Hospital trained the select boys to become naval officers. These pupils were referred to as the "King's Boys." They learned the principles of navigation in preparation for a career at sea. For a thorough account of this school, see Jones, *The Sea and the Sky*.

[12] Except for those very few selected students who went on to university, a majority of the pupils left Christ's Hospital as early as fourteen years of age to become clerks, workers, and apprentices in counting houses, the trades, and various social services.

Coleridge's scholastic abilities were recognized by his masters so that once he arrived at "the great school in London," he was swiftly placed in the Grammar School, where he eventually became a "Grecian."[13] Subsequently, it was not long before he was chosen by James Boyer, the Master of the Upper Grammar School, to be one of the select few to be groomed for Cambridge.[14]

In a January 1787 report, prepared during Coleridge's residence, for educational officials interested in founding a similar school in Ireland, Boyer outlined the Grammar School curriculum.[15] In this document, Boyer not only referred to the teaching of Latin and Greek grammar as well as the reading and translating of classical texts but also pointedly explained that those "young men" from the Upper Grammar School who had been chosen to attend university "upon Tuesday and Thursday afternoon" took tutorials at the Mathematical School in their last two years. Significantly, Boyer remarked that this instruction was "to their very great advantage, as a considerable knowledge of the Mathematics is necessary to the Student's advancement in the University of Cambridge" ("Particulars of Christ's Hospital 1787," 27).[16] Coleridge, therefore, during his final two years, walked over, at least twice a week, to the Mathematical School to be instructed by its Master, William Wales – a most extraordinary, good-humored person, who had been the navigator in Captain Cook's second voyage (1772–75). The specter of *Mathesis* was beginning to stalk Coleridge's intellectual pursuits.[17]

---

[13] Coleridge wrote to his brother Luke on May 12, 1787: "I suppose I shall be Grecian in about a year. Mr. Boyer says that if I take particular care of my exercises, etc., I may find myself rewarded sooner than I expected. I know not exactly what he means; but it is something concerning me in the first form" (*CL* 1:2). In one of his accounts of this time, Coleridge recalled, "Against my will, I was chosen by my master as one of those destined for the University" (*Christ's Hospital Recollections*, 95).

[14] A strict but insightful teacher, the mythical Boyer once told a homesick and weeping Coleridge: "'Boy! the school is your father! Boy! the school is your Mother! Boy! the school is your brother! Boy! the school is your sister! Boy! the school is your first-cousin, and your second-cousin, and all the rest of your relations! Let's have no more crying!'" (*Table-Talk*, May 27, 1830, 98–99, as quoted in *Christ's Hospital Recollections*, 99).

[15] I am grateful to Mike Barford of the Christ's Hospital Museum for bringing to my attention "Particulars of Christ's Hospital 1787" and for transcribing extracts from minutes of the Court of Governors (January 26, 1787 and April 20, 1787) in which the board discussed a request from the Administration of Ireland to receive an account of the foundation and establishment of Christ's Hospital.

[16] Leigh Hunt recalls that "The Deputy Grecians were in Homer, Cicero, and Demosthenes; the Grecians, in the Greek plays and Mathematics" (*Christ's Hospital Recollections*, 174).

[17] "Mathesis" is an archaic expression which referred not only to scientific learning but also, and increasingly so, to mathematics. The word came to England from the Anglo-Norman "Mathesis," which in turn was derived from late Latin and Ancient Greek. Later in this chapter, I quote Coleridge's use of the figure of "Mathesis" in a poem enclosed in an August 2, 1792 letter to his brother George.

Although not always enthusiastic about these lessons, Coleridge respected Wales and dutifully attended to the requirement – perhaps not always quite in the same sober and idealized spirit of the shipwrecked sailor in Book VI of Wordsworth's *The Prelude* who tucked Euclid's *Elements* under his arm and solemnly comforted himself by drawing geometric diagrams with a long stick in the sand (lines 160–74). Rather, Coleridge, if we are to believe him, apparently carelessly scribbled such figures on his breeches. In a humorous letter written on May 26, 1789 to his brother George, Coleridge charmingly asked for a new pair to replace those upon which he had scrawled geometric diagrams: "You will excuse me for reminding you that, as our Holidays commence next week, and I shall go out a good deal, a good pair of breeches will be no inconsiderable accession to my appearance. For though my present pair are excellent for the purposes of drawing Mathematical Figures on them ... yet they are not altogether so well adapted for a female eye" (*CL* 1:5).

True to its name, the instruction in the Royal Mathematical School depended heavily upon a thorough training in mathematics, a necessary skill when students were being prepared for careers in the navy or employment in the East India Company.[18] According to Wales's archived 1787 manuscript description of the curriculum, written just before Coleridge was attending his tutorials, it is clear that there would have been the assumption that Coleridge more or less adequately knew his arithmetic but lacked a thorough knowledge of and practice in working out the principles explained and demonstrated in Euclid's *Elements of Geometry* (first compiled in the third century and first translated into English in 1570). As I have mentioned, this was *the* standard geometry text in England during the eighteenth century as well as the first part of the nineteenth century.[19] Indeed, during the nineteenth century, just one edition of Euclid's *Elements* sold over a million copies.[20]

---

[18] The badge worn by the King's Boys on the upper left shoulder displayed a figure of Arithmetic holding a tablet inscribed with two rows of numbers; her hand rests on the head of a bluecoat boy next to her. Behind the boy is Geometry, holding an equilateral triangle and a pair of dividers. On the right of the badge is Astronomy holding an armillary sphere and a cross staff and wearing a pegasus, which is a winged hat (see Jones, *The Sea and the Sky*, 29).

[19] England was slow in adapting to non-Euclidean geometry that was already being developed on the Continent. It was not until the late nineteenth century that its mathematicians started incorporating this new perspective into their studies of geometry. For a fuller discussion of this matter, see Chapter 5 of this book.

[20] This figure concerning the number of copies sold comes from a catalogue accompanying a recent exhibit of William De Morgan's ceramics at the Guildhall Gallery, London. See *The London Mathematical Society and Sublime Symmetry* [produced in conjunction with the De Morgan Foundation for the exhibition "Sublime Symmetry: The Mathematics behind William De Morgan's Ceramic Designs"] (London: London Mathematical Society, 2017), 14.

## Part One: A Euclidean Culture

In Wales's account of his method of teaching mathematics, quoted below, one can perhaps recognize the origins of not only Coleridge's subsequent compulsive need to measure the particulars of his surroundings (discussed in the first chapter) but also his alertness to their angles and geometric shapes. Describing the curriculum of the Mathematical School in his unpublished 1787 report to the school's president, Wales wrote:

> I am ... particularly attentive in enquiring in to the learners reason for every step he takes, as well in stating as in working the question; firmly believing that if a boy be once well grounded in the nature and practice of this Rule he will seldom be at a loss in the application of Arithmetic to any of the common occurrences in life. I next teach the extraction of Roots, and the nature of arithmetical and geometrical progressions, in order to illustrate and explain the nature of logarithms; and lastly, proceed to the use of these artificial numbers.
>
> I proceed afterwards to explain the nature of the different kinds of extension; but particularly linear, plane, & angular extension; the nature and properties of geometrical figures; and the construction of some of the more useful geometrical Problems: but in this branch, illustration, rather than demonstration, is attended to. Plane Trigonometry succeeds: in which I exemplify, pretty fully, the various ways and cases of finding the sides and angles of plane triangles, right angled as well as oblique, from any three of them being given. ("Particulars of Christ's Hospital 1787," 40)

During their tutorial sessions, Coleridge and Wales would have probably been working out of a two-volume text prepared specifically for the "King's Boys" in 1772 and which Wales carefully revised and corrected. *The Elements of Navigation Containing the Theory and Practice with the Necessary Tables* opens with lessons in "Arithmetic," "Euclidean Geometry," and "Plane Trigonometry," before proceeding to matters that specifically concern those who are to be apprenticed at sea – to a study of "Spherics," "Astronomy," "Geography," "Plane Sailing," "Globular Sailing," and "Land and Marine Fortifications." One passage from the text's pages devoted to Geography suggests Coleridge's own sensitivity to the lines of motion in a landscape: "Rivers are streams of Water, flowing chiefly from the Mountains and running a long narrow channel, or cavities, through the land, till they fall into the sea, or into the rivers, which at last run with the sea."[21]

---

[21] J. Robertson, *The Elements of Navigation Containing the Theory and Practice with the Necessary Tables, and Compendium for Finding the Latitude and Longitude at Sea*, 2 vols., 5th ed., rev. William Wales, Master of the Royal Mathematical School, Christ's Hospital, London (London: C. Nourse, 1806), 2:332.

A letter Coleridge wrote to his brother George on March 31, 1791 while still at Christ's Hospital – a few months before going up to Cambridge – illustrates just how immersed Coleridge was in his study of Euclidean geometry. Displaying a facility with the mathematical idiom as well as a humorously ironic distance from, if not impatience with, such studies, Coleridge composed a humorous Pindaric ode based on Euclid's first proposition concerning the definition of an equilateral triangle. Playfully drawing on "the Nymph Mathesis from the visionary caves of Abstracted Ideas" and causing "her to unite with Harmony," he composed a poem entitled "Proposition the first and Problem the first." The initial verses offer enough of a glimpse to catch his spirited irreverent, yet significantly informed, familiarity with Euclid's first propositions:[22]

I

On a given finite Line,
Which must no way incline,
   To describe an equi=
   =Lateral TRI
   A EN GEE El E*
     *Poetice for Angle. [S.T.C.]

   Now let A B
Be the given Line,
Which must no way incline,
The great Mathematician
Makes this Requisition,
   That we describe an equi=
   =lateral Tri=
   =angle on it.
Aid us Reason! Aid us, Wit!

---

[22] When composing this poem, Coleridge, in the final verses, also used the structural makeup of the equilateral triangle to comment on his political ideas concerning equality and brotherhood:

   C A and B C and A B –
*All* are equal, each to his Brother.
Preserving the balance of Power so true:
Ah! the like would the proud Autocratorix [the Empress of the Russians] do!
   At taxes impending not Britain would tremble,
   Nor Prussia struggle her fear to dissemble,
     Nor the Mah'met-sprung Wight,
     The Great Musselman
     Would stain his Divan,
With Urine, the soft-flowing Daughter of Fright.

                                                                  (Third stanza)

# Part One: A Euclidean Culture 89

<pre>
                     2
          From the centre A. at the distance A B
          Describe the circle B C D.
          At the distance B A from B, the centre
          The round A C E to describe *bodily venture.*
              (Third Postulate see)
            And from the point C,
          In which the Circles make a pother
          Cutting and slashing one another
          Bid the straight lines a journeying go,
          C A, C B those lines will show
              To the points, which by A B are reckon'd;
              And Postulate the second
          For authority ye know.
                 A B C
              Triumphant shall be
              An Equilateral Triangle –
        Not Peter Pindar carp, not Zoilus can wrangle.
          *delendus fere – [S.T.C.]
                                              (CL 1:7–9)
</pre>

### The University of Cambridge

Once Coleridge entered the University of Cambridge in the autumn of 1791, the justification for the supplemental mathematics instruction at Christ's Hospital became strikingly apparent, for it soon became clear that mathematics comprised a significant, if not a defining, part of the university's curriculum. Initially reducing his classical study to an evening activity, Coleridge assumed the image of "the awkward Freshman, with his Euclid / And thin cap and gown, creeping like a snail / Unwilling to lecture" described in a January 1795 issue of the University of Cambridge's *The University Magazine*.[23] Consequently, after settling into his rooms at Jesus College in early November 1791, Coleridge explained to his brother George that in addition to attending "Mathematic Lectures, once a day – Euclid and Algebra alternately," he was reading "Mathematics three hours a day." After noting that he often deferred his reading of classics until after tea, he remarked that classical lectures were "seldom given" and when so were "very thinly attended" (*CL* 1:16) – such was the pressure to learn one's Euclid.

In a handful of subsequent letters, Coleridge occasionally expressed his frustration with this requirement and spoke of the tutorials and lectures as

---

[23] *The University Magazine*, January 1795, 62.

being dull and lacking in imagination. On one occasion, on April 2, 1792, pretending to have found a poem left in some lecture room, Coleridge forwarded it to his brother George. The verse's lines, portraying mathematics as a "loathsome strain" from which "the frighted Muses fly," reflect his momentary sense of the incompatibility between the imaginative and creative spirit and the dreary mathematical mind – an understandable attitude given the demands of his first year at Jesus College. The first six lines of the poem read:

> Where deep in mud Cam rolls his slumbrous stream,
> And Bog and Desolation reign supreme,
> Where all Boe[o]tia clouds the misty brain,
> The owl Mathesis pipes her loathsome strain,
> Far far aloof the frighted Muses fly,
> Indignant Genius scowls and passes by ...
>
> (*CL* 1:34)

Coleridge's irritation with the prominence given to Mathesis often occasioned a withering disrespect for his mathematics tutors. For instance, he thought John Newton, reputed to be a brilliant mathematician, uninteresting. Indeed, when Newton ("a very tall thin man, with little tiny blushing face") recovered from a "violent cold" – caught after falling into a deep, muddy hole while botanizing and emerging looking like a River God – Coleridge, in a flirtatious letter to Mary Evans, expressed how annoyed he and some of his friends were that his instructor had regained his health sooner than they hoped he might: "Verily I swear, that six of his duteous pupils myself as their General, sallied forth to the Apothecary's house with a fixed determination to thrash him for having performed so speedy a cure – but luckily for himself the Rascal was not at home" (*CL* 1:49–50). Similarly, in another February 1792 letter, this time to Mary's sister Anne Evans, he bitingly remarked: "but here I must interrupt my description [of Cambridge] to hurry to Mr. Costivebody's [*sic*] lectures on Euclid, who is as mathematical an Author, my dear Anne, as you would wish to read on a long summer's day" (*CL* 1:31). The reference is to Jacob de Costobadie (1758–1828), a Fellow of Jesus College.[24]

---

[24] Kathleen Coburn suggests that when Coleridge returned for the first time to Cambridge since his student days, he seems to have discharged an old debt to Costobadie "by paying Tiggin's widow Costobadie's debt for bell-ringing. It may be added that in the Frend controversy ... Costobadie was on the wrong side, in Coleridge's undergraduate view, which fact might help to account for his neglect of mathematics" (*CN* Notes 2:2894).

Indeed, a number of Coleridge's coterie and predecessors at Cambridge shared his impatience. These individuals often bewailed the crushing emphasis placed upon geometry that resulted in the necessity of "abandoning" their classical or literary studies.[25] Even William Frend, a tutor at Jesus and a brilliant mathematician, complained.[26] In 1787 he grumbled that mathematics "is the only knowledge which is made the test of a student's merit."[27] More particularly in 1795, a group of Coleridge's acquaintances,[28] who contributed to *The University Magazine*, objected to the fact that classical scholars not gifted in mathematical learning were rewarded insufficiently by the university and had less opportunity to show off their literary skills (see "Preface," February 1795, 2). The magazine's editors bemoaned the reality that those "chusing to offer no violence to nature" by neglecting mathematics in favor of their literary interests, received no "gift of so many laurels" usually bestowed by the university. Reinforcing its disapproval of the prominence of mathematics at Cambridge, *The University Magazine* also published a satirical poem both demonstrating and belittling Euclid's first proposition. The poem illustrates the editors' sense of the disparity between the creative imagination and the study of geometry. Its mocking tone recalls the poem, already quoted above, that Coleridge had, three years earlier, sent to his brother George. The 1795 *University Magazine* poem, written by "H" (unknown), like Coleridge's, demeans the rather plodding, unimaginative, "pothering" nature of the discipline.[29] The poem begins with a direct quotation from Euclid:

---

[25] In 1748–49 "one young Corpus student bemoaned the fact that he had to abandon the study of classics and turn his attention to the initiating steps which must be taken in mathematics." See John Gascoigne, "Mathematics and Meritocracy: The Emergence of the Cambridge Mathematical Tripos," *Social Studies of Science* 14.4 (November 1, 1984): 553.

[26] William Frend, in addition to writing about his liberal political and religious views, wrote *Principles of Algebra*, 2 vols. (London: Robinson, 1796).

[27] Gascoigne, "Mathematics and Meritocracy," 567.

[28] Coleridge's acquaintance with *The University Magazine* is supported by the fact that the publication was probably familiar to William Frend, Coleridge's acquaintance, especially since the magazine announced, under the heading "University Intelligence," that "Mr. Coleridge, of Jesus College, will shortly publish some sonnets" (February 1795, 133). The magazine was short-lived and came to an end by amusingly announcing on March 1, 1795: "Stolen or Strayed, this day, between *Magdalene Bridge* and the *Petty Curry*, on its road to the Press, the UNIVERSITY MAGAZINE. Had on when it disappeared a *Strait Waistcoat*. Whoever will give information thereof to its distressed owners, shall receive a reward of EIGHTEEN PENCE, or 3000 copies printed on very soft paper."

[29] Just as Coleridge's earlier geometric poem had political overtones, so too does this rendering of Euclid's first proposition. As a result, this poem also contains glancing political references to the idea of equality.

### The First Proposition in the First Book of Euclid, Poetically Rendered

With radius A B narrow bound
And centre A draw a circle round;
B = Φ the tiny circle name,
With B's centre firm, and radius same.
Swift as an arrow cuts the liquid sky
Describe the circle – A Φ and X.
With steady hand to Φ exact and fine
A and B next distinctly join.
Finish'd the work his welcome form displays,
Your future songs, ye sons of Science raise!
Sound, sound the Pean loud, ye valiant few,
While I the demonstration grand pursue.
Since equal radii in each circle flow,
Plain as the wig on C__k's tremendous brow
Should churlish justice forth the balance draw,
They satisfy Equality's strict Law.
Since then where monarch A 'midst the plain
Rules the proud sov'reign of his small domain,
Two radii of B Φ and ≡
A Φ, *A B* tower on high,
Equal they must be, tho' the critic train,
Bold to refute it, rack the sleepless brain.
Again, when B stands profoundly dull,
Blind as the dome of Clark's tyrannic skull,
In various lines two equal radii fly,
B and A, B too and Φ
A Φ, B Φ it then is clear
Each into A B equal are.
Therefore each line 'tis plain, without more pother,
Exactly equals are, both one and t'other.
H.

(*The University Magazine*, January 1795, 64)

The editors of *The University Magazine* would have agreed with an anonymous correspondent of *The Connoisseur* who, in 1774, was annoyed that at Cambridge, "Mathematics is the standard, to which all merit is referred; and all other excellence, without these, are quite overlooked and neglected";[30] they probably would have also empathized with Gilbert Wakefield, a student at Jesus in 1776, who longed to be emancipated from his mathematical studies so that he could have more leisure for his interest

---

[30] *The Connoisseur* 57 (1774): 19.

in theology,[31] and they would have agreed with William Heberden's 1792 criticism in his *Strictures upon the Discipline of the University of Cambridge* that the "public honours of the University ... are distributed merely according to mathematical merit."[32] Moreover, they certainly would have chuckled when one of Coleridge's friends from Christ's Hospital, Thomas Fanshaw Middleton, who, after matriculating from Pembroke College with second-rank mathematical honors, lampooned a Cambridge geometry professor by referring to him as "*Dr. Hexagon*," an individual "for ever explaining ... the properties of the Circle"; moreover, they would have been delighted with Middleton's satirical portrait of his tutor, "Mr. *Puzzlebooby*," who continually drew geometric figures in the sand and, furthermore, was about to publish a book containing no fewer than "three thousand four hundred and twenty one new Theorems in the higher part of Mathematics."[33] It goes without saying that Mr. Puzzlebooby cuts quite a different figure from Wordsworth's idealized depiction of the shipwrecked sailor in Book VI of *The Prelude* (see above).

If Coleridge had remained at Cambridge and sat the Senate House examinations, he would, to an even greater extent, have continued to experience the brooding presence of mathematical studies and suffered the pressure to ingest – thoroughly – all thirteen books of Euclid's *Elements*, not just the first six studied in the first two years, as well as reach a good understanding of Newton's *Principia*.[34] The university, to a

---

[31] Gascoigne, "Mathematics and Meritocracy," 566.
[32] Gascoigne, "Mathematics and Meritocracy," 553. William Heberden (1710–1801) was a graduate of St. John's College. He received his MA in 1782. He pursued a medical career and was a classical scholar.
[33] *The Country Spectator* [ed. Thomas Fanshaw Middleton], 3 (London: Gainsborough, 1792): 49. After he left Cambridge, Middleton became a curate in rural Gainsborough and feeling bored, in 1793, founded and edited *The Country Spectator* (obviously parodying Addison and Steele's publication), in which he sometimes mocked society. In a fictitious letter "from a Gentleman" in issue 3, Middleton satirized a gathering at Lowestoft in which two mathematicians from the university are present:

> But besides these great people [Lord and Lady Drinkpuddle, Lady Amelia Dubbletoe and Sir Thos Swimpuppy], our two Universities have favored us with the company of several persons, some of whom are remarkable for elaborate scientific research, and some for the refinement of their classical taste. That eminent Professor of *Cambridge, Dr. Hexagon*, is for ever explaining to the ladies the properties of the Circle; and the Revd. Mr. *Puzzlebooby*, Tutor of the Dr's. College, is mistaken by the common people for a *Conjurer* on account of the figures, that he is continually drawing his stick upon the sea-shore. He told me yesterday with exultation, that the University Press would soon groan with the weight of three thousand four hundred and twenty one new Theorems in the higher part of mathematics. (*The Country Spectator* 3 (1792): 49)

[34] Coleridge left Jesus College in December 1794 without sitting examinations. As those familiar with his biography know, he ran away and, using the pseudonym of Silas Tomkyn Comberbache, joined

greater extent than Oxford, promoted what came to be called the Mathematical Tripos, a series of examinations that lasted three days. After coming under increasing scrutiny, in 1901 this ritual was finally on the brink of major reform. In his *A History of the Study of Mathematics at Cambridge* (1899), W. W. Rouse Ball, using the moderator's book for 1778, preserved in the library of Trinity College, offers one a sense of the examination's contents. Ball explains:

> Each page is dated, and contains a list of the three subjects proposed for that day together with the names of the respondent and the three opponents. Of the three questions proposed by each respondent the first was invariably on a mathematical subject, and with one exception was always taken from Newton. In all but ten cases the second was also on some mathematical question. The last was on some point in moral philosophy.[35]

Ball also copies John Jebb's 1772 description of the examination – certainly an intimidating occasion and one that underlines the emphasis upon mathematical studies:[36]

> The moderator generally begins with proposing some questions from the six books of Euclid, plane trigonometry, and the first rules of algebra. If any person fails in answer the question goes to the next. From the elements of mathematics, a transition is made to the four branches of philosophy ... If the moderator finds the sets of questionists, under examination, capable of answering him, he proceeds to the eleventh and twelfth books of Euclid, conic sections, spherical trigonometry, the higher parts of algebra, and Sir Isaac Newton's *Principia*; more particularly those sections which treat of the motion of bodies in eccentric and revolving orbits ... Having closed the philosophical examination, he sometimes asks a few questions in Locke's *Essays on the human understanding*, Butler's *Analogy*, or Clark's *Attributes*. But as the highest academical distinctions are invariably given to the best proficient in mathematics and natural philosophy, a very superficial knowledge in morality and metaphysics will suffice. (Ball, *A History of the Study of Mathematics at Cambridge*, 191)

the fusiliers. Eventually his brother George rescued him from this impulsive act. If he had stayed on at Cambridge and, instead, become a "non-reading man" in order to matriculate, he would have had to demonstrate a knowledge of a bit of algebra, the first six books of Euclid, and some natural philosophy. Heather Glen has pointed out to me that after his time in Cambridge, when Coleridge was eventually living in the Lakes, his training in geometry might possibly have been reinforced or reawakened through his friendship with John Slee, who ran a famous mathematics academy in Tirril to which young men from Oxford and Cambridge came for tuition.

[35] W. W. Rouse Ball, *A History of the Study of Mathematics at Cambridge* (Cambridge: Cambridge University Press, 1899), 171.

[36] John Jebb had taken the examination in 1775 and had become a second wrangler. Besides W. W. Rouse Ball's book, Schneider's *Wordsworth's Cambridge Education* offers a thorough account of the curriculum at Cambridge.

Ball then reprints a group of questions from the 1786 Senate House examination. Three from the geometry section are quoted here:

> Question 10: Of right-angled Triangles containing a given Area to find that whereof the sum of the two legs AB + BC shall be the least possible [this and the two following questions are illustrated by diagrams; the angle at B is the right angle]. 11: To find the Surface of the Cone ABC [the cone is a right one on a circular base]. 12: To rectify the arc DB of the semicircle DBV. (196)

## Part Two: *Quod erat demonstrandum*

Notably, however, in spite of his intermittent discomfort with the university's stifling curriculum as well as his subsequent occasional reluctance to grind away at his mathematical studies, Coleridge did not ultimately turn his back on this legacy, but, instead, chose to accept, and at times embrace, a shared, deeply ingrained cultural conviction that one should take Euclid seriously – a persuasion that, as I have explained, was particularly prominent at the University of Cambridge. His relief when, in 1792, Middleton promised to continue "to read Mathematics with me" (*CL* 1:18)[37] was, therefore, not only motivated by a need to complete certain requirements but also provoked, and more significantly so, by a lasting recognition that a knowledge of Euclid's *Elements* was a prerequisite to comprehending both the phenomenological world and intellectual thought.[38] As Thomas Taylor in his *Philosophical and Mathematical Commentaries of Proclus* declared: "the mathematics are of the greatest utility to philosophy"; the study of the disciplines "prepares the intellectual apprehension of theology."[39] Mathematics, therefore, "must be considered desirable for its own sake, and for the contemplation it affords, and not on account of the utility it administers to human concerns" (1:67). Consequently, years after departing from Jesus College, Coleridge continued to respect the study of geometry not only for its practical applications – its aid in navigating the seas, surveying land, and engineering – but also for its assistance in comprehending the configuration of one's natural

---

[37] Thomas Fanshaw Middleton was received into Christ's Hospital on April 21, 1791. He eventually went to Pembroke College and took a BA degree and entered the church. He was a couple of years ahead of Coleridge.
[38] Indeed, in February 1808, Coleridge selected a copy of Euclid's "Euclid Graec. Et Lat." from Cuthell's book catalogue.
[39] Thomas Taylor, *The Philosophical and Mathematical Commentaries of Proclus; Surnamed, Plato's Successor, on the First Book of Euclid's Elements*, vol. 1 (London: Printed for the author, 1788), 63.

surroundings and its commentary on aesthetic matters, as well as its contribution to philosophic thought, the structure and arguments of which called upon mathematical constructions. As he noted in March 1805: "real metaphysicians and mathematicians are Friends, and Lovers; always look at each other with respect and welcome, and often walk arm in arm" (*CN* 2:2503; f. 69).

Coleridge would have agreed with William Whiston's 1714 introduction to an edition of Euclid's *Elements* that declared: "the Mathematicks are not foreign, not unuseful, or not unbecoming, but honourable and profitable to sound and certain philosophy."[40] And he would not have objected to Whiston's including a "General Preface," composed almost a century earlier, by Isaac Barrow (1630–77) – according to Coleridge: the "excellent Barrow" and "the last of the disciples of Plato and Archimedes among our mathematicians" (*CC* 6:51) – who believed that "all imaginable Geometrical figures" are inherent in every particle of matter.[41] Barrow, whose reverence for geometry enjoyed a wide audience, was often quoted as saying "God always acts geometrically."[42] In his preface to his work on Apollonius's *Conics* (1675), Barrow exclaimed: "How great a geometrician art thou O Lord! For while this Science has no Bounds; while there is for ever room for the Discovery of New Theorems, even by Human Faculties; Thou are acquainted with them all at one view, without any chain of Consequences, without any Fatigue of Demonstration."[43]

Steeped within a context for which geometry was not just an end in itself but also a passageway or a "vestibule"[44] to a deeper understanding of both the spiritual and the phenomenological world, Coleridge developed the practice not only of superimposing its figures onto his descriptions of the landscape but also, for years after he had given up his peripatetic activity, of applying its *modus operandi* to theological, political, aesthetic,

---

[40] Schneider, *Wordsworth's Cambridge Education*, 27. William Whiston succeeded Isaac Newton as holder of the Lucasian Chair at Cambridge. He held this position from 1702 to 1711. To give a sense of how many editions of Euclid there were, it is helpful to know that Whiston published several editions in Latin, ten editions in English (the last appearing in 1792), and one in Greek. See William Whiston. *The Elements of Euclid with Select Theorems out of Archimedes*, 11th ed. (Dublin: R. Jackson, 1791).

[41] Isaac Barrow, *The Usefulness of Mathematical Learning Explained and Demonstrated: Being Mathematical Lectures Read in the Public Schools at the University of Cambridge* (London: Printed for Stephen Austen, 1734), 75.

[42] Schneider, *Wordsworth's Cambridge Education*, 97.    [43] Whiston. *The Elements of Euclid*, 17.

[44] Thomas Taylor in his "Preface" to *The Philosophical and Mathematical Commentaries of Proclus* writes of the "middle nature" of geometry, a discipline that offers a "genuine passage to true theology" and is "the vestibule of divinity" (47).

or even literary questions.⁴⁵ There were the occasions when Coleridge drew an analogy between "The *idea* of a Supreme Being" and the "idea of infinite space in all the geometrical figures" (*CC* 7.1:200), discussed "the Trinity as I would a problem in Geometry" (*CC* 14.1:181), and equated the system of legislation to the composition of a geometric figure (*CC* 4.2:105). There were also other moments when he reflected upon the nature of Beauty or considered the relationship among Faith, Will, and Intelligence by commenting on the structures of a triangle and a circle (*CC* 11.2:1104). Furthermore, in a marginal comment on Shakespeare's works, he found a semblance between a geometric diagram and the rules of tragedy.⁴⁶ As Coleridge might have written after solving a geometric problem, *Quod erat demonstrandum*. ⁴⁷

Convinced, with some reservations, that geometry contained the structural foundation for any branch of knowledge and was applicable to all disciplines, Coleridge also used Euclidean figures, such as an equilateral triangle, to construct his arguments concerning the nature of belief and marriage.⁴⁸ Recognizing that geometry did not necessarily engage the reflective and discursive faculty, Coleridge, all the same, around 1824,

---

⁴⁵ There were innumerable occasions when Coleridge turned to geometry in order to explain an idea. In addition to the examples given in this text, see the passages in which he compares the "dips and declinations" of the human mind to "the application of Geometry to the forces and movement of the material world" (*CC* 6:78); begins his discussion concerning religion by proceeding, "like the Geometricians, with stating our POSTULATES"; and argues: "What *other* sense is conceivable, that does not destroy the doctrine it professes to interpret? Which will not convert it into its own Negative – as if a geometrician should name a Sugar-loaf an Ellipse, adding 'by which term I here mean a Cone'; and then justify the misnomer on the pretext, that the Ellipse is among the Conic Sections?" (*CC* 9:136).

⁴⁶ The analogy occurs in his marginal comments on Shakespeare's work:

> Dr Johnson has remarked that little or nothing is wanted to render the Othello a regular Tragedy but to have opened the play with the arrival of Othello in Cyprus, and to have thrown the preceding Act into the form of narration. Here then is the place to determine, whether such a change would or would not be an improvement, nay ... whether or not the Tragedy would by such an arrangement become *more regular*, i.e. more consonant with the rules dictated by universal reason or the true Common Sense of mankind in its application to the particular case. For surely we may safely leave it to Common sense ... Suppose a man had described a rhomboid or parallelogram, and a Critic were with great gravity to observe – if the lines had only been in true right-angles, or if the horizontal parallels had been but of the same length as the two perpendicular parallels that form the sides, the diagram would have been according to the strictest rules of Geometry. For (in all acts of judgement) it never be too often recollected and scarcely too often repeated, that rules are a means to end. (*CC* 12.4:863)

⁴⁷ This is the phrase conventionally added to solutions of problems in geometry.
⁴⁸ See, for instance, *CN* 3:3869 (f. 33), where Coleridge refers to "the wild attempt of the Platonists ... to explain the *final cause* of mathematical figures, and of numbers, so as to subordinate them to a *principle* of origination out of themselves ..."

used an equilateral triangle to work out the relationship among Faith, Practical and Speculative Thought; the resulting diagram is a bit difficult to understand. At the top of the triangle is the letter H, which stands for "the Apex of Humanity, or Faith as the Sum and Consummation of Will and Intelligence, the Practical and the Speculative–"; at the lower left angle of the triangle is ∏, which equals the "Practical"; and on the lower right angle of the figure is Ø, which stands for "Theoretical." A line descends from H down to the middle point of the triangle's base and is marked with a P, which stands for "Personal, or Indifference" (*CC* 11.2:1104). Earlier in a May 1808 notebook entry, Coleridge had already vividly elicited the same triangular figure when he attempted to work out for himself the dimensions of wedded love. Coleridge carried out this exercise at a time when, estranged from his wife, he was possibly recalling a night-long conversation with Wordsworth before his friend was to propose marriage to Mary Hutchinson.[49] The entire entry is worth replicating, for, in a rather exaggerated way, it demonstrates how Coleridge called upon the geometrical structure and process of reasoning to sort out or reason through a metaphysical question that at the moment was preoccupying him (see Figure 4).

Unintentionally, this notebook entry partially resembles "The Loves of the Triangles," a 1798 humorous poem written by George Canning and a group of friends for the *Anti-Jacobin or Weekly Examiner* that mocks Erasmus Darwin's *The Loves of Plants*, for both its substance and its "chunky style,"[50] by substituting geometric shapes where the plants should be.[51] It should be emphasized, however, that Coleridge emphatically did not consider his own geometric modeling to be parodic, for he genuinely subscribed, like most Cambridge men, to the idea that geometric structures and Euclidean paradigms underlay all natural phenomena. As a consequence, a knowledge of them was basic to an understanding of one's

---

[49] In her notes to this entry, Kathleen Coburn writes:

> The night-long conversation with WW is well substantiated; it took place at Keswick, 3 April 1802, when WW was on his way to propose marriage to Mary Hutchinson. The agony for Coleridge was multiple: not only was WW going to marry the sister of the woman Coleridge loved [Sara Hutchinson], but also ... WW was about to separate from Annette [Villon] and their child in order to marry – the sort of freedom for which Coleridge longed but which his conscience did not permit him. (*CN* Notes 3:3304)

[50] Patricia Fara, *Erasmus Darwin: Sex, Science, and Serendipity* (Oxford: Oxford University Press, 2012), 35.

[51] For a discussion of this poem, see Fara, *Erasmus Darwin*, 30–42. A text of "The Loves of the Triangles" is given in the "Appendix" to Fara's book, 259–80.

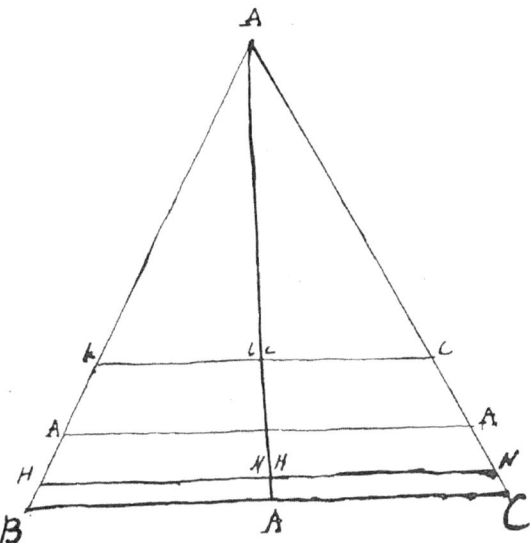

Let the Triangles ABA and ACA form the Triangle ABC. By this I represent wedded Love in its Ideal.

The Basis, BA + AC, signifies the ground of all Beings in God or Nature.

HN.HN = the common Basis of Human Nature.

AA = the *characteristic* Basis of Identity common both to B (the Woman) and to C (the man)/THAT in them both, which *in* both is the same; but which yet distinguishes them to each other from the rest of mankind.

Let bb, & cc, blending in the line A, signify, the qualities in each opposite to yet correspondent to, those of the other, viz. bb the qualities of B opposite yet correspondent to cc, the qualities of C opposite yet correspondent to bb in B.—(For instance; Feminineness in B thro' the whole Being, Head, Heart, and Person, the features, texture &c &c to Masculineness in C, so that the very same things, Eyes, Cheeks, &c are yet NOT the same, yet correspond; & even when different, as tender Dependence & protecting Courage, still correspond, as the Lock to the Key, or Sex to Sex—)

Then BAb + CAc = BCAbc. But b and c meet & become one in the bisection A—: that is, bc = equal A. Therefore Bb = A, and Cc = A: of course Bb = Cc.—They are one in Spirit, a unity in duplicity.—

[CN 3:3308 ff.9-10]

Figure 4  Samuel Taylor Coleridge's diagram of a triangle representing "wedded Love in its Ideal."
CN 3:3308 (ff. 9-10).

surroundings and even to a comprehension of one's own emotions – hence his lifelong fascination with geometric form.

Coleridge's acceptance of this orientation began, of course, from the fact that at the time when he was young and studying Euclid, he was also poring over Thomas Taylor's commentaries of Proclus, one of the books that was among those that the Christ's Hospital boys "had" at their "fingers's ends" (*CL* 6:843), reading classical texts at both Christ's Hospital and Cambridge, borrowing William Enfield's two-volume *The History of Philosophy* (1791) as well as Ralph Cudworth's *The True Intellectual System of the Universe* from the Bristol Library in 1795, and eventually studying German philosophy while at the University of Göttingen. Captivated by the works of Pythagoras, Plato, Plotinus, Proclus, the Cambridge Platonists, Descartes, Spinoza (with whom Coleridge found fault for "reducing all truth to geometrical truth" [*CC* 11.1:708]), Schelling, Schiller, and Kant, who "took possession of" him "as with a giant's hand" (*CC* 7.1:153), Coleridge, in one form or another, steeped himself in a culture that believed geometry led to an apprehension of the purer elements of truth that existed beyond all the static of a shifting, fluctuating, moving sensual world.[52]

In the mode of the Platonists, Coleridge understood that geometry, though technical, was a passageway – a "middle situation" – constructed to conduct a person from the phenomenological (the material) to the primary forms (the ideal) separated from time and place. It led one toward knowledge – but, of course, could not contain it. He would have agreed with Proclus's observation in Book 1 of his *Commentaries* that "It is necessary that the mathematical essence should neither be separated from the first nor last genera of things, nor from that which obtains a simplicity, essence, but that it should obtain *a middle situation* [italics mine] between substances destitute of parts, simple, incomposite and indivisible, and such as are subject to partition, and are terminated in a manifold composition

---

[52] Much of Coleridge's thought, of course, had its roots in his early reading of Book VII of *The Republic*, in which Plato proposed an educational scheme that devotes ten years to mathematics, the aim of which is to allow an apprehension of the purer elements of truth and provide a sense of permanence in a world of change. In a December 21, 1796 letter to John Thelwall, Coleridge exclaimed, "but I love Plato – his dear *gorgeous* Nonsense!" (*CL* 1:295). While at the University of Cambridge, Coleridge would, as mentioned above, have felt the lingering inheritance of what in the nineteenth century came to be called the "Cambridge Platonists." This was a group of theologians and philosophers at the university who were loosely linked. They not only held the philosophy of Plato and Plotinus in high regard but also drew upon a wide range of philosophical sources. The leading figures were Ralph Cudworth (1617–88), Nathaniel Culverwell (1619–51), Benjamin Whichcote (1603–93), and Henry More (1606–87).

*Part Two:* Quod erat demonstrandum    101

and various divisions" (Taylor, *The Philosophical and Mathematical Commentaries of Proclus*, 44).

Given Coleridge's sense of geometry's importance in guiding him to an understanding of metaphysical thought as well as the ordering of an external universe – that the universe is written with its characters – it is reasonable that he often later regretted not having paid more attention to his mathematical studies while at Christ's Hospital and Jesus College. As if echoing Wordsworth's sentiments in Book VI of *The Prelude* when the laureate admits that at St. John's he had devoted himself in the elements of geometric science "but a little way, / No farther than the threshold (with regret / Sincere I mention this)" (1805: lines 37–40), Coleridge, years after his Cambridge days, also expressed disappointment with his own neglect or heedlessness. In the 1821 fictitious letter to a second-year Cambridge undergraduate (mentioned in this chapter's opening), he, after defending geometric descriptions of the botanical world, confessed: "Often, my dear young friend, and bitterly, do I regret the stupid prejudice that made me neglect my mathematical studies, at Jesus. There is something to me enigmatically attractive and imaginative in the generation of curves, and in the whole geometry of motion" (*CC* 11.1:940). In a similarly contrite but more emphatic manner, Coleridge also wrote to his sons, Hartley and Derwent, regarding his "bitter regret" for not taking advantage of the "glorious opportunities" offered by "the famous Mathematician, WALES" and, at Jesus College, by "an excellent Mathematical Tutor, Newton, all *neglected* with great *remorse!*" (*CN* Notes 2:2894). (Recall that it was Thomas Newton whose recovery from a bad cold had irritated Coleridge and his friends, for sooner than they had wished, they would have to resume their tutorials with him.) Coleridge continued: "O be assured, my dear Sons! That Pythagoras, Plato, Speusippus, had abundant reason for excluding from all philosophy and theology ... those who were ignorant of Mathematics ... it *cannot* be *acquired* ... without the assistance of the technical! –" (*CN* Notes 2:2894).[53] No wonder, then, that Coleridge periodically recalled Plato's

---

[53] Persuaded of geometry's worth and application to many disciplines – not just to the structure of natural phenomena – Coleridge, in one of his later educational schemes, made sure that geometry played a role. For instance, when he thought of earning his living as a teacher, he wrote to the young man's guardian: "While your Son remains with me, he will, of course, be acquiring that knowledge and those powers of Intellect which are necessary as the *foundation* of excellence in all professions, rather than the immediate science of *any language* will engross one or two hours every day; the elements of Chemistry, Geometry, Mechanics, and Optics the remaining hours of study" (*CC* 13: lix). And in one of his marginalia describing the ways in which a scholar should be educated, Coleridge proposed that if the young man contemplated learning metaphysics, he should be

supposed motto above the entrance to his academy: "Let no man enter, who has not previously disciplined his mind by Geometry,"[54] and that around 1816, he expressed his longing for the genius of Johannes Kepler (1571–1630), whose knowledge of mathematical formulae helped him explain the multifarious phenomena of nature: "O for a flash of that same Light, on which the first position of geometric science that ever loosed itself from the generalizations of a groping and insecure experience, did for the first time reveal itself to a human intellect in all its evidence and all its fruitfulness" (*CC* 6:50).

## Part Three: A Temper of Mind

Coleridge's intermittent inclination to respect a geometrical perspective when observing a landscape, however, was not simply in deference to his training and his culture's mandate. It was also because he was attracted to a temper of mind that accompanied the geometric discipline – significantly, a mode of thinking that began with his early education and remained with him as he continued to shape and develop his thoughts in the ensuing years.[55] To begin with, the geometric idiom, with its reliance upon the order and connection of lines when classifying space, complemented his desire, as already noted in the previous chapter, to diagram what he gazed upon while walking through the countryside and trace the outline of a

path laid like two bows back to back 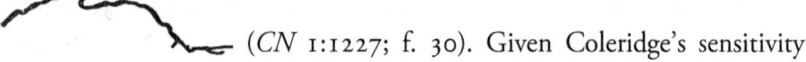 (*CN* 1:798; f. 33), a tarn that runs east to west "in something of this form" A. A. A. A. (*CN* 1:797; f. 22), or a "singular pike" seen through an inverted arch in the fells

(*CN* 1:1227; f. 30). Given Coleridge's sensitivity

---

prepared by "the elements of Geometry and universal arithmetic" (*CC* 13:lx). Coleridge was among those who fully understood that philosophy would languish without geometry.

[54] Coleridge refers to this motto in *The Watchman*, issue 1 (March 1, 1796), 34 (*CC* 2:33), and in one of his lay sermons (*CC* 6:173). See D. H. Fowler's *The Mathematics of Plato's Academy: A New Reconstruction* (Oxford: Oxford University Press, 1987), 200 for a discussion of the validity and sources of Plato's inscription. In Raphael's fresco *The School of Athens*, Geometry is clearly represented by the group at the right front.

[55] In this section of the chapter, it should be understood that the roots of the principles of attention, abstraction, and intuition attending the discipline of geometry were, in various degrees, present in his early training in geometry. When Coleridge later continued to read philosophic commentary in which geometry was mentioned, he became increasingly alert to their presence. As a result, throughout his life when discussing geometry, he continued to dwell on these principles.

to the existence of lines in a landscape, also discussed in the preceding chapter, the geometric figure was a natural extension of this orientation.

### Attention, Abstraction, and Intuition

There was, however, far more at play than his penchant to trace and connect the lines running throughout a scene in order to detect the shapes defining a landscape. Significantly, the geometric orientation also appealed to him throughout his adult life because it necessarily engaged and significantly sharpened the powers of attention, abstraction, and intuition, all of which increased his ability to see and organize what emerged before his eyes. As John Leslie observed in his 1809 edition of Euclid, the study of geometry, with its "invaluable exercise of patient attention and accurate reasoning" sharpens the observational skills.[56]

As already noted, during his walking years, Coleridge tramped from one detail to another and at every bend or step gazed upon yet another point of view subject to divisibility, time, angle of light, and gust of wind. Although invigorated by such dynamism, he was, as he later admitted, sometimes "frustrated and disheartened" by "the fluctuating nature" of what he saw, and, consequently, wished for moments of clarity and stability among a fluid landscape. Calling upon the powers of attention – what he later referred to as geometry's attendant that halts the wandering mind and fixes the "mental eye" (*CC* 14.2:456) – he was able to discover a quiet stillness and certainty in the midst of a scene composed of rushing clouds and dancing brooks that scatter as they progress into yet another manifestation of their being. How reassuring it was, as he later acknowledged, to note "the order and connection of Thoughts and Images" (*CC* 4.2:277) as well as receive the stamp of a geometric figure that stabilized the discursive stream of accidental details.[57] Moreover, how steadying to see "The woods

---

[56] John Leslie, *Elements of Geometry, Geometric Analysis, and Plane Trigonometry* (Edinburgh: James Ballantyne, 1809), v–vi. In *The Friend*, January 11, 1810, Coleridge writes:

> ATTENTION has for it's object the order and connection of Thoughts and Images, such of which is in itself already familiarly known. Thus the elements of Geometry require Attention only; but the analysis of our primary Faculties, and the investigation of all the absolute grounds of Religion and Morals, are impossible without energies of Thought in addition to the effort of Attention. (*CC* 4.2:277)

[57] In an earlier issue of *The Friend*, Coleridge had also stated that

> Attention has for its object the order and connection of Thoughts and Images, each of which is in itself already and familiarly known. Thus the elements of Geometry require attention only; the analysis of our primary faculties, and the investigation of all the absolute

on the left bank run up into semicircles & Triangles" (*CN* 1:360; f. 44), or pause and measure a cavern's elliptical opening as well as gaze upon the infinite variety of lines in a mountain that form segments of ovals and circles (*CN* 1:1489; f. 56). And how restful it was to see the stoniest parts of the fells "softened down by the semicircular Lines & bason-like concavities" (*CN* 1:1207; f. 3), to come upon "a *square* of cottages" after walking through a restless landscape (*CN* 1:1498; f. 6), and to behold "in the center of a view, a majestic single Rock, between a ∧ and a ⌒ in shape" (*CN* 1:1457; f. 12).

Attention, though not enough in itself to fully engage metaphysical and creative thought, did open a mental space in which the crucial powers of abstraction could step forward and bring Coleridge closer to the essential "truth" beneath the befuddling, pulsating, multifarious layers of experience (*CC* 6:20).[58] Subscribing to the view that mathematics gives knowledge of the world, Coleridge, therefore, often chose, in his landscape descriptions, to dwell upon the formal stabilizing geometrical figures that lay beneath the distracting accidents of physical phenomena.[59] As a result, as I have already mentioned, he shifted his perspective from the outer to the inner eye and dwelt upon the perpendicular shape of a deep ravine, a sheepfold in the shape of a parallelogram, a rock structured like an obtuse triangle with "segments of a circle forming an angle at their point of junction"(*CN* 1:1225; f. 26), a group of Scottish mountains resembling

grounds of Religion and Morals, are impossible without energies of Thought in addition to the effort of Attention. (*CC* 4.1:16)

[58] It should be mentioned that Coleridge, true to his continuous critical and ever-refining mind, was quick to point out that attentiveness alone had its limitations. He warned that though this temper of mind offered clarity, it was not enough in itself, for one also needed the power of thought to grasp a subject metaphysically. As he wrote in an 1810 issue of *The Friend*: "the elements of Geometry require Attention only; but the analysis of our primary Faculties, and the investigation of all the absolute grounds of Religion and Morals, are impossible without energies of Thought in addition to the effort of Attention" (*CC* 4.2:277). Expressing this conviction as well as recalling the numbing study of geometry at university that focused too exclusively upon attention, Coleridge declared it was no wonder that Cambridge had produced "so few men of genius & original power since the time of Newton." He remarked that not only did its curriculum "not call forth the balancing & discriminating powers (*that* I saw long ago) but it requires only *attention*, not *Thought* or Self-production" (*CN* 3:3670; f. 84).

[59] The highest perfection of natural philosophy would consist in the perfect spiritualization of all the laws of nature into laws of intuition and intellect. The phaenomena (*the material*) must wholly disappear, and the laws alone (*the formal*) must remain. Thence, it comes, that in nature itself the more the principle of law breaks forth, the more does the *husk* drop off, the phaenomena themselves become more spiritual and at length cease altogether in our consciousness. (*CC* 7.1:256)

"two sides of a spherical Triangle" (*CN* 1:1482; f. 40), and the ellipses and semicircles of the "bellying Foresails & Top sails" (*CN* 2:2029; f. 9). Moreover, sometimes, as if turning his back to the landscape so that he might view a prospect through a Claude mirror that simplified and abstracted the landscape's forms, Coleridge turned around to capture a view's geometric contours and observe that, for instance, "the Hill that is now to my left & makes an elliptical line to my back, curves in a circle-segment, while the Hill to my right ~~closes~~ folds round about it" (*CN* 1:1225; f. 28). And, while looking back at a mountain near Inverooran in Scotland, he notices a curving wall at "the extremity of this side of the Triangle" (*CN* 1:1482; f. 40).[60]

Abstraction allowed Coleridge to separate the wheat from the chaff and reduce the plethora of details (what he once referred to as the "immense heap of *little* things"[61]) and draw closer to a sense of a universal, permanent law.[62] His intermittent summoning of the Euclidean two-dimensional, shadowless geometric figures, such as the triangles, squares, ellipses, circles, and parallelograms in his notebook descriptions of landscape, momentarily released him from time. Purifying and clarifying his perception, abstraction drew him closer to realizing the truth; it allowed him to tease out the essence of things.[63] As such, it dispelled the frustrations and disheartening dilemma resulting from the "fluctuating nature of objects" (*CC* 6:20).

---

[60] Some evidence that occasionally Coleridge used the Claude glass is visible in his notebooks. For instance, in May 1804 he reported noticing "a sugar loaf Rock" and looking at it "thro' the Glass, but it appeared the same to the naked Eye, as I found by dropping the Glass every 2 or 3 seconds, only it shewed more noble & magnificent thro' the Glass – The *Green* only I cannot answer for – whether or not it depended on the Glass" (*CN* 2:2094; f. 46).

[61] In an October 14, 1797 letter to John Thelwall, Coleridge declared: "the universe itself – what but an immense heap of *little* things? – I can contemplate nothing but parts, & parts are *little* – -! – My mind feels as if it ached to behold & know something *great* – something *one* & *indivisible*" (*CL* 1:349). In a similar vein, Coleridge wrote a few days later to Thomas Poole: "Those who have been led to the same truths step by step thro' the constant testimony of their senses, seem to me to want a sense which I possess – They contemplate nothing but *parts* – and all *parts* are necessarily little – and the Universe to them is but a mass of *little things*" (*CL* 1:354).

[62] In his *Aids to Reflection*, Coleridge proposes: "In order to submit the various phenomena of moving bodies to geometrical construction, we are under the necessity of abstracting from corporeal substance all its *positive* properties" (*CC* 9:399).

[63] On a number of occasions, Coleridge criticized people for paying "An excess" of attachment "to temporal and personal objects." At such moments, he recalled Plato's directive: "Let no man enter … who has not previously disciplined his mind by Geometry" (*CC* 6:173). In his unfinished *Opus Maximum*, Coleridge, still thinking of Plato's idealism, wrote about geometry's role in purifying the mind, the discipline's being "the first step towards its [the mind's] emancipation from the despotism and disturbing forces of the senses" (*CC* 15:183–84). It should also be noted here that when examining George Beaumont's watercolors, Coleridge, as discussed in the previous chapter, was keen to abstract their content by identifying the lines that created inverted triangles, semicircular curves, semi-ovals, parallels, and perfect triangles.

Complementing Coleridge's attraction to the powers of attention and abstraction that necessarily attended the geometric frame of mind was the principle of intuition – an understanding that one has an *a priori* knowledge of the geometric figure. Rather than coming into being and then passing away, the idea of a square or a triangle always is. This intuition, I hasten to add, is not a phenomenon one carelessly refers to when one has a "sense" about something. Rather, it is a specific philosophic concept that one is born with a certain understanding or knowledge. In Plato's *Meno*, for instance, there is the well-known example of Meno's slave boy, who, never having been taught geometry, is able, after being guided by Socrates's questioning, to recollect or recover a knowledge concerning the composition of geometric figures that already resides in his mind and has been gotten from some previous life.[64]

Throughout his life, Coleridge was attracted to this concept so that later when he was writing his *Opus Maximum*, he was applying the idea of intuition to one's knowledge of God and writing, "We have a *pure* sensuous *intuition* of God ... in the same way as we <behold> mathematical figures; <ex. gr.>, the Point, Line, Triangles, Circle etc. of pure Geometry" (*CC* 15:275). Earlier, in the mid-1790s, however, already conditioned by his reading of Plato and by the Platonic sense in the *Timaeus* of a primary "ungenerated and indestructible" ideal as well the certainty of unchanging forms that exist beyond space and time,[65] Coleridge was naturally attracted to Immanuel Kant's insistence that mathematics is grounded in pure intuition. At times, wanting to reach for a spiritual certainty behind the fluctuations of phenomena as well as gain a knowledge of the eternally existent, he was drawn to the concept of intuition, and embraced the view that the individual manifestation of a geometric figure was but a copy of its idea, which one carries internally in one's mind before the experience of it. Introduced to Kant in the mid-1790s and then immersed in his philosophy when he went to Germany, Coleridge was often, throughout his adult life, to express – and often adamantly – the conviction that geometric truths are known with

---

[64] It is this image of Socrates and the slave boy drawing geometric figures in the sand that becomes a basis of Thomas Fanshaw Middleton's spoof (mentioned earlier in this chapter) of "Mr. Puzzlebooby," who is continuously drawing geometric figures in the sand. For a sensitive and subtle discussion of Plato's *Meno*, see Kathleen M. Wheeler's "Irony and Dramatic Art in Plato's Meno," in *Ironie in Philosophie, Literatur und Recht*, ed. Bärbel Frischmann (Würzburg: Königshausen & Neuman, 2014), 37–54. Among other points, she emphasizes the fact that geometry was part of the experience of grasping relations, of discovering patterns and laws. It contributed to the knowledge of relational apprehension.

[65] Plato, *Timaeus*, ed. J. Warrington (London: J. Dent, 1965), 61.

apodictic certainty.⁶⁶ They do not begin with a demonstrable proposition, but with a practiced idea. In his *Biographia Literaria* (1817), for instance, he repeatedly declared "Geometry is *always* and *essentially* INTUITIVE" (*CC* 7.1:174) and that "Geometry supplies philosophy with example of primary intuition" (*CC* 7.1:250).⁶⁷ The certainty that attended this understanding, of course, was as affirming as the frame of mind that permitted Coleridge to honor the accompanying, more abstract, quality of mind.

Indeed, it was Coleridge's oft-reiterated belief in geometry's attachment to the ideal world of intuition that made him impatient with the educational practice of teaching with three-dimensional models of geometric figures in order to visualize Euclidean concepts and make the study of them more palatable. (One can see these beautifully sculptured mid-eighteenth-century wooden models in the Whipple Museum at the University of Cambridge, in particular those rendered by George Adams.)⁶⁸ Longing to promote a more mindful approach to the applications of geometry, Coleridge thought these models numbing and restricting. As mere copies of the intuited geometric form that often "can never be fully realized in Nature" (*CC* 4.2:132), they ensnared the student in the imperfect world of the senses and, thereby, thwarted the development of abstract thought as well as advances in intellect.⁶⁹

---

[66] Thomas Beddoes would have been an invaluable source of knowledge about Kant as early as 1795. See Kathleen M. Wheeler, *The Creative Mind in Coleridge's Poetry* (Cambridge, MA: Harvard University Press, 1981), 10. Beddoes, moreover, for instance, in his *Observations on the Nature of Demonstrative Evidence, with an Explanation of Certain Difficulties Occurring in the Elements of Geometry and Reflection on Language* (London: J. Johnson, 1793), was writing about the "full evidence of intuition" (iii). John Thelwall, one of Coleridge's most frequent correspondents in 1796, belonged to F. A. Nitsch's Kantian Society in London and was perhaps another major source of information on Kant. For an insightful discussion of Coleridge's sense of Kant's understanding of Intuition, see Tim Fulford. *Coleridge's Figurative Language* (Houndmills, Basingstoke: Macmillan, 1991), 104–07.

[67] In a letter to Mr. Pryce of April 1819, Coleridge praised Kant for recognizing the "the pure a priori forms of the intuitive faculty" in mathematics (see *CL* 4:852).

[68] In the nineteenth century and into the twentieth century, there were geometry modeling clubs at Oxford and Cambridge. Arthur Cayley, a defender of Euclid and the Sadleirian Professor of Pure Mathematics at Cambridge, founded Cambridge's modeling club. See "Models of Geometric Surfaces" by Professor June Barrow-Green in *The London Mathematical Society and Sublime Symmetry*, 18–20.

[69] Among Coleridge's lay sermons is a passage that reveals his discomfort with using wooden models as a means of teaching geometry. He complained: "We too teach Geometry, but that there may be no danger of the pupil's becoming too *abstract* in his conceptions, it has been not only proposed, but the proposal has been adopted, that it should be taught by *wooden* diagrams!" (*CC* 6:173). Coleridge realized that it is not always possible to transform abstract notions derived from the pure intellect into concrete and distinct images. Lines are but copies of the original. In *Biographia Literaria*, Coleridge explained:

Worrying that these devices would detract from the intuitive, *a priori* disposition of geometry, Coleridge had severe words for those who promoted not only their use but also the inclusion of "gaudily" colored triangles and circles as well as folded-paper images of geometric figures in editions of Euclid's *Elements*. One consequence was that he lashed out at Thomas Beddoes, who, in his *Observations on the Nature of Demonstrative Evidence, with an Explanation of Certain Difficulties Occurring in the Elements of Geometry* (1793), promoted their use as what Coleridge labeled a "crutch" to understanding Euclid.[70] Moreover, in one of his public lectures, Coleridge dramatically protested: "we have invented wooden circles and tried to make the child to feel, in short we have tried to keep up his memory in the lumber room of his soul with guns and swords and all the implements of warfare, without observing that the arm was paralysed and the soul turned to a mere lumber room where inactive [images] remaining together brought forwards merely mists and vapours and self-conceit" (*CC* 8:394).[71]

## Part Four: Entangled Moments

I suggest, however, that despite an obvious and keen appreciation (demonstrated above in Coleridge's objections) for the disparity between the sensual world of experience and the realm of geometric abstraction associated with the pure, non-sensible Platonic Idea or Kant's understanding of intuited knowledge, Coleridge, when describing the landscape of his walks, softened the hardened and well-established distinction between the two modes of thinking by simultaneously celebrating the sights and sounds of a brook dancing over the rocks as well as the abstract geometric figure

> To the original construction of the line, I can be compelled by a line drawn before me on the slate or on sand. The stroke thus drawn is indeed not the line itself, but only the image or picture of the line. It is not from it, that we first learn to know the line; but, on the contrary, we bring this stroke to the original line generated by the act of the imagination, otherwise we could not define it as without breadth or thickness. Still however this stroke is the sensuous image of the original or ideal line, and an efficient means to excite *every* imagination to the intuition of it. (*CC* 7.1:250)

[70] Coleridge also declared that to use sense experience as a crutch for the learner is self-contradictory (*CC* 8:394).

[71] There were several attempts to make mathematical models. One is described in Samuel Cunn's *An Appendix to the English Translation of Commandine's Euclid* (London: Tho. Woodward, 1725). Wanting to remedy the inconvenience of not being able to exhibit to the eyes all the parts of a figure at once, Cunn devised a means by which he "caused Threads and Wires to be raised on Boards with Letters glewed on the particular Angles, and thereby have shown the several Propositions of the Solids" (6).

outlining a stone's surface. Rather than accepting, as so many of his contemporaries did, the differences between these dissimilar ways of regarding one's surroundings, he, instead, when describing a landscape, tempered this way of thinking by intertwining the experiential with the geometric so that neither detracted nor competed with the other. He does not separate the two. Rather than holding Euclid's *Elements* (the stone) in one hand and the shell (the poetic imagination) in the other as does the Arab in his dream (see Wordsworth's *The Prelude*, Book V, lines 71–98), he simultaneously clutches and conjoins the two. He goes a step further than what Theresa M. Kelley suggests when she proposes that these symbols of science and poetry in the Arab's dream are "both distinct, yet complementary."[72] Instead Coleridge thinks of their being intermingled. In so doing, he bestows a more complete portrait of what he saw as he trekked through the scenes of his rambles, and draws nearer to realizing "one beautiful Whole" (*CN* 2:1851; f. 72).

Significantly, in his notebook entries, Coleridge did not prioritize one mode of seeing or understanding over the other but, rather, momentarily dismissed the hierarchical order of perception – the senses being thought inferior to the Ideal – by valuing both the richness of the sensual world and the affirmation afforded by the certainty of the geometric figure. Refusing to deem one more elevated than the other, he disregarded the directive of the ancient philosophers who encouraged their followers to seek an emancipation from the senses so as to be free from their contamination and, therefore, reach a better understanding of an eternal, lasting truth.[73] For Coleridge a landscape's sensual delights and wonders were just as precious as its abstract geometric figures – an attitude clearly originating in "the sweet scenes of childhood" when, as a boy, he took pleasure in the willows bending over the smooth, transparent breast of the River Otter that flows through Nether Stowey ("Sonnet: To the River Otter"). Not wanting to dishonor either the feel, sounds, and sights of experience or the geometric state of mind with its attendant attention, abstraction, and intuition, he embraced and valued both. Disregarding the threat of the numbing, negative "loathsome strain" of Mathesis from which the "frighted Muses" take flight (expressed in his undergraduate verse quoted earlier), Coleridge readily combined these two seemingly contradictory modes of

---

[72] See Theresa M. Kelley, "Spirit and Geometric Form: The Stone and the Shell in Wordsworth's Arab Dream," *Studies in English Literature* 22 (1982): 569.

[73] As an example of this directive, consider Plato's despair about a person's distracting eyes and ears that infect the soul, and recall his mandate that we must be quit of the body, for in the company of the body, the soul cannot have pure knowledge.

perception to create exquisitely vivid passages from which the Muses do not fly and in which shadows of a birch's leaves play on a geometric shape. The result is a series of notebook observations replete with lush, striking and fluid images that stand along and intermingle with geometric figures.

Attracted to the transient and the perishing as much as he was to the existence of permanent, eternal forms, Coleridge composed many entries such as one he wrote after rambling near Bassenthwaite in November 1799. In this description, as in a myriad of others, he simultaneously engaged both the outward, sensual eye, sensitive to color and movement, as well as to the inner eye, conscious of a more permanent, intuited geometric form:

> From Ouse bridge, from the Inn Window, the whole length of Basenthwait, a simple majesty of water & mountains – / & in the distance the Bank rising like a wedge ◣ – & in the second distance the Crags of Derwentwater / What an effect of the Shadows on the water! / – On the left the conical Shadow, On the right a square of splendid Black, all the area & intermediate a mirror reflecting dark & sunny Cloud / – but in the distance the black Promontory with a circle of melted Silver & a path of silver running from it like a flat Cape in the Lake – The snowy Borrodale in the far distance / & a ridge, nearer mountains sloping down as it were to the faint Bank of the Basenthwaite. (*CN* 1:536; f. 43)

Similarly, in 1803, continuing to blend a fleeting impressionistic response with the more permanent geometric figure, he wrote:

> Thursday Morning, 40 minutes past One o'clock – a perfect calm – now & then a breeze shakes the heads of the two Poplars, (& disturbs) the murmur of the moonlight Greta, that in almost a direct Line from the moon to me is all silver – Motion and Wrinkle & Light – & under the arch of the Bridge a wave ever & anon leaps up in Light. – & the evergreens are bright, under my window /. The Moon now hangs midway over Cowdale Halse – in a line, ~~on~~ & resting on each of the divergi~~n~~gent Legs of its Triangle a fish-head-shaped Cloud – the whole area of the Triangle blue sky. (*CN* 1:1616; f. 73)

In a sense, when Coleridge portrayed the landscape of his walking, he suspended the notion of succession so that one mode of perception does not necessarily precede the other, either consciously or intuitively. Rather, Coleridge, in his portrayals of landscape, preferred to merge the two into one entangled moment or phrase in which one perspective intertwines with another. Hence, he saw "a yellow-green parallelogram" (*CN* 1:1627; f. 20), a "blue *Triangle*" (*CN* 1:1836; f. 67), and a "square of splendid Black" (*CN* 1:536; f. 43) – phrases that, given his strong objection to colored geometric figures in editions of Euclid's *Elements*, might, perhaps, seem to be out of character and to contradict one another. However, in the context of Coleridge's desire to obviate difference and hierarchy, neither condition superseded nor compromised the other but, rather, each dwelt with the other to create an indelibly vivid moment that does not limit the imagination.[74] In this intermingling, there can be change without loss. Difference disappears. In April 1806, after gazing at a column of smoke drifting through the air as well as the water traveling and falling in a waterfall, an ecstatic Coleridge remarked on what he phrased the coexistence of change and permanence by "an absolute annihilation of difference." His notebook reads: "The quiet circle in which Change and Permanence *co-exist*, not by combination or juxtaposition, but by an absolute annihilation of difference / column of smoke, the fountains before St. Peter's, waterfall / GOD! – Change without loss – change by a perpetual growth ... oh! It was aweful" (*CN* 2:2832; f. 92). It was this entangling that allowed him to fuse what is permanent with what is moving so that a "stone fence" "runs in a trembling circle round a green Lawn" (*CN* 1:549; f. 23). Just as motion is embedded in geometry – Euclid's sense that a point must travel to create a line – so is permanence a part of his experiential surroundings. As a result, Coleridge's notebooks are replete with descriptive passages in which participles propel static forms and reveal "a very wild, various, & angular outline, running in ridges, rising in triangles, sinking in inverting arches, or darting down in Nesses" (*CN* 1:1224; f. 24).

Perhaps it is helpful to conclude with a selection from a lengthy entry written in September 1803 when Coleridge was trudging back home through a rugged landscape after leaving William and Dorothy Wordsworth on their aborted tour of Scotland. In these passages, the terrain of the senses and the world of abstract forms tumble over each other to intertwine and knit their energy together. One form of perception does not exclude the other, but rather relaxes into the other so that neither the abstract nor the sensual experience enjoys priority. The first part of the entry describing a series of waterfalls calls upon the geometric

---

[74] One should be reminded of Kathleen M. Wheeler's "Coleridge's Theory of Imagination: A Hegelian Solution to Kant?," in which she discusses Coleridge's capacity to synthesize and his sensitivity to the interpenetration of opposites. See Wheeler, *The Interpretation of Belief: Coleridge, Schleiermacher and Romanticism*. ed. David Jasper (Houndmills, Basingstoke: Macmillan, 1986), 16–40. One also recalls Tim Fulford's discussion of Kant's *Critique of Pure Reason* in which he points out that when organizing sense data into coherent knowledge, "the *Critique* demonstrated that what we know through the evidence of the senses is in fact a synthesis of the manifold of sense impressions and the active power of the understanding to shape them into coherence." See Fulford, *Coleridge's Figurative Language* (Houndmills, Basingstoke: Macmillan, 1991), 104–05.

idiom yet continues to honor the movement and colors associated with the sense:

> The broader fall among the sublimest I have ever seen / it divides itself, I might say, it distinguishes itself into 3 falls, the one nearest the Great rock shoots out & leaves a large Cavern underneath where a man might stand & but for the *dashing in under* of the other part of the Fall shelter himself from a Storm under the ceiling of Foam – the 2 other parts <are divided> only at the very head by a tall pink rock, ~~from my~~ the one nearest the Shoot drives aslant the third which falls down in an opposite direction, and tho' they touch, preserve their Individuality / the Slanter covering all but the higher part of the third $\vee$ – the pink rocks seen every now & then at the bottom thro' the white Foam most *lovely*! – The Cone behind the Gavel, I saw it all / it was only a Jag of a noble rock rising up into a perfect acute Angled $\wedge$ behind the Gavel / or rather it is one of two cones in file rising up behind this $\wedge$, & yet another rises behind that Triangle & that Gavel / – first the Green Gavel, then, far lower than, but exactly like it in shape, a slender rocky Gavel, then higher perhaps even than the green Gavel this sharper & more perfect Gavel, then behind that a ridge having 2 sister Cones! (*CN* 1:1489; f. 55)

The second passage, which comes later in this long entry, eases into a splendid description of the light and shadows falling upon a stream – yet another reminder that for Coleridge the senses are no less significant than the organizing abstractions of a geometric figure:

> So having mounted a little & seen that there was not probably anything more to be noticed, I turned back – & now my mind being as it were leisurely and of[f] the stretch with what delight did I look at a floatage of Shadows on the water, made by the wavelets of the Stream, with what delight that most exquisite net at the bottom / sandy + pebbly river, all whose loops are wires of sunshine, gold finer than silk, beside yon Stone the Breeze seems to have blown them into a Heap, a rich mass of light, light spreading from the loop holes into the interstices. (*CN* 1:1489; f. 57)

## Conclusion

It is this entanglement of the geometric figure with the sights, movements, sounds, and colors of his natural surroundings which, as we shall see in the next chapter, metamorphoses into his poetry and, thereby, generates and sustains the momentum, structure, and tenor of Coleridge's verses celebrating the sublime and spiritual character of a landscape. Neither mode of seeing precludes or sullies the other but, rather, in their intermingling the two create a more complete and richer sense of the surrounding world. Therefore, what in his youth Coleridge perceived as blocking, or at best interfering with, creative thought and energy, does not. Indeed, the geometric idiom, with its linear and figurative structures, enters the composition to support the lush, fluid sensual images of the poem. The two modes work together to arrange and bring the verses' lines to life. Together they create a sense of the whole.

CHAPTER 4

# Ars Poetica

> The poet, described in *ideal* perfection, brings the whole soul of man into activity, with the subordination of its faculties to each other, according to their relative worth and dignity. He diffuses a tone, and spirit of unity, that blends, and (as it were) *fuses*, each into each, by that synthetic and magical power to which we have exclusively appropriated the name of imagination
>
> (*CC* 7.2:15–16)

> For the first condition – namely, simplicity while it distinguishes Poetry from the ~~laborious~~ arduous processes of Science laboring towards an end not yet arrived at, & supposes a smooth and finished Road on which the Reader is to walk onward easily, with streams murmuring by his side, & Trees & Flowers, & human dwellings to make his journey as delightful as the Object of it is desirable ...
>
> (*CN* 3:3287; f. 9)

In October 1803, while on a journey up north, Coleridge passed by a thatch roof that being so full of weeds resembled "a Hill-bank." Struck by the thatch's wild demeanor, he remarked on its scraggy, overgrown appearance and then notably added: "This I assuredly shall introduce into Verse" (*CN* 1:1585; f. 55) – a comment that prompts one to reflect upon the relationship between Coleridge's experiences while wandering through a landscape and his writing of such poems as "A Beck in Winter," "Sonnet: To the River Otter," "Frost at Midnight," and "This Lime-Tree Bower My Prison," as well as the lesser-known verses occasioned by his walking.[1]

---

[1] It needs to be said that Coleridge rarely, if at all, wrote a poem based upon one particular ramble described in his notebooks (for instance, there is nothing like Wordsworth's "I Wandered Lonely as a Cloud," which specifically refers to a passage in Dorothy's journal), but rather Coleridge called upon his memory of various experiences and observations while wandering through a landscape. Indeed, Coleridge is often more a poet in his notebooks than in his poetry that occasionally echoes conventional modes and portrays a dependency on tradition. It should also be mentioned that there are several poems, other than those mentioned above, that emerged from his walking. Robin Jarvis points out, for example, that "'Kubla Khan' was composed in the course of a long

More particularly, Coleridge's remark provokes one to ponder just how the footfall of his rambles, his alertness to the lines of motion in a landscape, and his intermittent geometric perspective – all attendants of his rambling as well as topics discussed in the preceding chapters – contributed to the topography of these selected poems so that they retained some memory or vestige of his wandering. One wonders what remnants of his sensitivity to the tread and feel of his feet as well as to his lineal and geometric sensibilities remained to help sculpt these verses. Though such a query does not address the many acknowledged complexities of Coleridge's creative process – the foibles of his personal life, his philosophical reading, his political views, changes in his circumstances, his literary models, and alterations in his theological beliefs – it does introduce additional ways of discussing the composition of these poems composed during the decade of his walking. The following discussion will add yet another dimension to what critics, most particularly Robin Jarvis in his *Romantic Writing and Pedestrian Travel* (1997), have already explored when addressing the connection between Coleridge's excursive walking and his writing as well as his physical immersion in the landscape.[2]

## The Tread and Feel of His Feet: The Peripatetic Rhythms of His Verse

When writing his poetry describing a landscape, Coleridge frequently called upon the kind of striking, moving images that had rapidly tumbled over each other in his notebook entries. Wanting their liveliness to resonate in his verses, he drew attention to "the wild streamlet of the West" ("Sonnet: To the River Otter"), to a stone fence that "flings its narrow slip of grey" ("Perspiration"), to a village spring that over a "rough rock bursts and foams along" ("Lines: To a Beautiful Spring in the Village"), and to the "bare bleak mountain speckled thin with sheep" ("Lines written at Shurton Bars"). Though few of these images necessarily

---

unaccompanied coastal walk to Lynton and back" and that *The Ancient Mariner* "was conceived during a walk of several days to Dulverton in the company of Wordsworth and Dorothy" (*Romantic Writing and Pedestrian Travel*, 127).

[2] It should be acknowledged that when thinking generally of poetry, various commentators point out a connection between the rhythm of one's bodily movements and poetic meter. The parallel between the pace of human feet and poetic feet is not imaginary but, rather, present. Robert Macfarlane, for instance, in his evocatively lyrical *Old Ways*, repeatedly acknowledges the relationship between thinking and walking, between footfall and understanding, between writing and walking (29). Thinking of Edward Thomas's poetry based upon his rambling, Macfarlane observes how the "shod feet" of the traveler and "the scratch of the pen nib" expire into one another (340).

recollect a specific notebook entry, each calls to mind the distinctive tenor of a passage's vivid details.³

I want to suggest, however, that it was not so much the evocation of these particulars as it was the specifically recollected rhythm or imprint of his feet moving through a landscape that significantly contributed to the ways in which Coleridge shaped the contours of his nature poems and bestowed upon them a feeling of immediacy as well as a consciousness of an evolving present. Appropriately, he once observed to William Sotheby that among the senses a poet "must have" is "the eye of a North American Indian tracing the footsteps of an Enemy upon the Leaves that strew the Forest" (*CL* 2:810). On many occasions he heeds this directive, for his nature poems are alert to the steps and the feel of his rambling. Like the large flock of brown linnets that initially scatter and eventually reassemble into "one beautiful Whole," these poems respond to the repeated disturbance of his footfall and ultimately shape their dispersed words and images into a unified entity. His poems reunite the thoughts and impressions diffused by the tread of his feet (*CN* 2:1851; f. 72).⁴

As a result, Coleridge's early verses often call attention to the pace of his walking – to his "many a weary step" with which he gains, for example, the summit of Bala Hill ("On Bala Hill"). In these poems, he describes a landscape that "At every step" widens to his "sight" so that "Wood, Meadow, verdant Hill, and dreary Steep" follow "in quick succession of delight" ("Life"). Throughout the verses' lines, "with slow foot" he wanders near a "sweet stream" ("Lines: To a Beautiful Spring in a Village"), counts "the echoings of my feet" ("Lines written at Shurton Bars"), and remembers their plunging "into the gentle river" where the "river-swans have heard my tread" ("Lewti").

---

³ Kathleen Coburn, for instance, suggests that the image of the alder tree in the opening of "Lines Written at Dove Cottage" ("Over the broad tho' shallow, rapid Stream, / The Alder, a vast hollow Trunk ...") refers to alder trees seen on Coleridge's Scottish tour with the Wordsworths (see *CN* 1:1489; f. 51). She proposes that possibly Coleridge was going over the tour notes with Dorothy Wordsworth and came across the image.

⁴ The whole entry reads:

> Friday evening, Jan. 20, 1804. Observed in the garden of Eaton House the flight of the Brown Linnets, a large flock of whom I had repeatedly disturbed by my foot-fall as I walked by the thicket / 1. Twinkling of wings. 2. Heavy & swanlike rise & fall, yet so that while one was rising, another was falling – & so 4. Their sweet straight onward motion / they swam on, not with *speed* or haste, much less *hurry*, but with easy natural Swiftness – & their graceful wheel round one half of a circle or more, & then cut straight the diameter of it – 4. Their change of position amongst themselves / right to left, hindward to the front, vanguard to the rear – these four motions all at once in one beautiful Whole, like a Machine –. (*CN* 2:1851; f. 72)

These passing references to his footfall, however, are not what actually capture the sensation of trudging through a landscape. Rather, it is the uneven, erratic rhythms of these verses that suggest the stride of his walking and, thereby, introduce a sense of sequential immediacy into his poetic line. To accomplish this effect, Coleridge revisits the erratic, interrupted tread of his notebook passages, such as one describing an August 1802 fell walk:

> I pass along for a furlong or so upon the road, the river winding thro' the narrow vale, & then turn off to my left athwart a Cove on Donnerdale Fell – a very rocky Fell, yew-trees on the Rocks / (each crag a lownding-place for sheep) the outer line running in the segment of a circle so as to form the cove athwart which I went – this outline most wildly saw-toothed / and sheep-tracks every where – O lovely lovely Vale! – (*CN* 1:1225; f. 26)

As if desiring his poetry to replicate this entry's sense of immediacy, he summons the dashes, breaks, slashes, and exclamatory phrases visible throughout his notebook descriptions. He transfers enough –a vestige – of these devices into his nature poems so as to catch the successive moments of exertion, rest, and amazement attending his wandering. As a result, his poems often breathe to this physical memory and, thereby, reveal his keen appreciation for what Jarvis recognizes as the kinetic muscular foundation of poetic rhythm.[5] One senses the movement of Coleridge's steps as he progresses along the verses' lines. Rarely do these nature poems, therefore, travel to the regular measure of the Dame's cheery song set to the predictable clip-clop pattern of Dobbin's foot as the horse "jogs the accustom'd road along" ("Songs of the Pixies"), but, rather, they reverberate with and take shape from the irregular tread of his rambling. Although much of his education would have been spent analyzing the meter of the poetry he was studying, and even though he had a keen sense of meter and often conducted metrical experiments, when it came to these verses, it was not traditional meter that ruled but rather the rhythm of his walking.[6]

---

[5] To see Robin Jarvis's comments on the relationship between the rhythm of a poem and walking, see "'Indolence Capable of Energies': Coleridge the Walker" in his *Romantic Writing and Pedestrian Travel*, 126–54. See also Andreas Mayer's *The Science of Walking*, in which Mayer states that in the eighteenth century there is a belief that when one walks, step by step, there is also a "march of ideas." There is an "interlacing of outer and inner man" (68).

[6] It is perhaps not necessary to be reminded of Coleridge's keen sense of meter. A cursory glance at his notebooks finds him marking the rhythm of poetic lines and conducting metrical experiments. So much of his education would have been spent analyzing the meter of the poetry he was reading. In his "Preface" to *Christabel* (1797), Coleridge seems in part to be recalling the uneven, individual

In this respect, it is interesting to note that long after his rambling days were over, Coleridge assigned himself the exercise of transforming two lines of prose – he thought they could be found in either "a book of topography or a descriptive tour" – into "a descriptive poem" that vividly captures the sensation of journeying past wind-blown pines silhouetted against an evening sky ("[Ars Poetica]," *CP* 2:1006). As if evoking his earlier walking excursions, he not only arranged the lines of prose into the pattern of a poem but also resuscitated the dashes and caesuras that had once appeared in his notebook entries.[7] These marks and interruptions transform the relatively static, though rather lovely, "Behold you rows of pines, that shorn and bow'd / Bind from the sea-blast, seen at twilight eve" into a breathing and moving poetic fragment – "into a semblance of poetry" – that gives the illusion of tracking the beholder's progress as he observes the astonishing scene:

> "You row of bleak and visionary pines,
> By twilight-glimpse discerned, mark! how they flee
> From the fierce sea-blast, all their tresses wild
> Streaming before them."
>
> (*CP* 2:1006)

As I have already mentioned, with the exception of a handful of critics, little attention is paid to this aspect of Coleridge's art. And, perhaps, for good reason, for there is scarcely a passage in his notebooks or in his critical writing which overtly comments upon the specific link between the act of

---

footsteps through a continually moving landscape as well as his shifting emotional reactions to a scene when he explains the irregularity of this poem's rhythm:

> I have only to add that the metre of Christabel is not, properly speaking, irregular, though it may seem so from its being founded on a new principle: namely, that of counting in each line the accents, not the syllables. Though the latter may vary from seven to twelve, yet in each line the accents will be found to be only four. Nevertheless, this occasional variation in number of syllables is not introduced wantonly, or for the mere ends of convenience, but in correspondence with some transition in the nature of the imagery or passion. (*CP* 1:215)

One also cannot overlook Coleridge's playfully instructive "Metrical Feet: Lessons for a Boy," in which he typically uses the analogy of a walker's long and short strides to illustrate the set, conventional arrangements of stressed and unstressed syllables that his sons would have been required to know when studying poetry (see *CP* 1:401–02).

[7] It is interesting to note that in a November 20, 1798 letter to Thomas Poole, Coleridge remarked on a conversation that Wordsworth had with the German poet F. G. Klopstock. According to Coleridge, in that conversation "Wordsworth explained his definition & ideas of harmonious Verse, that it consisted in the arrangement of pauses & cadences, & not in the even flow of single Lines – Klopstock assented" (*CL* 1:442).

walking and composing poems.[8] One notable exception occurs in an October 1803 entry, written while on a long fell ramble in the Lakes. In this entry he chronicles a moment in which the course and measure of his strides, a "healthy man's walk," between a bridge and a pile of stones prompts him to contemplate organizing a poem:

> Go & build up a pile of three [stones], by that Coppice – measure the Strides from the Bridge where the water rushes down a rock in no mean cataract if the Rains should have swoln the River – & the Bridge itself hides a small cataract – from this Bridge measure the Strides to the Place, build the Stone heap, & write a Poem, thus beginning – From the Bridge &c repeat such a Song, of Milton, or Homer – so many Lines I ~~will~~ must find out, may be distinctly recited during a moderate healthy man's walk from the Bridge thither – or better perhaps from the other Bridge – so to this Heap of Stones – there turn in – & then describe the Scene – O surely I might make a noble Poem of all my Youth nay *of all my Life* – (*CN* 1:1610; f. 72)

This passage exemplifies Coleridge's tendency, already discussed at the beginning of this book, to adopt the surveyor's mode of counting the footsteps between one spot and another and then marking that distance with the building of a pile of stones, but more significantly, it exhibits his willingness to attend to the correlation between the pacing of his footfall and that of his poetic line – hence, his preference to modify conventional poetic meter by introducing the idiosyncratic rhythms of his notebook entries.

A number of poems, written during his walking period, display this inclination. In "Lines: Composed while climbing the Left Ascent of Brockley Coomb, Somersetshire, May 1795," Coleridge, for example, refers to the speaker's uneven footfall and the emerging scenery as he scrambles up the coomb to gain "the topmost site" (*CP* 1:94). Starting his many lines with a stressed syllable, he marks each new sighting or sound (the warbling, the far-off sound of the cuckoo, a flock of birds) as if registering the downward thrust of his boot as it presses on during the

---

[8] It should be pointed out that in March 1808, Coleridge compared the laborious process of science to the smooth road of a poem upon which a reader walks. The notebook entry reads:

> simplicity, while it distinguishes Poetry from the ~~laborious~~ arduous processes of Science laboring towards an end not yet arrived at, & supposes a smooth and finished Road on which the Reader is to walk onward easily, with streams murmuring by his side, & Trees & Flowers, & human dwellings to make his journey as delightful as the Object of it is desirable, instead of having to toil with the Pioneers, & painfully make the road, on which others are to travel, precludes every affectation – & so on / (*CN* 3:3287; f. 9)

climb. And, toward the end of the poem when reaching his destination, he reproduces the rests his speaker takes by breaking up the sonnet's iambic pentameter line, and then, once at the summit, as if catching his breath, he inserts a dash and a series of exclamatory phrases that require the reader to inhale and tarry ("I rest: – and now have gain'd the topmost site / Ah!") so he too might enjoy the "luxury" of the prospect and thoughts of the speaker's loved one.[9] Step by step, the poem inserts the reader into the poem's continuous present. The first eleven lines offer a sense of the poem's peripatetic pulse:

> With many a pause and oft reverted eye
> I climb the Coomb's ascent: sweet songsters near
> Warble in shade their wild-wood melody:
> Far off the unvarying Cuckoo soothes my ear.
> Up scour the startling stragglers of the flock
> That on green plots o'er precipices browze:
> From the deep fissures of the naked rock
> The Yew-tree bursts! Beneath its dark green boughs
> (Mid which the May-thorn blends its blossoms white)
> Where broad smooth stones jut out in mossy seats,
> I rest: – and now have gain'd the topmost site.
> (*CP* 1:94, lines 1–11)

During his rambling years, Coleridge composed other poems that invite the reader to participate in the bodily exertion of making his way through both the poem and the unfolding scenery.[10] As a result, a reader, while treading these poems' lines, keeps pace with Coleridge as he listens to "the echoings" of his feet ("Sonnet On Quitting School for College," *CP* 1:29),

---

[9] Coleridge's simile to describe the effects of too much regularity is particularly graphic and reflects his sense of poetic rhythm being a bodily sensation. He states that the effects of disproportionate meter are "like that of leaping in the dark from the last step of a stair-case, when we had prepared our muscles for a leap of three or four" (*CC* 7.2:66).

[10] Walking helps shape the pace of other poems, such as "To a Young Friend On his proposing to domesticate with the Author" (1796), a poem in which Coleridge looks forward to a time when he and Charles Lloyd might ramble at different paces together over "jutting rocks," up "a path sublime" and then "oft pausing" descend by a "downward slope" to "some lone mansion, in some woody dale" (*CP* 1:155–57, lines 3, 17, 45, 46). Walking's varied rhythms are audible in other poems, such as a section in "The Picture or the Lover's Resolution" (1802), when Coleridge follows the successive "wild" footsteps of the speaker as he climbs and descends in order to frame his narrative about the determination of a lover:

> Through weeds and thorns, and matted underwood
> I force my way; now climb, and now descend
> O'er rocks, or bare or mossy, with wild foot
> Crushing the purple whorts; ...
> (*CP* 1:369, lines 1–4)

complains of the track's rough condition, or rests to admire a prospect. "Devonshire Roads," an early poem composed in August 1791, overtly recognizes this relationship when it opens with the image of "The indignant Bard" composing an ode while dragging his way through Plimtree Road (a place eight miles north of Ottery St. Mary's) and cursing the dreary path's muddiness in which his sandal gets stuck. The abrupt pace of the first few lines catches the speaker's dilemma caused by his feet "crusted in filth and stuck in mire":

> The indignant Bard composed this furious ode,
> As tired he dragg'd his way thro' Plimtree road!
> Crusted with filth and stuck in mire
> Dull sounds the Bard's bemudded lyre;
> (*CP* 1:27, lines 1–4)

And when in January 1804 he set himself the task of composing a poem by reducing "many minute descriptions of natural objects" into blank verse, he also honored the pace of his rambling.[11] "A Beck in Winter" is the result. Though the poem does not specifically mention Coleridge's actual rambling (until the last line, which recalls his having once safely trod a path), the rhythm of its consecutive images suggests the progress of a walk.

> Over the broad tho' shallow, rapid Stream,
> The Alder, a vast hollow Trunk, & ribb'd
> Within / all mossy green with mosses manifold,
> And Ferns still waving in the river breeze,
> Sent out, like Fingers, ~~five~~ 7 projecting Trunks,
> The shortest twice 6 of a tall man's Strides,
> One curving upward, and in its middle growth
> Rose straight with grove of Twigs, a pollard Tree
> The rest more brookward, gradual in descent,
> ~~Two in~~ One on the Brook, & one befoam'd its waters,
> One ran along the bank, with elk-like Head
> And pomp of Antlers / – but still that one
> That lay upon or just above the brook
> And straight across it, more than halfway o'er
> Ends in a broad broad head, & a white Thorn
> Thicket of Twigs – & here another Tree
> As if the winds & waves had work'd by art
> That it, with similar Head, & similar Thicket
> Bridging the Stream compleat / thro' these two Thickets

---

[11] Significantly, Robin Jarvis points out that after Coleridge retired from his peripatetic life, he almost abandoned writing in blank verse (*Romantic Writing and Pedestrian Travel*, 139).

> The Shepherd Lads had cut & plan'd a Path /
> O sweet in summer / & in winter Storms
> I have cross'd the same unharm'd
>
> (*CN* 1:1837)[12]

This poem not only selectively recalls various details seen on his rambles but also advances with the measure of the speaker's progress as he continually remarks on his surroundings while passing by a rapid stream, trees, ferns, and a path once cut by the tread of "Shepherd Lads" – notably, the tree trunks are measured by a person's stride ("The shortest twice 6 of a tall man's Strides"). The lines' dashes and diagonal slashes that, as already discussed, created the compelling cadence of Coleridge's notebook descriptions reappear to honor the rambler's pauses and draw attention to the breezes, winds, and waves that shape each visible detail. Moreover, as in the walker's continuous passage, no full stop interrupts the poem. One moment follows another to unfold the speaker's progress.[13]

The development of the poems mentioned above brings to mind Coleridge's reference to a serpent, in chapter 14 of *Biographia Literaria*, that makes its way along a path by pausing and half receding so as to collect the force with which to carry itself forward – a phenomenon that represents how one forms one's thoughts. As he wrote:

> The reader should be carried forward, not merely or chiefly by the mechanical impulse of curiosity, or by a restless desire to arrive at the final solution; but by the pleasureable [*sic*] activity of mind excited by the attractions of the journey itself. Like the motion of a serpent, which the Egyptians made the emblem of intellectual power; or like the path of sound through the air; at every step he pauses and half recedes, and from the retrogressive movement collects the force which again carries him onward. (*CC* 7.2:14)

So too do the irregular, back-and-forth, here-and-there movements of his footsteps propel him and his ideas along his poetic lines. Indeed, it is the resulting energy from this movement that helps distinguish Coleridge's verses, such as "Sonnet: To the River Otter" (1793), from "The River Itchin," "River Wainsbeck," and "The River Charwell," three poems written by William Lisle Bowles, who is said to have motivated

---

[12] This version of the poem published in Coleridge's notebooks varies slightly and is shorter than the fragment that appears in E. H. Coleridge's edition of the collected poems. See *CP* 2:998–99.

[13] In her notes, Kathleen Coburn remarks: "It is rather poignant to see this effort of very detailed description in blank verse written probably on one of the last two nights in Dove Cottage before departure. It refers I think to an alder seen on the Scottish tour (*CN* 1:1489 *ff* 53–54) and possibly he was going over the tour notes with Dorothy Wordsworth who was writing up her journal" (*CN* Notes 1:1837).

Coleridge to compose this sonnet.[14] Bowles was a poet whom he warmly admired during the mid-1790s for introducing him to a style of poetry that allowed him to honor his "love of nature" and "the sense of beauty in forms and sounds" (*CC* 7.1:17). The opening lines of a sonnet "To the Rev. W. L. Bowles," first printed in 1794, express Coleridge's gratitude. The following lines come from the second version, published in 1796:

> My heart has thank'd thee, BOWLES! for those soft strains,
> Whose sadness soothes me, like the murmuring
> Of wild-bees in the sunny showers of spring!
> 
> (*CP* 1:85, lines 1–3)[15]

Such was his reverence for Bowles's poetry that when he was seventeen, Coleridge transcribed forty copies of Bowles's sonnets and presented them to his friends at Christ's Hospital School.[16] One can see why initially he was attracted to these verses that speak of the slow wanderings of a

---

[14] W. K. Wimsatt in his much-anthologized essay "The Structure of Romantic Nature Imagery," in *The Verbal Icon: Studies in the Meaning of Poetry* (Lexington: University of Kentucky Press, 1954). 103–16, couples William Lisle Bowles's "To the River Itchin" with Coleridge's "Sonnet: To the River Otter" (see 105–10). Wimsatt suggests that both poems and their description of nature are more vivid than those written in the age of Pope – that each speaker in these sonnets keeps "his eye more closely on the object" (108). In the discussion that follows in this chapter, however, I qualify Wimsatt's argument and discuss the ways in which Coleridge's poem is significantly far more vivid than Bowles's.

[15] The first version of the sonnet "To the Rev. W. L. Bowles" that was first published in December 1794 reads:

> My heart has thank'd thee, BOWLES! for those soft strains
>   That, on the still air floating, tremblingly
>   Wak'd in me Fancy, Love, and Sympathy!
> For hence, not callous to a Brother's pains
> 
> Thro' Youth's gay prime and thornless paths I went;
>   And, when the *darker* day of life began,
>   And I did roam, a thought-bewilder'd man!
> Thy kindred Lays an healing solace lent,
> 
> Each lonely pang with dreamy joys combin'd,
>   And stole from vain REGRET her scorpion stings;
>   While shadowy PLEASURE, with mysterious wings,
> Brooded the wavy and tumultuous mind,
> 
> Like that great Spirit, who with plastic sweep
> Mov'd on the darkness of the formless Deep!
> 
> (*CP* 1:84)

[16] In chapter 1 of *Biographia Literaria* (1817) Coleridge recalls his indebtedness to William Lisle Bowles. When at Christ's Hospital, his "patron and protector" John Middleton, before leaving for the University of Cambridge, presented him with a copy of twenty sonnets by Bowles. Coleridge recalls: "I had just entered on my seventeenth year, when the sonnets of Mr. Bowles, twenty in number, and just then published in a quarto pamphlet, were first made known and presented to me, by a school-fellow who had quitted us for the University ... I refer to Dr. Middleton, the truly

sequestered stream, the mossy-scattered rocks, the dark woods, the willowed edges of a river, and the tinges of light on the sedge – all details that could have populated his notebooks.[17] But I suggest that there is a distinct difference, for Bowles's sonnets celebrating these natural images soon retreat into a reflective, weary mood that dispatches the poem into a time gone by and conveys little sense of an unfolding, imminent present that drives and impels Coleridge's nature poetry. The opening six lines of Bowles's "To the River Itchin" exemplify this withdrawal to a still past:

> Itchin! when I behold thy banks again,
> Thy crumbling margin, and thy silver breast,
> On which the self-same tints still seem to rest,
> Why feels my heart a shivering of pain!
> In it, that many a summer's day has past
> Since, in life's morn, I carolled on thy side![18]

How unlike Coleridge's "Sonnet: To the River Otter" (originally composed in 1793), which, although also referring to days remembered, resuscitates for a moment his playing by the River Otter as a child. The poem does not suffer from a defect of stillness but, rather, step by step, revives the energy of physically being there so that the images of the water, the "crossing plank," and the "bedded sand" once more rise into the here and now. The poem re-engages the "continual present tense of pure phenomenality"[19] that is supremely audible in his notebooks:

> Dear native Brook! wild Streamlet of the West!
>   How many various-fated years have past,
>   What happy and what mournful hours, since last
> I skimm'd the smooth thin stone along thy breast,
> Numbering its light leaps! Yet so deep imprest
> Sink the sweet scenes of childhood, that mine eyes
>   I never shut amid the sunny ray,
> But straight with all their tints thy waters rise,
>   Thy crossing plank, thy marge with willows grey,

---

learned, and every way excellent Bishop of Calcutta." A few paragraphs later he wrote: "My obligations to Mr. Bowles were indeed important!" (*CC* 7.1:13, 15).

[17] Eventually Bowles's influence on Coleridge naturally declined as his reading expanded, but in those early poems written during Coleridge's walking years, the example of Bowles lingered. Indeed, Coleridge's interest in Bowles remained so that he continued to include it in his 1797, 1803, 1828, 1829, and 1834 collections of his own poetry.

[18] *The Poetical Works of William Lisle Bowles*, ed. George Gilfillan, vol. 1 (Edinburgh: James Nichol, 1855), 1.

[19] Harold D. Baker, "Landscape as Textual Practice in Coleridge's Notebooks," *ELH* 59.3 (1992): 667.

And bedded sand that vein'd with various dyes
Gleam'd through thy bright transparence! On my way,
   Visions of Childhood! Oft have ye beguil'd
Lone manhood's cares, yet waking fondest sighs:
   Ah! That once more I were a careless Child!
                                                    (*CP* 1:48)

It is, of course, this fluid immediacy that reflects Coleridge's sensitivity to the lines of motion in a landscape made visible by his feet sequentially treading the paths of his excursions. It is these lines that shape the contours of his poems.

## The Lineal

When composing his nature poetry, Coleridge, as if extending the path made by the tread of his feet, occasionally also resuscitated his keen sensitivity to the lines of motion that run through and diagram the landscapes described in his notebooks. As discussed in the second chapter, throughout the notebook entries depicting an unfolding scene, he habitually remarked on and actually traced (with a pencil) the outline of a hill's fissures, the moving contours of a mountain, the course of a waterfall, or the "moving pillar of clouds, flame & smoke, rising, bending, arching, and in swift motion" (*CN* 1:781; f. 9). And he singled out the beeches "spreading their green arms" (*CN* 1:411; f. 23), the curving path of a flowing river, the threads of water shooting down a slope, and "the endless endless lines of motion of the Trees" (*CN* 1:1495; f. 66). These lines were integral to his finding his way among the fluidity and continuous changes in the evolving landscape of his walks.

A residue of this impulse is discernible, for example, in "Sonnet: To the River Otter" (quoted above), which dwells upon various selected lines of motion traversing or bordering this body of water: the stone skimming on its surface, the crossing plank, the margin of the river, and the veins that run through the embankment's sand. Together these lineal images build the scaffolding upon which Coleridge constructs both the poem and a memory of his childhood. Similarly, in "The Beck in Winter" (also quoted above), Coleridge charts both the brook's and the poem's course by tracing and measuring the lines of an alder tree with its "ribb'd" and "~~five~~ 7 projecting Trunks" ("like Fingers") that shoot out, rise straight, curve, descend, and run along the bank. As was his tendency, Coleridge surveys and portrays this scene by isolating and attending to the length and angles of its defining lines. These help him gain his bearing by delineating the topography of the moment.

Without wanting to overdo the point, I suggest that it is not just these images that exemplify Coleridge's sensitivity to the lines of motion. Rather, it is also his occasional close attention to the pattern of a poem's lines within the boundaries of a page – to their graphic arrangement. For this reason, when reworking his verses, he not only continually altered words and removed or added sections but also often compulsively attended to their layout – to the way a poem sits on a page.[20] Jack Stillinger, who has carefully monitored the alterations Coleridge made in the numerous revisions of his poems, notes, for instance, that the most interesting differences among the versions of "Kubla Khan" "have to do with the organization of its lines."[21] This consideration, of course, was a matter that he completely disregarded when jotting down his notebook entries, which, in their hurry-scurry to catch the vitality of a moment or the drama of a landscape, ignored any concern for where a line begins or ends. As already discussed, in these journals, the words and his scrawling handwriting stretch out, even spill over a page's margins.

Obviously, once Coleridge turned to his poetry, the lineal and spatial organization of his thoughts mattered. As if honoring his surveying impulses as well as poetic convention, he took this aspect of his art seriously and became, as Stillinger remarks, "a precise calculator of the page-space that his writing would occupy in print."[22] Appreciating that lines are essential to the shaping and constructing of a poem and perhaps taking a cue from Euclidean geometry, he carefully considered how each poetic line emerged from one point and traveled to another. And again perhaps thinking of Euclid, he recognized how these lines congregated to

---

[20] Jack Stillinger in his *Coleridge and Textual Instability: The Multiple Versions of the Major Poems* (New York: Oxford University Press, 1974) points out, for instance, that between 1796 and 1829, Coleridge drafted and worked on sixteen separate manuscript and printed versions of "The Eolian Harp" by periodically removing and marking paragraph spacing; he deleted lines and rearranged the order of words to create twelve versions of "This Lime-Tree Bower My Prison"; and he wrote ten distinct versions, ranging from seventy-three to eighty-five lines, of "Frost at Midnight." Indeed, Stillinger argues, it is extremely rare to find a presentation copy of a poem that does *not* contain alterations in Coleridge's hand (109). Coleridge was not unaware of this impulse. For example, in a February 1797 letter to Joseph Cottle, he complained of "torturing" a poem (*The Destiny of Nations*) and himself with corrections (*CL* 1:309). And a couple of months later, still exasperated, he admitted to Cottle, "I should not think of devoting less than 20 years to an Epic poem. Ten to collect materials ... the next five in the composition of the poem – & the five last in the correction of it" (*CL* 1:320–21).

[21] Stillinger, *Coleridge and Textual Instability*, 73. Stillinger looked at the sixteen versions of "The Eolian Harp," done between 1796 and 1828, and determined that many of the changes had to do with not only the number of lines (between fifty-one and sixty-four) but also the paragraph divisions. In other words, Coleridge made changes not only in the length of lines but also in their separation.

[22] Stillinger, *Coleridge and Textual Instability*, 28.

generate the very surface and shape of a poem.[23] One is reminded of a passage from chapter 12 of *Biographia Literaria* in which Coleridge writes: "The first and most simple construction in space is the point in motion, or the line" (*CC* 7.1:249–50). For this reason, no wonder a spider he observed on St. Herbert's Island enchanted him, for when watching the spider shooting out its thread in order to spin its web, Coleridge must have called to mind his own creative process. He too lived along and followed the lines of his thoughts as well as those visible in his surroundings so he could weave his poems and hang their words upon their threads like "dew drops" quivering "on the Spider's web" ("The Picture or the Lover's Resolution," *CP* 1:370, line 35).[24]

At this point, it might be helpful to return to "Sonnet: To the River Otter" and look at the difference between its 1796 lineal organization and the 1834 published version quoted above. In the first rendering, which appeared in *The Watchman* (issue 5 [April 2, 1796], 133–34) under the title "Recollection," every line hugs the left-hand margin so that the poem, more or less, seamlessly glides along; image after image drifts into the other. A selection from the 1796 "Recollection" illustrates the point:

> How many various-fated years have past,
> What blissful and what anguish'd hours, since last
> I skimm'd the smooth thin stone along thy breast
> Numb'ring its light leaps! Yet so deep imprest
> Sink the sweet scenes of childhood, that mine eyes
> I never shut amid the sunny blaze,
> But strait, with all their tints, thy waters rise,
> The crossing plank, and margin's willowy maze,
> And bedded sand, that, vein'd with various dyes,
> Gleam'd thro' thy bright transparence to the gaze –
> (*CP* 2:1024, lines 17–26)

---

[23] One is tempted to consider the idea of "surface reading" and attend to what is evident rather than to what is either hidden or in hiding – what, in the geometric sense, has length and breadth but no thickness, and therefore covers no depth. Such a reading attends to a surface which insists on being looked at rather than seen through. Such a reading suggests that we can think about abstract things only because we can understand them in terms of concrete spatial experience. See Stephen Best and Sharon Marcus, "Surface Reading: An Introduction," *Representations* 108 (Fall 2009): 1–21.

[24] In an October 1803 entry, Coleridge records the moment he saw "a large Spider floating in the air":

> On St. Herbert's Island I saw a large Spider with most beautiful legs floating in the air on his Back by a single Thread which he was spinning out, and still as he spun, heaving in the air as if the air beneath were a pavement elastic to his Strokes / – from the Top of a very high Tree he had spun his Line, at length reached the Bottom, tied his thread round a piece of Grass, & re-ascended, to spin another / a net to hang as a fisherman's Sea net hangs in the Sun & Wind, to dry. – (*CN* 1:1598; f. 67)

The 1834 "Sonnet: To the River Otter," quoted earlier, however, displays quite a different affect, for, because of Coleridge's frequent alterations, it has evolved into a sixteen-line sonnet with intermittently indented lines. The resulting white spaces create intervals between the scene's details so that each particular becomes more visible; each is released from the paradoxically fluid regularity of the 1796 version and stands on its own. These gaps stimulate and offer room for the shaping spirit of the imagination. The result is that one is more conscious of the poet's gaze, step by step, as well as of every line of motion: the stone skimming across the water, the plank crossing over the river, the willow trees lining the river's margin, and the streaking sand. As Jarvis observes when speaking generally about the correlation between Coleridge's walking and writing, "The reader is never allowed to forget the nuances of motion and perspective in the retarded seriality of these descriptions."[25] Like the spider's thread, these images, one at a time, shoot out as straight as the River Otter's waters rise to construct the poem so that one experiences not only the form of the poem but also its forming. Reading the poem involves one in the actual process of its making as if one were walking side by side with the poet. The result is close to what Angela Leighton in *On Form: Poetry, Aestheticism, and the Legacy of a Word* observes when she writes that "Form is not a body but an agent. It forms," and suggests that this difference "between 'forming forms' and 'formed form' appears throughout Coleridge's writing, and underpins much of his theory of imagination."[26] Lines 4–11 from a later version demonstrate this point by inviting the reader to witness the shaping, line by line, of his childhood memories.

> I skimm'd the smooth thin stone along thy breast,
> Numbering its light leaps! Yet so deep imprest
> Sink the sweet scenes of childhood, that mine eyes
>     I never shut amid the sunny ray,
> But straight with all their tints thy waters rise,
>     Thy crossing plank, thy marge with willows grey,
> And bedded sand that vein'd with various dyes
> Gleam'd through thy bright transparence! . . .
>                                              (*CP* 1:48, lines 4–11)

As a poet, Coleridge knowingly displays each line and vein of those early experiences so that none is either lost or kicked aside by "the hurrying

---

[25] Jarvis, *Romantic Writing and Pedestrian Travel*, 136.
[26] Angela Leighton, *On Form: Poetry, Aestheticism, and the Legacy of a Word* (Oxford: Oxford University Press, 2007), 7.

foot." The effect reminds one of a passage in chapter 12 of *Biographia Literaria* when Coleridge talks about a genius's ability to reveal the veins and tints of a pebble so as to expose its splendor and rescue it from "common observation." The selection reads:

> Like the moisture or the polish on a pebble, genius neither distorts or false-colours its object; but on the contrary brings out many a vein and many a tint, which escape the eye of common observation, thus raising to the rank of gems, what had been often kicked away by the hurrying foot of the traveller on the dusty high road of custom. (*CC* 7.2:148–49)

While working on "Sonnet: To the River Otter," Coleridge seems to do just this, for he isolates and displays the forming lineal images of his childhood by polishing each line so that it exposes the "vein'd" sand and together with the other lines creates a gem of a poem.

Perhaps there is no more explicit or visible example of his early preoccupation with the lineal's role in shaping the substance and form of a poem than when he reworked the placement of a poem's lines in one of Thomas Dermody's sonnets – the kind of adjustment that, as we have seen, Coleridge attended to when he revised his own "Sonnet: To the River Otter." Dermody was a precocious Irish poet born in 1775. As if experimenting with poetic form and actively considering how to construct a poem through its lineal arrangement, possibly in November 1796 Coleridge, who had earlier borrowed *Anthologia Hibernica* from the Bristol Library, selected and altered Dermody's "Sonnet II" from volume 1 – with the intent, one supposes, of improving it.[27] Being interested in and often studying the art of many other poets – a practice encouraged ever since he was studying under his classics master at Christ's Hospital School and often demonstrated within his letters to friends in which he would discuss the nature of poetry – he selected this poem so as to contemplate poetic diction and form. Dermody's version of "Sonnet II" follows:

---

[27] If one peruses the titles of Coleridge's poetry, one often finds that he adapted poems written by others. For instance, see "Adaptation of Robert Southey's Sonnet 'Pale Roamer thro' the Night,'" "Adaptation of Charles Lamb's Sonnet *Written at Midnight, by the Sea-side*," "Adaptation of Charles Lamb's Sonnet 'Was it some sweet device of faery land ... ?,'" "Metrical Adaptation of Gessner," "Adaptation of Ben Jonson's *The Poetaster*," "Adaptation of Hagedorn," "Adaptations from a Shakespeare Sonnet," "Adaptations of Lines from Daniel's *Civil Wars*," "Adaptations of Milton's Lines on Shakespeare," "Adaptations of Ben Jonson," and "Adaptation of Donne's *To Sir Henry Goodyere*." One discovers, however, that most of the adaptations have to do with word or phrase changes and not with the arrangement of lines.

> Lonely I sit upon the silent shore,
> Silent, save when the dashing surges break
> 'Gainst some steep cliff, in low, and sullen roar,
> Or the hoarse gulls on night's still slumber shriek,
> Soft streams in tremulous vibrations o'er
> Ocean's broad, frownless front, the lunar ray,
> Borne in full many a dimpling wave away,
> Or strew'd in a glittering points, and seen no more.
> *Tranquility* has spread her raven plume
> Streak'd with faint grey, and shadowey blue, around,
> While *Silence* (catching the dull, frequent sound
> Of yon dim sail whitening the distant gloom,)
> Lies in her cell abrupt, where the howling sprite
> Starting terrific from his floating bier
> Ne'er enters, nor the swart hags of the night
> Who drink the sob of death with ruthless ear.
>                                         (*CC* 16.1:300–01, lines 1–16)[28]

When Coleridge adapted this poem, he not only altered the wording of the first few lines to make the action of the sea's swell and the moon's trembling rays more immediate but also, and just as significantly, experimented with the difference a line makes by altering Dermody's linear arrangement. Indeed, the last eleven lines are word for word what Dermody wrote. In this latter section, the layout is the only change. Coleridge's reworked version follows:

> Lonely I sit upon the silent shore,
>     Silent, save when against the rocky Bay
> Breaks the dead Swell; the Moon soft-trembles o'er
>     Ocean's broad, frownless front, with streamy ray,
>     Borne in full many a dimpling wave away,
> Or strew'd in glittering points, and seen no more.
> TRANQUILITY has spread her raven plume
>     Streak'd with faint grey, and shadowy blue, around;

---

[28] The remaining lines of Dermody's sonnet that Coleridge chose not to adapt read:

> Brooding below, on many a corse, that lies
> Hideous, and bare, deep, deep, from human eyes,
> And hoarded treasures, whose pernicious charms
> Urg'd o'er the grim profound the daring oak,
> Ah! from their gulphy bed can gold revoke
> It's martyrs pale, or hush the shrill alarms
> Of elemental fate, when battling high,
> The world of water centres in the sky!
>                                         (*CC* 16.1:300–01)

> While SILENCE (catching the dull, frequent sound
> Of yon dim sail whitening the distant gloom)
> Lies in her cell abrupt, where howling SPRITE
>   Starting terrific from his floating bier
> Ne'er enters, nor the swart hags of the night
>   Who drink the sob of death with ruthless ear.
>                             (CC 16.1:300–01)

As one readily sees, in Coleridge's reworking, no longer does the poem continuously return to a set left-hand margin. The resulting intermittently indented lines introduce spatial intervals that, as in the 1834 version of "Sonnet: To the River Otter," effectually draw more attention to the landscape's details – to its lines of motion. One at a time, these images, such as the moon's streaming rays, the strewed glittering points, and streaks of "faint grey," graphically survey the scene – a result enhanced by Coleridge's alteration of the first five lines in which he introduces a strong, onomatopoeic presence that audibly breaks the silence of the shore. His modified version has far more life; its imagery, more potency.

## A Geometric Frame of Mind

In certain ways, Coleridge's attention to line in his verses connects to a larger understanding that a poem, like a geometric figure, is basically an arrangement of lines in space – a circumstance that prompts one to consider to what extent, if at all, he recognized a relationship between the two and, consequently, invoked the geometric idiom when composing his so-called nature poems. One recollects, of course, that when describing a landscape in his notebook entries, Coleridge had repeatedly summoned such figures as squares, triangles, spheres, ovals, and circles to grasp the shape of what was appearing before his gaze. Consequently, as we have seen in the previous chapter, it is not unusual to read entries that picture a vale as being completely land-locked by segments of circles folding in behind each other (*CN* 1:510; f. 52) as well as to find references to a triangular bay, a huge pyramidal crag, the "convex semicircle of the bare knobby crag" (*CN* 1:549; f. 24) or "one beautiful Ellipse" (*CN* 1:1160; f. 36). As I have suggested, these geometric forms offered him a stable resting place, for they organized and abstracted and momentarily kept still what was continuously emerging before his eyes as he wandered through a landscape. They were his guide. Moreover, they honored his sense that nature is ordered geometrically.

Coleridge, however, does not initially give the impression of having transposed these geometric figures into his verses, for there are no explicit references to them. Rather, when composing his nature poetry, he seems to have set aside these abstracted forms in favor of the more vibrant, successive three-dimensional particulars that recreate the ambiance of a landscape and prompt the metaphysical overtones of a poem. His poems concentrate on the sounds, movement, textures, shadows, and reflected light that "clothe" a scene and shape its meaning. As a result, it is the singular experience of "the roaring dell," the trembling yellow leaves," the "purple shadow," and the gleaming dark branches that catches the attention.[29] And appropriately so, for, as Coleridge once tellingly remarked, the "chief differences" between geometry and poetry are "that in geometry it is the universal truth itself, which is uppermost in the consciousness, in poetry the individual form in which the truth is clothed" (*CC* 7.2:185–86). Indeed, it does appear that, in these poems, the individual sensory forms predominate and actuate each line. From a reader's perspective, the immediacy of each vibrant and moving image easily overwhelms the urge to search for or acknowledge an abstracted geometric figure that has no depth, shadow, breadth, or sound.

I suggest, however, that Coleridge's desire to create a unified, synthetic whole (a poem) out of these fleeting sensory experiences prompted him, from time to time, to continue to call upon the geometric figure. Acutely aware that an understanding of the phenomenal world can be enhanced by geometrical reasoning and that mathematics is the natural language of pattern and form, he did not completely set this orientation aside and, therefore, was not always averse, when writing his verses, to thinking geometrically. As already established, he understood that a knowledge of Euclid was a prerequisite to comprehending both the sensory world and intellectual thought. Consequently, it was not unusual for him to observe, as he once did in October 1803, a dance of flies and let his mind metamorphose the chaos of their myriad and confusing motions into an abstract, unifying conceptual shape. The notebook entry reads:

> Nothing affects me much at the moment it happens – it either stupefies me, and I perhaps look at a merry-make & dance the hay of Flies or listen entirely to the loud Click of the great Clock / or I am simply indifferent, not without some sense of philosophic Self-complacency. – For a Thing at the moment is but a Thing of the moment / it must be taken up into the mind, diffuse itself thro' the whole multitude of Shapes & Thoughts, not

---

[29] These particulars come from "This Lime-Tree Bower My Prison."

one of which it leaves untinged – between ~~each~~ wch & it some new Thought is not engendered / this a work of Time / but the Body feels it quicken with me – (*CN* 1:1597; f. 67)

Significantly, the same impulse was occasionally at work when he converted a myriad of sensory images into the shape of a poem. Turning to the geometric figure gave him a means not only to confer a larger sense of spatiality but also to create an impression of unity and to exercise a synthetic power, which connected one point, line, or detail to another. It collected, within its boundaries, the sensory particulars and thoughts, and demonstrated how these fleeting particulars mutually support each other. It helped him structure – even diagram – a poem's argument. Therefore, as he had when later working out the relationship among Faith, Will, and Intelligence or the meaning of married love via the figure of a triangle (pictured in Figure 4 in the previous chapter), he occasionally employed the structure of the geometric shape to bring his thoughts together and imaginatively apprehend a pictorial unity.[30]

To reach a better understanding of how this inclination works, it is helpful first to turn to "Frost at Midnight," originally published in 1798. The poem opens with Coleridge, late on a winter's night, watching over Hartley, his "cradled infant," slumbering "peacefully" (line 7). Soon Coleridge's thoughts wander from the quiet solitude of the present to his own restricted schooldays ("For I was reared / In the great city, pent 'mid cloisters dim" [lines 51–52]), and then his attention turns to imagining his child's freer future when he will see and hear the affirming shapes and sounds of an unenclosed landscape. He anticipates a time when Hartley will

> wander like a breeze
> By lakes and sandy shores, beneath the crags
> Of ancient mountain, and beneath the clouds,
> Which image in their bulk both lakes and shores
> And mountain crags . . .
> (*CC* 16.1:456, lines 54–58)

Eventually the poem concludes by returning to the present and to the initial images of the frosty night.

---

[30] Robin Jarvis suggests: "the multiplication of perspective and accompanying figurations places extra strain on the eventual discovery of an aesthetic 'whole,' suggesting perhaps that Coleridge is not concerned with a conventional pictorial unity, but rather with a unity that is the synthesis of temporarily sequenced perception, and which can only be imaginatively apprehended" (*Romantic Writing and Pedestrian Travel*, 133).

"Frost at Midnight" was actually reworked at least ten times. One change is to be found in the poem's conclusion, which in the first published version reads:

> Like those, my babe! Which, ere to-morrow's warmth
> Have capp'd their sharp keen points with pendulous drops,
> Will catch thine eye, and with their novelty
> Suspend thy little soul; then make thee shout,
> And stretch and flutter from thy mother's arms
> As thou wouldst fly for very eager-ness.
> 
> (*CC* 16.1:456, n. 74)[31]

In the second (at the Pierpont Morgan Library) and subsequent versions, Coleridge deleted the last six lines of what is quoted above so as to conclude with details that take the reader back to what had opened the poem – to the frost and the "silent icicles / Quietly shining to the quiet Moon":

> Or if the secret ministry of frost
> Shall hang them up in silent icicles,
> Quietly shining to the quiet Moon.
> 
> (*CP* 1:242, lines 72–74)

This rendering of the poem's conclusion is not only shorter but also tighter. As if still heeding the directive of his Christ's Hospital master, Rev. James Boyer, Coleridge tamed and purged the "swell and glitter both of thought and diction" (*CC* 7.1:7) by eliminating the lines describing Hartley's vigorous movements in his mother's arms as well as such ornamental phrases as "with pendulous drops" so as to return simply, and even linguistically, to the initial "silentness" of the frost, as well as to the repeated phrase "secret ministry" (*CP* 1:240–42, lines 1, 10, 72) that had already opened the poem.[32] All, in a sense, has come full circle.[33] This is a circularity that is not only noticed by several commentators but

---

[31] For a discussion of the various versions of "Frost at Midnight" see Stillinger, *Coleridge and Textual Instability*, 52–54.

[32] In *Biographia Literaria*, Coleridge writes: "In the after edition (of 1794 collection), I *pruned the double* epithets with no sparing hand, and used my best efforts to tame the swell and glitter both of thought and diction ..." (*CC* 7.1:7).

[33] In chapter 1 of *Biographia Literaria* Coleridge pays tribute to Rev. James Boyer:

> I learnt from him, that Poetry, even that of the loftiest, and, seemingly, that of the wildest odes, had a logic of its own, as severe as that of science; and more difficult, because more subtle, more complex, and dependent on more, and more fugitive causes. In the truly great poet, he would say, there is a reason assignable, not only for every word, but for the position of every word. (*CC* 7.1:9)

also, and more importantly, consciously orchestrated by Coleridge, who once explained that "The last six lines I omit because they destroy the *rondo* [italics mine], and return upon itself of the Poem." (*CC* 16.1:456, n. 74) – a pattern that allows for what Tim Fulford notices to be the fluidity of the "relation of past to present."[34]

Indeed, the "rondo" in this poem embraces and creates a whole out of the poem's various lines of direction and moments in time. By means of this structure, Coleridge transforms what might ordinarily be considered to be a consecutive sequence of events into a "*circular* motion" that annuls the usual understanding of the linear passage of time. In so doing, he leaves behind the chronological straight line and, in his words, assumes the image of "the snake with it's Tail in it's Mouth." As he later explained to Joseph Cottle in 1815, when speaking generally about the art of poetry: "the common end of *all narrative*, nay of *all* Poems is to convert a series into a *Whole*: to make those events, which in real or imagined History move in a *strait* Line, assume to our Understanding a *circular* motion" (*CL* 4:545). Consequently, although "Frost at Midnight" starts in the present tense, continues after each paragraph to go back and forth between various moments in his childhood, and then anticipates a future that returns to the present – like arrows each paragraph shoots out in various chronological directions – the poem does not scatter but rather re-collects itself just as the snake brings its tail into its mouth. The poem's many "*strait*" lines, such as the stark, parallel repetition of "Sea, hill, and wood" (lines 19–20) and the parallel image of the "stranger" (lines 26, 41), the lines of the still thin blue flame (line 19), and "the bars" of his Christ's Hospital rooms (line 25), as well as the shining icicles, not only represent the experience of the moment but also comment and "flow back" upon each other. In the end, their shifting lineal direction resembles what Coleridge was to describe in chapter 12 of *Biographia Literaria* when thinking of Euclid's explanation of how a line becomes a circle. He writes that if a line is not "determined by a point without it ... then it must flow back again on itself," and "there arises a cyclical line, which does inclose a space. If the strait line be assumed as the positive, the cyclical is then the negation of the strait. It is a line, which at no point strikes out into the strait, but changes its direction continuously" (*CC* 7.1:250).

In the end, the poem's encompassing evolving geometric figure becomes the medium through which Coleridge transcends a temporal, earthbound context in order more readily to embrace "The lovely shapes and sound

---

[34] Fulford, *Coleridge's Figurative Language*, 49.

intelligible / Of that eternal language, which thy God / Utters, who from eternity doth teach / Himself in all, and all things in himself" (lines 59–62). As explained in the previous chapter, Coleridge understood that the geometric figure could serve as the intermediary to a more universal and unified sense of the world. As a "vestibule" of deeper understanding, it functions to help him reach one beautiful whole.[35]

Another poem that illustrates Coleridge's sensitivity to the shaping influence of the geometric form is "This Lime-Tree Bower My Prison," written in 1797 and first published in 1800. When he composed this poem, he appears to have called upon the triangular geometric figure in order to help him unite what initially seems separated or disconnected. As is well known, the poem begins with Coleridge describing being left alone and behind because of an accident that has left him unable to ramble with his friends up to a nearby hill-top. Ernest Hartley Coleridge in his edition of the poems explains: "In the June of 1797 some long-expected friends paid a visit to the author's cottage; and on the morning of their arrival, he met with an accident [Sara had accidentally spilled boiling milk on him], which disabled him from walking during the whole time of their stay. One evening, when they had left him for a few hours, he composed the following lines in the garden-bower" (*CP* 1:178).

The poem opens with Coleridge's abrupt complaint: "Well, they are gone, and here must I remain, / This lime-tree bower my prison!" (lines 1–2). Initially he thinks only of his loss, but not so much in terms of lacking his friends' company as of his being barred from the experience of the "Beauties and feelings" (line 3) he would have had enjoyed if he had been able to be gazing at what they are now seeing. Wistfully, he imagines his acquaintances wandering "in gladness" (line 8), and, true to form, recalls the details and the movement belonging to the landscape that they now traverse. He recollects such landmarks as the place "Where its slim trunk the ash from rock to rock / Flings arching like a bridge," as well as such particulars as the trembling yellow leaves, and "the dripping edge / Of the blue clay-stone" (lines 18–19). Given his sensitivity to the tread of his feet, he also remembers the feel of walking on "springy heath" (line 7). In the midst of this reminiscence, his attention turns to Charles Lamb who, living in London, has not been able to enjoy this privilege and has "hunger'd after Nature, many a year, / In the great City pent" (lines 29–30). Thinking of this circumstance, Coleridge finds consolation in

---

[35] See Chapter 3 for a discussion of geometry serving as a medium to comprehending and realizing a larger, more universal understanding.

the fact that now his friend can "stand, as I have stood, / Silent with swimming sense; yea, gazing round / On the wide landscape" (lines 38–40). In the course of such thoughts, his sense of being deserted and denied the pleasure and comfort of such a prospect precipitously dissipates. He at once feels as if he is "there" with his friend: a "delight / Comes sudden on my heart, and I am glad / As I myself were there!" (lines 43–45). Moreover, the garden bower where he sits is no longer a prison but rather becomes a place that reveals the soothing, sensual delights of his immediate surroundings. Coleridge realizes that, even though he is left alone, enclosed at home, Nature has not abandoned him: "Nature ne'er deserts the wise and pure" (line 60):

> Nor in this bower,
> This little lime-tree bower, have I not mark'd
> Much that has sooth'd me. Pale beneath the blaze
> Hung the transparent foliage; and I watch'd
> Some broad and sunny leaf, and lov'd to see
> The shadow of the leaf and stem above
> Dappling its sunshine! And that walnut-tree
> Was richly ting'd, and a deep radiance lay
> Full on the ancient ivy, which usurps
> Those fronting elms, and now, with blackest mass
> Makes their dark branches gleam a lighter hue
> Through the late twilight: and though now the bat
> Wheels silent by, and not a swallow twitters,
> Yet still the solitary humble-bee
> Sings in the bean-flower!
> (*CP* 1:180–81, lines 45–59)

This section prefaces the poem's concluding lines in which Coleridge sees the "last rook" of the evening "Beat its straight path, along the dusky air,/ Homewards" (lines 68–70). The rook's direct straight line of flight negates the distance between him and his friend by connecting Coleridge to Lamb, who is simultaneously gazing at the same bird "creeking" (line 74) over his head. In this epiphanous moment, he and Lamb are as one, bound together by the "gladness" (line 27) of nature.[36] The isolation that Coleridge had experienced at the poem's beginning is no more.

Unlike "Frost at Midnight," this poem does not end where it begins but rather, as I have suggested, employs a triangular composition, a structure that Coleridge often favored when working through his ideas and

---

[36] In *Romantic Writing and Pedestrian Travel*, Robin Jarvis observes: "the rook, passing out of the gaze of one and into the gaze of the other, rhetorically, unites the friends in a shared worship" (150).

responses to experience. As already mentioned, in his notebooks he frequently evoked this geometric figure when portraying parts of a landscape, such as the occasion he noticed "a small Dip in the shape of an inverted Triangle – the Sea, & a triangle of Green Coast" (CN 1:1223; f. 23), remarked on the mountains "rising in triangles" (*CN* 1:1224; f. 24), or perceived a hilly ridge in the form of "an inverted obtuse-angled triangle" (*CN* 1:1225; f. 28). Later, following the example of his philosophical training, he sometimes utilized the figure in his more speculative writing, when he not only drew and used the triangle to think through and literally diagram his ideas concerning the nature of belief and marriage (see Chapter 3) but also called upon its form when pondering Shakespearean rules of tragedy or reflecting upon the relationship between Faith, Practical and Speculative thought.[37] Moreover, in a more personal, humorous mode, Coleridge even applied the triangular figure to diagram a visit with friends who lived near Nether Stowey. In a summer 1807 letter to Mary Cruikshank published in Joseph Cottle's *Reminiscences of Samuel Taylor Coleridge and Robert Southey*, he summons the figure to recollect their happily drinking two bottles of port together:

> I confess that Mr. B. and Myself disobedient to the voice of the ladies, had contrived to finish two bottle of Port between us, to which I added two glasses of mead. All this was in consequence of conversing about John Cruikshanks' [*sic*] coming down. Now John Cruikshanks' idea being regularly associated in Mr. B's mind with a second bottle, and S. T. C. being associated with John Cruikshanks [*sic*], the second bottle became associated with the idea. And afterwards with the body of S. T. C. by necessity of metaphysical law, as you may see in the annexed figure, or diagram.[38]

Coleridge's original, and certainly more casual, diagram is visible in an August 1807 letter to Mary Cruikshank (see *CL* 3:23).[39] (see Figure 5).

Given these examples, it is tempting to recall Coleridge's occasional *modus operandi* and diagram, as a triangle, "This Lime-Tree Bower My Prison." Such an exercise abstracts the outline of the poem's overall structure. It helps demonstrate how the three initially disconnected elements in the poem – Coleridge imprisoned in the garden bower, the landscape of the hill-ridge, and the friends who have left him behind to wander in that landscape – eventually join to establish a "beautiful

---

[37] See, for instance, *CC* 11.1:1104.
[38] Joseph Cottle, *Reminiscences of Samuel Taylor Coleridge and Robert Southey* (New York: Wiley and Putnam, 1843), 81.
[39] In the "Afterword" of this book I briefly discuss Coleridge's diagram of this event.

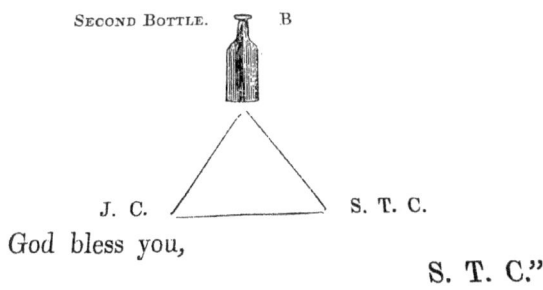

Figure 5  Samuel Taylor Coleridge's diagram from an August 1807 letter to Mary Cruikshank, published in Joseph Cottle's *Reminiscences of Samuel Taylor Coleridge and Robert Southey* (1843).

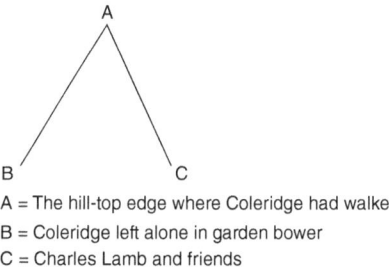

A = The hill-top edge where Coleridge had walked
B = Coleridge left alone in garden bower
C = Charles Lamb and friends

Figure 6  Author's diagram of an open triangle illustrating "This Lime-Tree Bower My Prison."

Wholeness." This sense of harmony at the poem's end comes when the rook's straight flight connects these three disparate spheres to form a complete triangle. The poem then moves from a consciousness of a painful division to a state of mind that not only unites Coleridge with Lamb but also combines the beauties and feelings of the unbounded hill-top with the soothing, sensual delights of his lime-tree bower. The geometric figure, as is its wont, connects various points and removes distance to make everything immediate.

At the risk of being parodic, a geometric diagram of the poem might help demonstrate this impulse. The first figure shows an incomplete or an open triangle (see Figure 6). At the top is A, the hill-top ridge where Coleridge has walked and where Charles Lamb and friends now ramble. In the lower left angle of the triangle is B, where Coleridge sits alone in his lime-tree bower. And in the lower right angle is C where Lamb and friends are, separated from Coleridge. Nothing connects them, for initially each

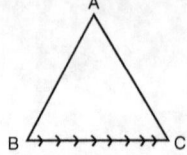

A = The hill-top ridge
B = Coleridge alone in Lime-tree Bower
C = Charles Lamb
B→→→C = The Rook's straight path that connects B (Coleridge) to C (Charles Lamb)

Figure 7   Author's diagram of a complete triangle illustrating "This Lime-Tree Bower My Prison."

has gone his separate way. Coleridge remains isolated at home. However, both B and C are linked to A – to the hill-top ridge – either through recollection or, in the case of Coleridge's friends, by their immediate physical presence. Both have their attention on A. But as yet there is no sense of a whole – the triangle is incomplete, for there is no line extending between B and C. Rather, there is the acute sense of separation as well a severance from the comforting presence of nature. Coleridge feels imprisoned, while Lamb enjoys the freedom of the landscape's open wildness.

In the second figure, the broken triangle is now complete (see Figure 7). The "last rook" of the evening has beaten "its straight path, along the dusky air" (lines 68–69) to make a line that links Coleridge to Lamb. The bird flies between the two, connecting point B to point C. Coleridge sees the rook and imagines that Lamb witnesses it too. All, in Coleridge's mind, has become whole: The two friends are united through this mutual seeing and so too is the natural world, for the poem ends with both the line of flight that binds the two friends as well as with the conviction that Nature, whether experienced on the hill-top edge or seen from the bower, "ne'er deserts the wise and pure" (line 60). What initially had seemed cut off is now, like the triangle itself, one whole figure that connects one part to another and keeps "the heart / Awake to Love and Beauty!" (lines 63–64), even in absence.

Then there is the poem's image of the glorious sun's orb across which the rook flies. Aware of this bird's passage across the sky, Coleridge is no longer confined to the prison or "blindness" (line 5) of a practically sunless landscape but in looking up is released so he can share with Lamb the sight of the sinking sun and participate in the "deep radiance" (line 52) of his surroundings. The final geometric figure of this poem might, therefore, be

*A Geometric Frame of Mind* 141

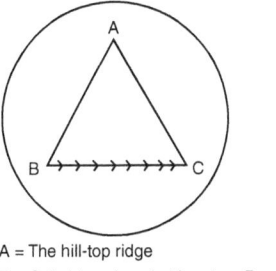

A = The hill-top ridge
B = Coleridge alone in Lime-tree Bower
C = Charles Lamb
B→→C = The Rook's straight path that
          connects B (Coleridge) to C (Charles Lamb)

Figure 8   Author's diagram of the sun's radiant orb encircling the complete triangle in "This Lime-Tree Bower My Prison."

of the sun's presence encompassing and brightening the completed triangle (see Figure 8).[40]

But, of course, this exercise, though contributing to an understanding of the poem's larger structure, if taken on its own, is misleading; it neither grasps nor appreciates the fuller organic and pulsating life of this poem. Obviously, Coleridge would agree with this criticism. He disapproved of those readers who, "determined to understand" a poem, laboriously launch upon an exposition that is "not very dissimilar to that, with which he would construct a diagram, line by line, for a long geometrical proposition" (*CC* 7.2:127) – *mea culpa*.[41] Furthermore, he worried when he himself gazed at a mountain and all he saw was a triangle. Fearing that "the poet is dead in me," on March 25, 1801 he wrote to William Godwin:

> You would not know me – ! all sounds of similitude keep at such a distance from each other in my mind, that I have *forgotten* how to make a rhyme – I look at the Mountains (that visible God Almighty that looks in at all my windows) I look at the Mountains only for the Curves of their outlines; the

---

[40] I am indebted to Jim Chandler for suggesting that I diagram the poem in relation to the sun itself. I have attempted to honor his observation.
[41] The whole quotation reads:
> Such descriptions too often occasion in the mind of a reader, who is determined to understand his author, a feeling of labor, not very dissimilar to that, with which he would construct a diagram, line by line, for a long geometrical proposition. It seems to like taking the pieces of a dissected map out of its box. We first look at one part, and then at another, then join and dove-tail them; and when the successive acts of attention have been completed, there is a retrogressive effort of mind to behold it as a whole. The poet should paint to the imagination, not to the fancy. (*CC* 7.2:127)

> Stars, as I behold them, form themselves into Triangles ... The Poet is dead in me – my imagination (or rather the somewhat that had been imaginative) lies, like a Cold Snuff on the circular Rim of a Brass Candle-stick, without even a stink of Tallow to remind you that it was once clothed & mitred with Flame. (*CL* 2:714)[42]

Though this suggests a way of understanding the poem's larger structure, it is easy to see that this exercise does not adequately demonstrate Coleridge's sense of what it is to be a poet and "bring the whole soul of man into activity" (*CC* 7.1:cvii).[43] This limitation is yet another reminder that the topography of his poems is not just determined by the outline of its structure but rather finds its vibrancy in the arrangement and selection of its internal, sensual details – a condition that recalls the potency of his notebook entries that intermingle the geometric figure with the surrounding sights, movements, sounds, and colors to create a fuller sense of the landscape that emerges before his consideration.

### The Brown Linnets, the Serpent, the Spider, the Flies, the Snake, and the Rook

In the end, even though alert to abstract geometric figures, Coleridge's nature poetry primarily grounds itself within the realm of the poet's physical contact with the earth. As Coleridge wrote to William Sotheby in September 1802: "A Poet's *Heart & Intellect* should be *combined, intimately* combined *& unified*, with the great appearances in Nature – & not merely held in solution & loose mixture with them, in the shape of formal Similes" (*CL* 2:864). Following his own directive and perhaps also heeding John Aikin's 1777 plea to put an end to the "perpetual repetition" of tired hackneyed poetic phraseology when calling upon natural images, Coleridge's poems attend to the actual feel of treading the ground beneath his boots and to an immediate, singular depiction of all his walking

---

[42] These expressions of discontent bring to mind Coleridge's complaint during his Cambridge days when he, as well as many of his colleagues, feared that the dreary mathematical mind or the figure of Mathesis might destroy the creative spirit (see Chapter 3).

[43] Approaching the poem within the perimeters of "fancy" clearly reduces an understanding of the poem's imaginative reach. Indeed, the diagrammatic exercise risks repeating what Coleridge and his colleagues feared during their undergraduate days when they worried that the emphasis upon mathematics in the curriculum would chase away the creative muse. For an excellent discussion of the differences between fancy and imagination as well as the metaphysical content of this poem, see Wheeler, *The Creative Mind in Coleridge's Poetry*, a study of Coleridge's poetry that discusses how Coleridge's theories of mind and imagination function within the poems and help shape their design.

revealed.[44] In this regard, it is perhaps no coincidence that when he wrote to Sotheby about the character of poetry, he often placed his remarks within letters that also recounted what he had seen during a recent walk among the fells – "Close under my feet as it were" (*CL* 2:858).[45] It is fitting, therefore, to find analogies, as I have done in this chapter, between his mode of composing and his references to the motions made by the brown linnets swarming in flight, the serpent's muscular movements, the spider weaving its web, the dance of flies, the curled snake, and the rook flying in a straight line across the evening sky.[46] These organic metaphors are yet another demonstration of Coleridge's keen sense of the vital connection between the temperament of the natural and the poetic realm. They are prompted not only by a larger cultural preoccupation that was showing an inordinate curiosity in the surrounding natural world but also by his receptiveness to the actual sights, sounds, movements, and textures of the terrain he observed during his walking years.[47]

---

[44] John Aikin, *An Essay on the Application of Natural History to Poetry* (London: J. Johnson, 1777), 2. Aikin was a contemporary of Johnson, Wordsworth, and Coleridge. He was an important dissenting critic at the end of the eighteenth century and turn of the nineteenth century. His training in science and medicine influenced his thinking. In another quotation from his *An Essay on the Application of Natural History to Poetry*, Aikin writes: "Yet, if it be admitted that the grand and beautiful objects which nature every where profusely throws around us, are the most obvious store of materials for the poet, it must also be confessed that it is the store which of all others he has the most sparingly touched" (4).

[45] In another letter to William Sotheby from the summer of 1802, Coleridge continued to surround his discussion of the nature of poetry by placing his remarks within the context of watching the sun on Bassenthwaite. In this letter, he asks Sotheby to imagine

> now before your eyes – Over Bassenthwaite the Sun is setting, in a glorious rich *brassy* Light – on the top of Skiddaw, & one third adown it, is a huge enormous Mountain of Cloud, with the outlines of a mountain – this is of a starchy Grey – but floating fast along it, & upon it, are various Patches of sack-like Clouds, bags & woolsacks, of a shade lighter than the brassy Light of the clouds that hide the setting Sun – a fine yellow-red somewhat more than sandy Light – and these the highest on this mountain-shaped cloud, & these the farthest from the Sun, are suffused with the darkness of a stormy Color. – Marvellous creatures! how they pass along! (*CL* 2:819)

[46] Another instance of an organic metaphor can be found in a July 19, 1802 letter to William Sotheby, when Coleridge explained:

> when I wished to write a poem, beat up Game of far other kind – instead of a Covey of poetic Partridges with whirring wings of music, or wild Ducks *shaping* their rapid flight in forms always regular (a still better image of Verse) up came a metaphysical Bustard, urging it's slow, heavy, laborious, earth-skimming Flight, over dreary & level Wastes. (*CL* 2:814)

[47] This cultural fascination prompted Coleridge, for instance, to spend hours with Erasmus Darwin's volumes, to take a course on natural history from Johann Friedrich Blumenbach, who wrote *A Manual of the Elements of Natural History*, trans. R. T. Gore (London: W. Simpson & R. Marshall, 1825 [1779–80]), and to read such texts as Pliny's *Naturalis Historia*, William Bartram's *Travels through North and South Carolina, Georgia, East & West Florida* (Philadelphia: James & Johnson, 1791) (Coleridge owned the second edition of 1794), and Thomas Pennant's *British Zoology*, 4 vols. (London: Benjamin White, 1796).

Because of this orientation, Coleridge's peripatetic poems breathe and progress with every step as well as with the emerging lines and shadows created by the shifting light and with the interrupted quietness of the night. They dwell among what Coleridge refers to in "Frost at Midnight" as "the numberless goings-on of life" (line 12) that assemble and find some semblance of order within the timeless geometric form. As in the notebook entries depicting a landscape, both perspectives work together so that neither the phenomenal sensual world nor the realm of geometric abstraction interferes with the other. Rather, collectively, they create one graceful and intelligent whole that never loses touch with the feel of the ground or the sight of a "beautiful white cloud-like foam" darting off from the vessel's side and the "pure evening blue" of the Ratzeburg evening sky (*CC* 7.2:168, 193).

CHAPTER 5

# *Youth and Age*
## *Coleridge and the Shifting Paradigm of Geometric Thought*

In the year 1756, a communication was made by M. La Sage to the Academy of Science at Paris, stating that he had discovered an error in the Elements of Euclid ... his reasoning was approved by the Academy, and has ever since been deemed conclusive, I think I shall perform a service of some utility to the Public, if I am able to refute this charge, and to vindicate the honor of Euclid. It has indeed become so fashionable of late to question the accuracy of the Elements, and to alter them in the most arbitrary manner, that it behoves every one, who has any regard for the memory of the venerable author, or for the credit of Geometry itself, to exert his best endeavours to check the growing spirit and to confine it within the bounds of decency.
(John Warren, Fellow and Tutor of Jesus College, Cambridge, *A Treatise on the Geometrical Presentation of the Square Roots of Negative Quantities*, 1828)[1]

### Part One: Youth and Age

> Verse, a breeze mid blossoms straying,
> Where Hope clung feeding, like a bee –
> Both were mine! Life went a-maying
>    With Nature, Hope, and Poesy,
>       When I was young!
> ("Youth and Age," lines 1–5)

The first chapter of this book opens with a passage in which Coleridge likens himself not only to a wild leaf in autumn, blowing this way and that, but also to a Chamois-chaser who, as if driven by a *"bottom-wind,"*

---

[1] John Warren, *A Treatise on the Geometrical Presentation of the Square Roots of Negative Quantities* (Cambridge: J. Smith, 1828), 7.

adventurously scrambles along the mountain tops in pursuit of his goal.[2] This 1803 self-portrait not only reflects the youthful vivacity of Coleridge's mind but also recalls the almost reckless manner in which he, during his rambling years, bounded ahead like a chamois-hunter – no matter what the consequences. A notebook entry from a fell walk in August 1802 illustrates his daring:

> I descended from Sca fell and went backward from Wastdale to another Point, a great mountain of Stones, from a pound to 20 Ton / climbed up them, and am now lownded on the other side, with *Hollow Stones* beneath me, the frightfullest Cove, with huge Precipice Walls ... O for a better & less *hazy* day – ... I pass along Scafell Precipices; & came to one place where I thought could descend, & get upon the low Ridge that runs between Sca Fell & Bowfell, & look down into the wild *savage, savage* Head of Eskdale / Good heavens! what a climb! dropping from Precipices and at last should have been crag fast but for the chasm – (*CN* 1:1218; ff. 15, 17)

Over sixteen years later much had changed. In his late forties, Coleridge was no longer as carefree or as physically able. Consequently, when he again invokes the metaphor of the chamois-hunter in an August 1820 instructive letter to his son Hartley, gone is his sense of himself as a person carried by the wind, impulsively vaulting across rugged ground while hunting his game. Instead, a more measured persona emerges in which he, though still thinking himself on a quest, rather than subjecting himself to the forces of nature and rushing through the landscape without regard for any "noble purpose," deliberately, step by step, constructs a road across the mountains. Purposefully, as if working out a geometric proof, he makes his way so that he might later retread and create a path of thought. Coleridge advises Hartley:

> There is no way of arriving at any sciential End but by finding it at every step. The End is the Means: or the adequacy of each Mean is already it's end. Southey once said to me: You are nosing every nettle along the Hedge, while the Greyhound (meaning himself, I presume) wants only to get sight of the Hare, & FLASH! – strait as a Line! – he has it in his mouth! ... But,

---

[2] The passage, quoted at the beginning of Chapter 1, is from a letter to Thomas Wedgwood. It reads:

> like a Leaf in Autumn; a wild activity, of thoughts, imaginations, feelings, and impulses of motion, rises up from within me – a sort of *bottom-wind*, that blows to no point of the compass, & comes from I know not whence, but agitates the whole of me; my whole Being is filled with waves, as it were, that roll & stumble, one this way, & one that way, like things that have no common master. I think, that my soul must have pre-existed in the body of a Chamois-chaser. (*CL* 2:916)

the fact is – I do not care twopence for the *Hare*; but I value most highly the excellence of scent, patience, discrimination, free Activity; and find a Hare in every Nettle, I make myself acquainted with. I follow the Chamois-Hunters, and seem to set out with the same Object. But I am no Hunter of *that* Chamois Goat; but avail myself of the Chace in order to a nobler purpose – that of making a road across the Mountains, on which the Common Sense may hereafter pass backward and forward; with desperate Leaps or Balloons that scar indeed but do not improve the chance of getting onward. (*CL* 5:98)

This alteration in Coleridge's sense of himself probably originated in his early thirties when the increasingly painful and debilitating consequences of his opium addiction were bringing an end to the challenging rambles belonging to his earlier life, though there were occasional determined moments, for example in 1809 when, as if still the youthful chamois-hunter, he walked twenty-eight miles across the mountains between Grasmere and Penrith in pursuit of the person who had agreed to publish *The Friend*.[3] This expedition, however, was fraught with disaster; he twisted his ankle, slipped, and sprained his knee.

Eventually in October 1810 Coleridge left Grasmere for good and fell into a more sedentary life in London, where he devoted his energy to a variety of ambitious endeavors, such as working on literary, theological, philosophical, and political projects, as well as preparing and giving several series of public lectures. Indeed, his last visit to the Lakes in 1812 was not for the pleasure of roaming through its landscape but to lecture and collect copies of *The Friend* from the printer. By the time Coleridge was forty-three and had joined Dr. Gillman's household at Moreton House, Highgate, on April 15, 1816, his physical life had significantly diminished.[4] Essentially, his wandering days were over. As Earl Leslie Griggs, the editor of his letters, observes: "old age came upon him prematurely and ill-health often incapacitated him" (*CL* 5:xxxiii).

Because of these alterations, his correspondence no longer resonates with the animated descriptions of his rambling. More and more

---

[3] *The Friend* was a weekly periodical containing Coleridge's essays and published between 1809 and March 1810. In a February 1809 letter to Daniel Stuart, Coleridge describes this lengthy walk: "I received a letter from Penrith, that Brown was both able and willing to print & publish the Friend – in consequence on Sunday I walked from Grasmere over the Mountain (O *Heaven!* what a *Journey* hither – and arrived at last *limping*, having sprained my knee in leaping a Brook & slipping on the opposite bank twisted my left leg outward" (*CL* 3:180). Barbara E. Rooke, the editor of *The Friend* in *The Collected Works*, remarks that in 1809 "more than once Coleridge walked over the mountains, in rain and fair weather" to reach the printer's establishment in Penrith (*CC* 4.1:lviii).

[4] Dr. James Gillman accepted Coleridge as a patient and as a friend. Coleridge remained with Dr. and Mrs. Gillman until his death on July 25, 1834.

frequently its contents refer to his traveling by coach – sometimes humorously, such as the occasion when he found himself squashed by a "lusty Traveller having great Coats on, or rather *huge* Coat." He quipped, "I was terribly cramped, my shoulders in a pillory and my legs in the stocks" (*CL* 3:40). Only sporadically does Coleridge mention taking walks – and these occasions, of course, bear little resemblance to his former expeditions. In a May 1819 letter he alludes to "Strolling down Milfield Lane, my favorite Walk" (*CL* 4:940); in January 1826 he writes of leaving the house "for two or three turns in the sunshine" (*CL* 6:547), and two years later, Coleridge comments on taking a walk "for the purpose of a long conversation on family matters with my daughter" (*CL* 6:704). Given these instances, it is almost surprising that just six years before his death, he mentions visiting Charles Lamb and taking "a great deal of exercise," even attempting a hike that might have extended to twelve miles (*CL* 6:765). It appears, therefore, that when his health permitted it, the impulse to ramble was still with him.[5] But rarely was there the sense of freedom or daring exploration attending such outings. Rather, some ailment often compromised or overwhelmed them. For example, on his 1828 amble with Lamb, Coleridge was soon bothered by a "pair of tight-healed Shoes so that on the next morning" he "walked tho' in much pain about 3¼ miles across the fields to fall in with the Edmonton Stage – and on getting out of the Stage on Snow-Hill" experienced "great difficulty ... from the almost torture that every step gave me" (*CL* 6:765).[6] Eventually and sadly, when he was close to death, Coleridge's attempts even to move from his bed to his chair were difficult. In a July 5, 1834 letter to Mrs. Dashwood, Coleridge describes requiring "the support of both the Maids" (*CL* 6:986). As he once wrote to an unknown correspondent, with the advance of years, the spider "spins it's thread narrower and narrower, still closing in on us, till at last it shuts us up within four walls, walls of flues and films, windowless" (*CL* 5:414).

---

[5] It should be mentioned that in 1828 he also went on a month's tour of the Netherlands and the Rhine with Dorothy and William Wordsworth. The traveling, however, was primarily by coach.

[6] The remainder of Coleridge's letter is devoted to his attempts to find relief for his damaged foot:

> not knowing what better to do, I went into the Druggist's Shop midway Skinner Street & Holborn, & breast-plated both heels with Diacolon Plaister – and not doubting the rest and the mere guarding against friction would bring all right, I kept on the plaister in the next 24 hours & more – when an inflammation of the left leg warned me to have my heels looked to – and in miserable plight they were – and it was some days before by poultices & keeping my Limbs in a horizontal position I could bring them to heal. (*CL* 6:765)

Under the care of Dr. Gillman, there were periods in which Coleridge endeavored to regain some of his physical strength. At the doctor's direction, both Coleridge and Mrs. Gillman, from 1819 to 1833, periodically traveled to Ramsgate – to the seashore – where both of them could benefit from the healing powers of the sea air and their plunges into the ocean as well as a "regular devotion of the Daylight to Exercise" (*CL* 5:180).[7] Because of his declining physical vitality, these activities were inevitably modest. At times, Coleridge spoke of "creeping along the coast" (*CL* 4:674) and, just two years before his death, described himself as shuffling through life and "crawling up the Hill towards Belle Vue" (*CL* 6:947).

During these periods by the sea, occasionally remnants of his old self re-emerged, but when they did, they tended, as I have suggested, to reside within a cautionary mode. For instance, in a November 1824 letter to Dr. Gillman about his recent bathing at Ramsgate, Coleridge counted, as had been his former practice, the paces of his feet, enumerated his swimming strokes, and, in spite of the rain, mentioned the pleasure of throwing himself forward into the sea. However, these older habits and freer moments were soon qualified by his cautionary remarks about swimming out of one's depth:

> I am at present in my best sort and state of health; bathed yesterday, and again this morning in spite of the rain and in so deep a Bath, that having thrown myself forward from the first step of the machine Ladder & only taken two strokes after my re-emersion, I had at least ten strokes to take before I got into my depth again – so that it is no false alarm when those who cannot swim are warned that a person may be drowned a very few yards from the machine. (*CL* 5:392)

Indeed, it took the drama and excitement of witnessing a shipwreck off the coast of Ramsgate in November 1824 to arouse some remnant of the energetic descriptive prose belonging to his earlier notebook entries. This vestige, however, is tempered by the fact that he is watching the spectacle from his window and not out amid the blasting wind. Coleridge described the event to Dr. Gillman:

> The gales have been tremendous – at the moment the Waves at the mouth of the Pier look like a surf-cliff, and it is fearful to watch the Skiffs, how they are tossed and twisted & what hair-breadth escapes several of them have

---

[7] For a book that looks into the places associated with Coleridge's visits to Ramsgate, see Allan Clayson. *Wish You Were Here: Coleridge's Holidays at Ramsgate 1819–1833* (Ramsgate, Kent: A. & C. Clayson, 2001).

from being dashed against the pier-head. At day-break this morning a West Indian was descried that had struck on Goodwin Sands – and long before the time must have gone to pieces. Had she been made of Iron, she could not have stood out. The Breakers were distinctly visible from our window; and with a glass had the appearance of a very high & bold Coast. No Boat could possibly approach to her: and if the Crew are saved, it will be little short of a miracle ... The Night but one after, it blew great guns the whole night – and last night up to the present moment the South West Wind has left Bedlam loose on the air. To move only the length from the second pillar from our house [and] back again required the utmost effort of my strength. A torrent of water would scarcely have pressed with a more *compact* force. (*CL* 5:396)

Perhaps for these reasons, as the years proceeded, the organic, natural world profoundly visible in his early notebooks and letters became less and less prominent. Rarely did Coleridge remark on a "glorious Sunset" (*CL* 4:779) or a beautiful "Country road," or mention a wood "full of Birds" and nightingales (*CL* 4:868). And only briefly, in November 1826, did he mention the "Lowness and slowness of the shooting stars," as well as the haunting shadow cast by the Ramsgate pier (*CC* 11.1:135). These passages are sparse. Gone are the extended intimate descriptions of his immediate surroundings. Only a residual memory of them remained to support his fashioning of a metaphor, such as the time Coleridge compared the development of youth to "Caterpillars, with the future of a Butterfly ... unfolding within them" (*CL* 5:296), associated the connecting "Dots in Frog-spawn" with the act of recollection, or pointed out the similarity between the descent from poetry to prose and a skylark descending "from the purple Clouds to the Corn field" (*CL* 6:635).

Once in a while, in his fifties, one senses some nostalgia for a former time. From Ramsgate he wrote to Thomas Allsop and longingly declared: "Not a day has past [*sic*] since we left Highgate, in which I have not been tracing you in Spirit up and down the Dells and Glens of Derbyshire, while my feet only have been in commune with the sandy beach here at Ramsgate" (*CL* 5:179). And in 1823, when Coleridge sent Edward, his nephew, directions on how to travel to the Lake District, he momentarily departed from his adopted guidebook prose to recall a poignant former experience: "if you could return by Crummock & thro' the vale of Newlands, the inverted arch of which (on the $\underset{a\quad\quad b}{\smile}$ points (A B) of which I once saw the two legs of a rich Rainbow, so as to form with the Arch a perfect Circle) *faces* Greta Hall, you will have seen the very

Pith & Marrow of the Lakes" (*CL* 5:286).⁸ And there was a moment when his heart swelled at the thought of the so-called "bottom-wind" which "all above and around in Stillness and Sunshine" warmed the northern Lakes (*CL* 5:23).

A poem "Youth and Age" that Coleridge began composing in 1828 and continued working on and expanding through 1832–33 (when he would have been around sixty years of age) expresses his wistful sense of the "change 'twixt Now and Then." The second stanza of the published 1832 version reads:

> When I was young? – Ah, woful When!
> Ah! for the change 'twixt Now and Then!
> This breathing house not built with hands,
> This body that does me grievous wrong,
> O'er aery cliffs and glittering sands,
> How lightly then it flashed along: –
> Like those trim skiffs, unknown of yore,
> On winding lakes and rivers wide,
> That ask no aid of sail or oar,
> That fear no spite of wind or tide!
> Nought cared this body for wind or weather
> When Youth and I lived in't together.
> (*CP* 1:439–40, lines 6–17)

Eventually, because of the loss of his former physical immersion in his surroundings, Coleridge dwelt more exclusively within the workings of the mind and his interest in metaphysics. Though, during his walking years, he had always concerned himself with such matters, he now increasingly devoted his energy to working out his thoughts concerning social and political problems, the differences between understanding and reason, the abstracting powers of the intellect, and the dynamics of human relations, as well as the intricacies of literary, religious, and philosophical thought

---

⁸ A selection from the directions sent to Edward reads:

> There is an Inn at Patterdale where you might sleep so as to make one day of it from Penrith to the Lake Head via Lowther & Hawes water; & thence to Keswick would take good part of a second. There is one consideration in favour of this Plan – that from Carlisle to Penrith or even to Lowther you might go by coach, & I question whether you could reach Greta Hall by the Caldbeck Route in one day. When at Keswick, I would advise you to go to Wastdale thro' Borrodale, & if you could return by Crummock & thro' the vale of Newlands, the inverted arch of which (on the points (A B) of which I once saw the two legs of a rich Rainbow, so as to form with the Arch a perfect Circle) *faces* Greta Hall, you will have seen the very Pith and Marrow of the Lakes, & especially as your Route to Chester or Liverpool will take you that lovely road thro' Thirlmere, Grasmere, Rydal (where you will of course pay your respects to Mr Wordsworth), Ambleside & the striking half of Wyndemere. (*CL* 5:286)

that transcend, though never completely forget, the evidence of physical phenomena. Throughout, his interest in and indebtedness to the geometric idiom explored in this book remained evident. This context continued to be valuable not only for its own sake but also as a tool to help him contemplate the relation – the order and connection – among things as well as reach necessary and universal truths. In a sense, he depended on the series of deliberate steps supplied by the discipline of geometry to help him reach the temple of knowledge and contemplate philosophical, theological, and religious questions.[9] For Coleridge, geometry was never an end in itself; it was not what was hunted. Rather, its methods and propositions prepared and supplied the means in which the end is visible. Its series of proofs and structures helped construct a systematic thoroughfare along which Coleridge could tread, time and time again, the landscape of metaphysical thought. In this way, as he had told Hartley, he could make a "road across the Mountains" (*CL* 5:98). As a result, one finds him still calling upon the Euclidean idiom to work out the idea of Christian love (see the use of the triangle in a September 1821 letter to Thomas Allsop), writing to his son Derwent about the fact that space was to the Divinities as "Space to the Diagrams for the Geometricians," explaining to his nephew Edward about the art of contemplating "Things" by means of a triangle, and expounding, in a letter to James Gillman, Jr., on how geometry increases the quality of knowledge (*CL* 6:537, 597, 635). And one discovers him calling upon the triangle to sort out the changing dimensions of wedded love (*CN* 3:3308) or in 1815 diagramming "the line of *Being*" and "the surface of *Becoming*" by using a roughly drawn circle (*CN* 3:4226).[10] The strength of Euclid, it seems, endured.

### Part Two: A Sustaining Paradigm

Coleridge's ongoing reliance on his training in Euclidean geometry is predictable, for he was, in his later years, surrounded by a culture in which Euclid was still considered to be one of the most sustaining paradigms of thought and methods of describing physical space. Throughout Coleridge's lifetime, multiple editions of the *Elements* continued to be published and to guide the teaching of geometry in the schools and

---

[9] In *Table Talk*, Coleridge wrote: "Geometry is a means to an end – a series of steps to a temple" (*CC* 14.2:455).

[10] Coleridge drew this diagram after reading Henrich Steffens's *Grundzüge* concerning the Vital Powers and the Scientific Construction of Nature. See Kathleen Coburn's note to notebook entry *CN* 3:4226.

universities.[11] Remarkably, until the mid-1880s, Euclid seemed never to have reached a saturation point. In England, his *Elements* had almost no rivals. As a textbook, it endured to train students not only in pragmatic matters but also in correct reasoning.[12] The prevailing opinion was, as I have discussed earlier in this book, that a knowledge of Euclidean geometry was a necessary prerequisite to all disciplines and deemed relevant to the many professions.[13] As a result, prefaces to the various editions of the *Elements* published while Coleridge was alive often spoke of its contents as a foundation for many subjects. For instance, the "Preface" to the sixteenth edition of Robert Simson's *The Elements of Euclid: The First Six Books Together with the Eleventh and Twelfth* (1814) declared that studying Euclid was of "the greatest use in the art both of peace and war,"[14] a conviction that echoed John Love's introduction to his 1792 edition of *Geodaesia or the Art of Surveying and Measuring of Land Made Easy*, which spoke of geometry as a "wholesome and innocent exercise, that we seldom find a man that has once entered himself into ... can ever after wholly lay aside, so natural is it to the minds of men."[15] Similarly, in the 1806 "Preface" to *The Elements of Land Surveying*, A. Crocker proclaimed that the study of Euclid "gives a habit of close and demonstrative reasoning." Crocker asserted that "even philosophy without geometry, is like medicine without chemistry." He continued: "The greater number of modern philosophers reason inconclusively, only because they are unacquainted with geometry" ("Preface," n.p.). Later, in the mid-1800s, Lord Palmerston went as far as to declare that studying Euclid offered excellent training for a diplomat. As Alice Jenkins points out, until the mid-nineteenth century the guiding opinion was that a knowledge of Euclid was not only essential for all professions and most trades but also necessary to developing a person's

---

[11] Many commentators remark that second only to the Bible in the number of editions published, Euclid's *Elements* was one of the most influential works ever to be written.
[12] On the Continent, however, by the late eighteenth and early nineteenth centuries, Euclid was no longer used as a standard textbook to teach geometry. In "Attempts Made during the Eighteenth and Nineteenth Centuries to Reform the Teaching of Geometry," Florian Cajori points out, for instance, that "in the latter half of the eighteenth century, Euclid ceased to be used as a text-book in France." See Cajori, "Attempts Made during the Eighteenth and Nineteenth Centuries to Reform the Teaching of Geometry," *American Mathematical Monthly* 17.10 (October 1910): 182.
[13] This sense that mathematics leads toward knowledge has one of its roots in Plato's *Timaeus*, which states that "every branch of knowledge ... in some way involves mathematics. Mathematics is a good starting point for a journey to the Form of the Good." *Timaeus*, ed. Warrington, 25.
[14] *The Elements of Euclid: The First Six Books Together with the Eleventh and Twelfth*, ed. Robert Simson, 16th ed. (London: F. Wingrave, 1814), n.p.
[15] John Love, *Geodaesia or the Art of Surveying and Measuring of Land Made Easy* (London: G. G. J. & J. Robinson, 1792), "Preface," n.p.

moral development as well as his mind in correct reasoning. She remarks: "A great deal of early nineteenth-century rhetoric about education and learning proposed geometry as the purest and most rational kind of knowledge" imbued "with moral as well as intellectual qualification."[16]

In addition to the many editions of the *Elements*, tangible proof of Euclid's continuing influence and importance in late eighteenth-century and early nineteenth-century England are the mathematical copybooks (briefly mentioned in Chapter 1) which children assembled while attending all manner of schools, from the humblest to such elite institutions as Rugby School. These manuscript exercise books were not only an indispensable tool to support the learning of Euclidean geometry but also items a pupil could take with him once he left school and progressed to either a trade, university, or a profession. They served as an aide-memoire as well as a reference.[17] Recently I purchased one of these at a rare book fair in London. It had once belonged to a Thomas Luckin. His vellum-bound mathematical notebook, dated July 31, 1810, contains, among other forms of mensuration, basic geometrical problems that Luckin studied so as to be prepared for his future work running his establishment, S. Luckin and Sons – Fishmongers and Fruiterers – in Great Dunmow, Essex.

Luckin's manuscript book is one of many surviving copybooks, assembled by pupils in the eighteenth century and up to the second half of the nineteenth century, in which, among other modes of calculation, schoolchildren laboriously wrote out and diagrammed Euclid's definitions and postulates.[18] Some of these are elaborate and reveal more advanced training, such as Charles Shea's, compiled in 1802 while he was a student in the Royal Mathematical School at Christ's Hospital.[19] Shea's manuscript features his own watercolor illustrations as well as his carefully executed

---

[16] Alice Jenkins, *Space and the March of Mind* (Oxford: Oxford University Press, 2007), 168.

[17] In *Figuring It Out: Children's Arithmetical Manuscripts 1680–1880* (Oxford: Huxley Scientific Press, 2012), 51, John Denniss points out that the aim of a copybook was to have a sufficient number and variety of work examples for every role, so that any given problem could be directly matched to one found in the copybook.

[18] Jacqueline Stedall in her *The History of Mathematics: A Very Short Introduction* (Oxford: Oxford University Press, 2012) remarks that before his death in 2005, the mathematics educator John Hersee collected over 200 mathematical copybooks written by pupils in schools throughout England and Wales between 1704 and 1907 (49–71). These are now housed as the John Hersee Collection in the University of Leicester Library, Special Collections. Recently this collection has been digitized.

[19] Charles Shea, admitted to Christ's Hospital in 1797 and a pupil in the Royal Mathematical School, left the school in 1802 and soon found himself "a witness to a victory by the East India Company over the French Navy, the Battle of Pulo Aura (Pulau Aru) in February 1804" (Jones, *The Sea and the Sky*, 200). For a discussion of Shea's career, see Jones, *The Sea and the Sky*, 200–02.

copies of Euclid's definitions and diagrams (see Chapter 1). Perhaps the most extensive assemblage of these copybooks is housed at the University of Leicester Library. In that library's John Hersee Collection are a few elaborately ornamented examples, such as P. W. B.'s "Mensuration" (Item B1) rendered in 1818, which also contains watercolor sketches as well as meticulously presented pages featuring such categories as "Problems of Geometry preparatory to Trigonometry." Many others in this archive are less decorative but are uniformly written in what we would now consider a skilled calligraphic hand. For example, there are the adroitly inscribed pages of John Keale's copybook possibly of 1762 (Item K3) outlining a series of "Geometrical Problems." These display a flourishing, well-trained hand. And there are the beautifully lettered pages presenting Euclid's geometrical "Definitions" that introduce James Sharp(e)'s 1782 notebook (Item 51b; see Figure 9).

More examples of this ornate style can be found in Montagu Cholmeley's 1790 copybook (Item C5), William Davis's of 1803 (Item D1) and Thomas Clark's of 1807 (Item C4). Clark's typically begins with a page devoted to "Geometric Definitions."[20] A few even reveal the distracted, wandering hand of the pupil, such as the back cover of Davis's copybook, which exhibits various doodles – including a rough drawing of a bird, smudges, twirling pen strokes, and crossings-out – some of which could have later been penned by another child.

Putting these books together appreciably immersed these students in a process of learning that reinforced the heart of geometry, which was to instruct a person on how to organize information and think in rational ways. Most pupils did not receive a ready-assembled blank notebook but had to compile it themselves. As a result, they had to learn not only how to fold paper, make gatherings, sew them together in a vellum or cardboard binding, and trim the edges but also how to arrange the layout of each page and determine the order of the gatherings.[21] Therefore, just as in

---

[20] The Special Collections at the University of Leicester Library received these manuscript notebooks in January 2012. Although the collection is housed in the library, it is owned by the Mathematical Association, of which John Hersee was President from 1992 to 1993. John Hersee (1930–2005), whose interest in mathematical education prompted him to collect these notebooks (over 200 of them), received first-class honors in mathematics from the University of Oxford; he started his career as a schoolmaster and eventual taught mathematical education in Bristol. He was involved in both national and international mathematical curriculum development as well as in the Mathematical Association.

[21] For an instructive article on these copybooks assembled by pupils in Scotland, see Matthew Daniel Eddy's "The Nature of Notebooks: How Enlightenment Schoolchildren Transformed the Tabula Rasa," *Journal of British Studies* 57.2 (March 29, 2018): 275–307.

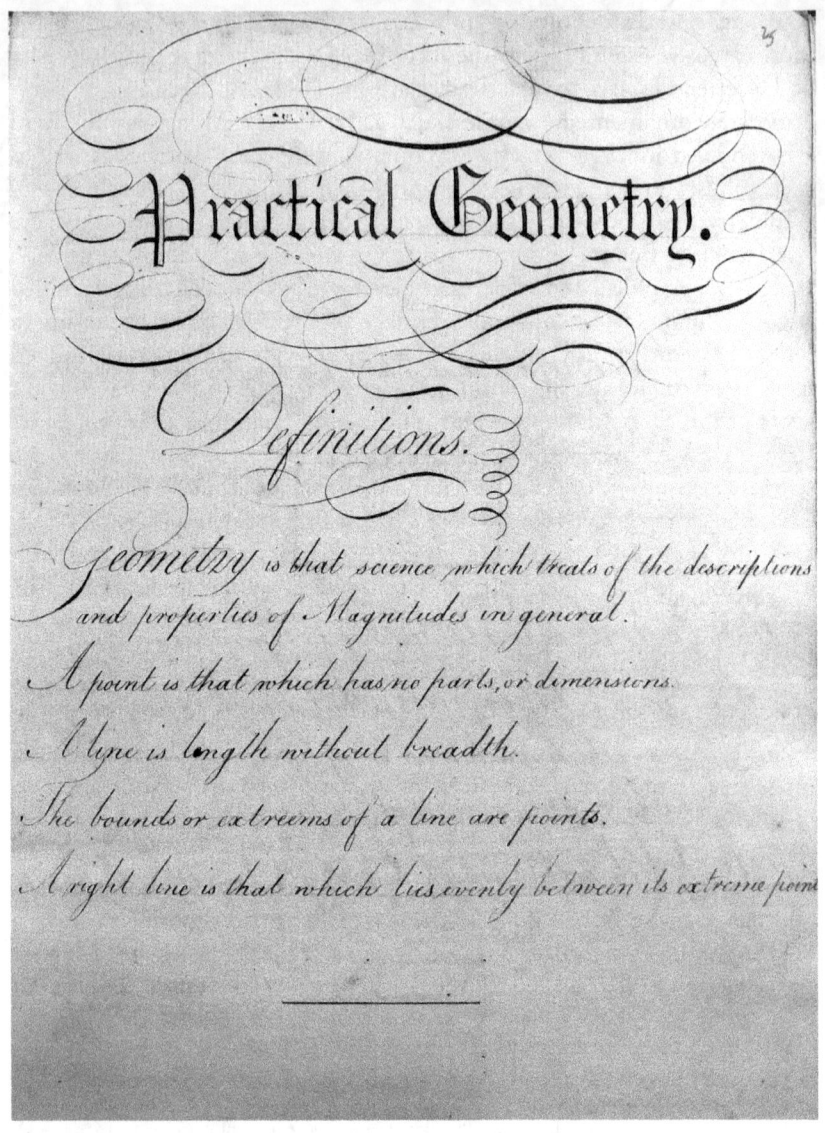

Figure 9   Page from James Sharp(e)'s 1782 copybook.
Library of the Mathematical Association at the University of Leicester, John Hersee Collection, MA/HE/1/S/1/B. By permission of the Mathematical Association [James Sharp]

geometry, young scholars when assembling these copybooks studied how to manage space. Compiling them was a form of visual training that made students consider the layout of a blank page – a reminder, perhaps, of Coleridge's repeatedly close attention to the arrangement of lines in his poetry and his concern with how the poem appeared on a page (see the discussion in the previous chapter).

Well into the nineteenth century, such was the priority given to a schooling in Euclid's basic geometry that in 1871, a dedicated group of teachers founded the Association for the Improvement of Geometrical Training (the AIGT). In 1894 the association was renamed the Mathematical Association. In its early years much of the organization's energy focused upon various debates concerning preferable methods of teaching geometry, developing syllabi and pedagogical techniques that allowed students more readily and genuinely to understand Euclid's *Elements*, especially the first six books. There was a fear that a proper learning of Euclid was being sacrificed to the artifice of rote memory, therefore resulting in a wearisome and bewildering comprehension of his system. For instance, in 1868, James Maurice Wilson, senior mathematics master at Rugby School, complained that "there are scores of schools where boys learn and say their Euclid like declensions."[22] As a result, to make the material more palatable and, most particularly, to allow students better to comprehend Euclid's theorems, texts were produced that used colored diagrams and folded paper figures – a trend that, as we have seen in Chapter 3, escaped neither Coleridge's notice nor his displeasure. Even before the efforts of the AIGT to make geometry more approachable, Coleridge had worried lest these methods detract a student's mind from abstract thought.[23] Recall, for instance, the vehemence with which he disapproved of Thomas Beddoes's desire to teach Euclid's basic principles

---

[22] Sloan Evans Despeaux, "A Voice for Mathematics," in *Mathematics in Victorian Britain*, ed. Raymond Flood, Adrian Rice, and Robin Wilson (Oxford: Oxford University Press, 2011), 170. Before teaching at Rugby School, James Maurice Wilson had been a fellow of St. John's College, Cambridge. In a lecture in Edinburgh, Wilson remarked: "There will always be danger enough of a boy's preferring the labor of almost committing it [knowledge of Euclid] to memory." See Wilson, *A Lecture on Mathematical Teaching, Especially Geometry* (Rugby: W. Billington, 1870), 8.

[23] For a detailed article on the developing of syllabi in the AIGT, see Simon Newcomb's "The Fundamental Definitions and Propositions of Geometry, with Especial Reference to the Syllabus of the Association for the Improvement of Geometrical Training," *Nature* 21.535 (January 29, 1880): 293–95. In his *Observations on the Nature of Demonstrative Evidence*, Thomas Beddoes wrote: "The more I consider the subject, the more I am inclined, in the spirit of Mr. Harris, to believe not only in the possibility, but the rendering the elements of geometry palpable. If they be taught at an early age – a plan in which I think I see many advantages – models would make the study infinitely more engaging" (vii).

by appealing to pupils' sensory understanding and letting them learn by using three-dimensional wooden models of geometric figures.[24] From Beddoes's perspective, these models would lay a good foundation by making "the study infinitely more engaging" (vii).[25] Beddoes believed that the idea of a triangle, for instance, is "acquired by the exercise of the senses" (*Observations on the Nature of Demonstrative Evidence*, 7). He was convinced that the mind needed the assurance of this reality. Coleridge, however, was not convinced of this benefit, and years later was to continue to criticize the use of various gimmicks. For instance, in his posthumous publication *Logic*, a work based on his 1822–23 lectures, Coleridge despaired: "Common sense would condemn the teacher of geometry who should present his circles, triangles, etc. to the scholar in gaudy and variegated colours" (*CC* 13:15) – a criticism he surely would have repeated had he also commented on a 1725 edition of Euclid in which threads and wires were "raised on Boards with Letters glewed [*sic*] on to the particular Angles," so as to illustrate "the several Propositions of the Solids" (Cunn, *An Appendix*, 6), or had he lived to peruse Oliver Byrne's popular 1847 edition of Euclid featuring colored diagrams as well as W. D. Cooley's 1860 *The Elements of Geometry Simplified and Explained*, in which three-dimensional folded paper figures replicated the construction of Euclid's theorems.[26]

---

[24] See Chapter 3 of this book, which mentions Coleridge's objections to Thomas Beddoes's desire to use geometric models when teaching basic geometry. In Chapter 3, I discuss the seeming paradox of Coleridge's objection to using sensual props to learn geometry.

[25] Thomas Beddoes, however, was aware of the Continental mathematicians who had turned away from Euclid. Indeed, in his *Observations on the Nature of Demonstrative Evidence* (1793), he wrote that Euclid's *Elements* are not in "any way necessary to lay a good foundation in mathematics, for there are few, I will venture to guess, of the eminent mathematicians of Europe, that have been initiated by the study of Euclid" (x).

[26] W. D. Cooley once wrote about this text: "In 1860 there was published for me, by Messrs. Williams and Norgate, a little volume entitled *The Elements of Geometry Simplified and Explained*, adapted to the system of empirical proof, and by exhibiting the truth of theorems by means of figures cut in paper." Cooley continues, however, to explain that even though the basic text is Euclid's, he has unfortunately rearranged the order of some of Euclid's theorems:

> It contains in 35 theorems the quintessence of Euclid's first six books, together with a supplement not in Euclid. There was no gap in the sequence or chain of reasoning, yet the 32d and 47th propositions of Euclid were, respectively the 3d and 17th of my series. This book proved a failure ... but it will be sufficient here to state but one [reason for the failure], namely, that it came forth ten years before its time (As quoted in Cajori, "Attempts Made during the Eighteenth and Nineteenth Centuries to Reform the Teaching of Geometry," 196)

See also W. D. Cooley, "Elementary Geometry," *Nature* 4 (1871): 485–86.

## Part Three: The Euclid Debate

Even though Euclid's tenacious hold on the English imagination continued throughout the eighteenth century and into the first half of the nineteenth century, mathematicians were beginning to interrogate the ultimate authority of Euclid. Since a number of these arguments were circulating around Coleridge, it is helpful, despite the risk of distorting intricate and technical mathematical calculations and perspectives, to give some general sense of their content. In one way or another, these challenges to Euclid may seem merely tangential to Coleridge's thoughts, but on reflection they can be shown to amplify the direction that Coleridge's own geometric imagination was taking. As I shall eventually go on to suggest, when describing the landscape of his surroundings, Coleridge often upset or modified the scaffolding of his Euclidean training and embraced what in the end I refer to as a wild geometry – an impulse that obliquely places him among those who were Euclid's rivals and were on their way to creating a non-Euclidean geometry. Before discussing Coleridge's place in these debates, I want first, however, to give some sense of the questions surrounding Euclid's certainty.

### Euclid and His Modern Rivals

Beginning in the late eighteenth and early nineteenth centuries, a few English and Scottish geometers were gradually joining their European counterparts in questioning various sections of Euclid's *Elements* so that during Coleridge's lifetime there were rumblings about the text's restrictions and inaccuracies.[27] Jeremy Gray in his *Plato's Ghost: The Modernist Transformation of Mathematics* explains that the "problem with the very apparatus of Euclid's geometry" was that what once was obvious "seemed harder and harder to define." There were "gaps" in Euclid's reasoning that were "harder and harder to fill."[28] As the decades passed, debates

---

[27] Among these critics was Thomas Beddoes, who admitted that "it is high time to discard Euclid's Elements" (*Observations on the Nature of Demonstrative Evidence*, x). Given this sentiment, it is interesting to note that in *A Short Account of the History of Mathematics* (London: Macmillan, 1908), W. W. Rouse Ball speaks of the complete isolation of the English school of geometry from the Continent (339–440). I would like to suggest, however, that this was not necessarily the case. When one starts to read various British mathematical treatises and introductions to Euclid written in the late eighteenth and early nineteenth centuries, one soon realizes that indeed there was an awareness of the various adjustments being made to Euclid's theories and that British mathematicians were more alert to the questioning of Euclid's postulates on the Continent than Ball recognizes.

[28] Jeremy Gray, *Plato's Ghost: The Modernist Transformation of Mathematics* (Princeton, NJ: Princeton University Press, 2008), 19.

concerning these matters gained momentum so that eventually British geometers were catching up with and joining their European counterparts. Circulating among this group were discussions about the order in which Euclid presented his system of geometry; consequently, a number of British mathematicians began carefully considering both the form and arrangement of Euclid's propositions so that they could be presented in a more perfectly logical sequence.

One difficulty was with Euclid's fifth postulate concerning parallel lines.[29] For thousands of years many attempts had been made to prove this postulate, for unlike the first four, the fifth parallel postulate was not self-evident; it did not logically follow from what preceded it. Questioning of Euclid's system actually harkens back to the eleventh century, when Omar Khayyám recognized the possibility of omitting Euclid's fifth postulate. This postulate concerning parallel structures continued to resonate through the centuries so that in the thirteenth century, Nasir al-Din ai-Tui attempted to contradict the parallel postulate.[30] During Coleridge's lifetime, this long struggle was alive and well in both Europe and Britain. As Gray points out, "hardly a year on the subject went by without someone writing a book on the subject."[31]

As a result of this questioning and primarily through the efforts of the Continental mathematicians, Euclidean geometry was being modified. There developed, for instance, a spherical geometry with no parallels – what generally became associated with "non-Euclidean geometry."[32] Eventually in Britain, such was the impetus to revise Euclid that, by the 1880s, a growing number of geometers were actively campaigning for the *Elements* to be amended and brought up to date with the work of eminent Continental mathematicians who were proposing substitute propositions

---

[29] Parallel lines, according to Euclid, are lines that however far they are extended will never meet because they are everywhere equidistant.

[30] One of the better-known attempts to tackle this postulate is Playfair's Axiom. John Playfair proposed replacing Euclid's fifth postulate with his own. In 1795 Playfair brought out a revised Euclid containing this proof. Charles Dodgson eventually became involved in the debate and in 1888 published *A New Theory of Parallels* (London: Macmillan). In this treatise, Dodgson addressed those who attempted "to dispose with Euclid's celebrated 12th Axiom" (xvi) and concluded that these "suffer from the same defect as Euclid's Axiom (xx). The quotations in this chapter are from the third edition (London: Macmillan, 1890).

[31] Jeremy Gray, *Ideas of Space: Euclidian, Non-Euclidian, and Relativistic* (Oxford: Clarendon Press, 1979), 76.

[32] For a readable history of this preoccupation with Euclid's theory of parallels, see Gray, *Ideas of Space*, 29–50. Gray states that the "most fullblooded attempt upon the parallel postulate during the eighteenth century was that of Gerolamo Saccheri (1667–1733), who published his *Euclid Vindicated from Every Blemish* in Milan in 1733. In it he dealt with the postulate and claimed in the end to have established it" (54).

and verifications.³³ Significantly, their drive to embrace these alternate geometries gathered enough strength so that in 1888 both Oxford and Cambridge accepted proofs in their final examinations that occasionally differed from Euclid's.³⁴

Concerned that these adjustments to Euclid needed to be incorporated into the teaching of geometry, J. M. Wilson of Rugby School, in 1870, produced a textbook which, in addition to campaigning against the learning of geometry by rote memory, integrated many of these challenges.³⁵ On January 20 of that same year, Wilson also delivered "A Lecture on Mathematical Teaching, Especially Geometry" at the Royal High School, Edinburgh. In this talk, though readily admitting his reverence for Euclid (indeed, in his eyes, a "second to Aristotle"), Wilson compellingly proclaimed that Euclid's system had its weaknesses: that Euclid "fails in method," that "his system is artificial, and not natural," and that there are "numerous faults in his definitions" as well as "inconsistencies."³⁶ Asserting that geometry was "not exempt from the universal law of stability and change" (*A Lecture on Mathematical Teaching*, 2) and that "Truth has nothing to fear from discussions" (1), Wilson notably insisted that more attention should be given to mathematicians like Adrien-Marie Legendre in France (1752–1833), who at the same time as honoring Euclid was also questioning, altering, and supplanting the ancient geometer's rules and propositions.³⁷ With these thoughts, Wilson joined others in Britain who were beginning to recognize the

---

[33] Arguments for a non-Euclidean geometry eventually flourished in Russia and the Continent during the late eighteenth and early nineteenth centuries. Some of the names associated with this movement are Nikolai Ivanovich Lobachevsky, János Bolyai, and Karl Friedrich Gauss. Coincidentally, Bolyai and Gauss were attending the University of Göttingen in the late 1790s, approximately the time when Coleridge was there in the spring and summer of 1798. Gauss, for instance, was studying mathematics at the university between 1795 and 1798. There is absolutely no evidence, however, that their paths ever crossed.

[34] For a discussion of this, see Tony Crilly's "The Rise and Fall of the Mathematical Tripos" in *Mathematics in Victorian Britain*, ed. Raymond Flood, Adrian Rice, and Robin Wilson (Oxford: Oxford University Press, 2011), 17–84.

[35] See James Maurice Wilson's *Elementary Geometry Books I–V Containing the Subject of Euclid's First Six Books Following the Syllabus of Geometry Prepared by the Geometrical Association* (London: Macmillan, 1878).

[36] James Maurice Wilson, *A Lecture on Mathematical Teaching, Especially Geometry* (Rugby: W. Billington, 1870), 9–13.

[37] Adrien-Marie Legendre assisted with the Anglo-French survey (1784–90) in order to calculate, precisely, the distance between the Paris Observatory and the Royal Greenwich Observatory. He was best known for his *Éléments de géométrie* (1794), in which he reorganized and simplified many of Euclid's propositions. In 1822, David Brewster published an English translation of Legendre's geometry.

desirability of revising Euclid if the discipline were to be kept vital and defended from mechanical applications of half-understood processes.

To demonstrate just how effective and concerning these arguments were, it is helpful to be reminded that at the same time as Wilson was holding forth, other English mathematicians were entering the debate concerning the validity of Euclid's continuing worth. One was Charles L. Dodgson, who, as a mathematics lecturer at Christ Church, Oxford, was producing a short tract, *Euclid and His Modern Rivals*, in order to defend Euclid against these challenges.[38] This whimsical, yet utterly earnest, four-act "play" started out as a pamphlet in 1876 and was eventually published as a book by Macmillan in 1879.[39] Featuring three characters (Minos, a nineteenth-century mathematician; the ghost of Euclid; and Rhadamanthus, a phantasm of a German professor, Herr Niemand [German for "Nobody"], who speaks on behalf of Euclid's rivals), Dodgson's text systematically examined each of Euclid's critics, among whom are not only the Continental mathematicians but also Wilson, the mathematics instructor at Rugby School quoted earlier. In the course of a lively repartee among these characters and their questioning of various Euclidean theories, Dodgson not only exhibits his awareness of the various non-Euclidean arguments, but also, with certain reservations, simultaneously expresses his continuing reverence for Euclid. He, it seems, was determined to demonstrate that this classical geometer's fundamental ideas were neither outdated nor obsolete, especially in the teaching of basic geometry. Indeed, such was Dodgson's veneration for Euclid that he dedicated the book to his memory. As a result, throughout the tract, Euclid's phantom eloquently argues for the validity of his *Elements*, and

---

[38] Charles L. Dodgson in his "Prologue" to *Euclid and His Modern Rivals* (London: Macmillan, 1879) writes:

> The object of this little book is to furnish evidence, first, that it is essential, for the purpose of teaching or examining in elementary Geometry, to employ one text-book only; secondly, that there are strong *a priori* reasons for retaining, in all its features, and specially in its sequence and numbering of propositions and in its treatment of parallels the Manual of Euclid; and thereby, that no sufficient reasons have yet been shown for abandoning it in favour of any one of the modern Manuals which have been offered as substitutes. (ix)

[39] The opening of the dialogue immediately catches the whimsical tone of *Euclid and His Modern Rivals*: It begins with stage directions showing Minos:

> *discovered seated between two gigantic piles of manuscripts. Ever and anon he takes a paper from one heap, reads it, makes an entry in a book, and with a weary sigh transfers it to the other heap. His hair, from much running of fingers through it, radiates in all directions, and surrounds his head like a halo of glory, or like the second Corollary of Euc. I. 32.* (Dodgson, *Euclid and His Modern Rivals*, Act I)

concludes the drama by addressing his interrogators and readers with this final thought:

> Let me carry with me the hope that I have convinced you of the importance, if not necessity, of retaining any order and numbering, and my method of treating straight Lines, angles, right angles, and (most especially) Parallels. Leave me these untouched, and I shall look on with great contentment while the changes are made – while my proofs are abridged and improved – while alternative proofs are appended to mine – and while new problems and theorems are interpolated. (Dodgson, *Euclid and His Modern Rivals*, 199)

To support this sentiment, Dodgson added an appendix in which he quotes two prominent English mathematicians, Isaac Todhunter and Augustus De Morgan. Though sometimes agreeing with the various challenges to Euclid, these mathematicians, like Dodgson, believed that if one were to abandon Euclid, there would be little agreement as to how he would be replaced and by whom.[40] If Dodgson's *Euclid and His Modern Rivals* is any indication, it seems, therefore, that in spite of the growing number of challenges to Euclid's system, there remained in Britain, up into the second half of the nineteenth century, a deep-seated loyalty to the *Elements*. For example, Arthur Cayley (1821–95), who held the Sadleirian Professorship of Pure Mathematics at the University of Cambridge, ardently campaigned to prevent the abolition of Euclid at Cambridge. It was only after Cayley's death in 1895 that his successor Andrew Forsyth agitated for the abandonment of Euclid.[41]

## Part Four: Coleridge and the Alternate Paradigms

Coleridge was by no means actively involved in the various arguments and technical discussions brewing among mathematicians on the Continent

---

[40] Isaac Todhunter admitted that Euclid was falling out of favor on the Continent, but asserted that "it would be rash to throw away certain good in order to grasp a phantasmal of benefit" (Dodgson, *Euclid and His Modern Rivals*, 209). In the "Preface" to his *The Elements of Euclid for the Use of Schools and Colleges* (rev. ed. London: Macmillan, 1882), first published in 1862, Todhunter wrote, "If Euclid were once abandoned, that any agreement" as to "who should replace him" would not be possible (vii). In his appendix to Dodgson's pamphlet, Augustus De Morgan (1806–71) picturesquely asked the question: whether Euclid's text be "as many suppose, the best elementary treatise on geometry, or whether it be a mocking, delusion, snare, hindrance, pitfall, schoal, shallow, and snake in the grass" (Dodgson, *Euclid and His Modern Rivals*, 201). Although he was open to revising Euclid, he, like Todhunter, Dodgson, and many others, continued to value Euclid's *Elements*. De Morgan, however, did dare to suggest that certain parts of Legendre's system, particularly his work on solid geometry, might profitably substitute for parts of Euclid.

[41] For a discussion of Cayley's position see Amitrouche Morkteft's "The Euclid Debate," in *Mathematics in Victorian Britain*, ed. Raymond Flood, Adrian Rice, and Robin Wilson (Oxford: Oxford University Press, 2011), 321–34.

and eventually in Britain. However, he must have been somewhat aware of the various ongoing debates about Euclid's validity as well as the numerous, but often futile, attempts to find an appropriate substitute for the *Elements*. Coleridge was, after all, persistently responsive to Continental thought. His was never, as his studies in Germany and the range of his lifelong reading demonstrate, an insular point of view. Furthermore, as already discussed in this and previous chapters, he was conversant with the various philosophical treatises about the nature of geometry. Moreover, periodically he conversed about the character of geometry with people like Stephen Peter Rigaud, an historian of mathematics. Later in life, he might also have been alert to the disputes at Cambridge that were gradually calling attention to the validity of Euclid's ascendency – though, as mentioned earlier, these never really came to the fore until the latter part of the nineteenth century.[42]

### Coleridge and the Geometry of Visibles

In particular, during the period of Coleridge's lifetime, the proposal of one British philosopher and mathematician to modify Euclid's spatial perspective caught Coleridge's attention – and that was Thomas Reid's. Reid was the Scottish philosopher whose *An Inquiry into the Human Mind: On the Principles of Common Sense* (first published in 1764) enjoyed much notice and seems especially to have gained Coleridge's respect.[43] In particular, section IX, "Of the Geometry of Visibles," garnered attention and came, retrospectively, to be seen, by some, as an early expression of a non-Euclidean geometry in Britain.[44] It should be pointed out, however, that

---

[42] Kathleen Coburn's note to a notebook entry (*CN* Notes 3:4266) suggests: "It is tempting to associate all this [a long entry about the paradoxes of mathematics] with Coleridge's conversations with Stephen Peter Rigaud, historian of mathematics, on 21 April 1811" and with a "return to the subject in a letter of Sept. 27 1815. *CL* 4:588–89."

[43] Thomas Reid (1710–96). In 1752 Reid was appointed Professor of Philosophy at King's College in Aberdeen. He founded the Aberdeen Philosophical Society. After the publication of his *An Inquiry into the Human Mind*, he was appointed the Professor of Moral Philosophy at the University of Glasgow, a position he held until 1781. He is known for his integral role in the Scottish Enlightenment. Two of Reid's uncles were professors of mathematics; Reid himself devoted much time to studying the subject. After his *Inquiry* first appeared in 1764, during the eighteenth and nineteenth centuries it went through multiple editions. The text is still being published. One of the most recent is Derek R. Brooke's critical edition published in 1997 by the Pennsylvania State University Press. The quotations in this chapter are from the seventh edition published by Anderson and Macdowall, and James Robertson in Edinburgh, 1818. In two issues of *The Friend*, Coleridge compliments Reid's genius. See *CC* 1:423 and 2:33.

[44] Reid's "geometry of visibles" came to be regarded as one of the first expressions in Britain to challenge Euclidean thought, a number of years before the late nineteenth-century publications of

Reid, like many others, though questioning the dominance of Euclid's concepts, did not set out to discard Euclid's *Elements* and often registered his regard for the text. And most certainly he did not consciously identify himself with the non-Euclidean forces of the Continental mathematicians, even though, as Norman Daniels observes, he "discovered a non-euclidean geometry some 60 years before the mathematicians."[45]

Interested in the nature of perception and eighteenth-century theories of vision as well as mathematics, Reid, in section IX of his *An Inquiry*, argued that the visual field is governed by principles other than those outlined by the familiar theorems of Euclid.[46] He reasoned that:

> When the geometrician draws a diagram with the most perfect accuracy; when he keeps his eye fixed upon it, while he goes through a long process of reasoning, and demonstrates the relations of several parts of his figure; he does not consider, that the visible figure presented to his eye, is only the representative of a tangible figure, upon which his attention is fixed; he does not consider that these two figures have really different properties, and that which he demonstrates to be true of the one, is not true of the other. (Reid, *An Inquiry*, 115)

Reid maintained that even though Euclidean geometry is the appropriate geometry for the objects we touch in the space around us,[47] it is not the correct geometry for immediate, external objects of sight, "the visible

---

the Russian mathematician Nikolai Ivanovich Lobachevsky, as well as those of the German Bernhard Riemann (of the University of Göttingen) and then Karl Friedrich Gauss on the Continent.

[45] Norman Daniels, "Thomas Reid's Discovery of Non-Euclidian Geometry," *Philosophy of Science* 39.2 (June 1976): 220.

[46] Reid was sensitive to the fact that "the visible appearance of things ... varies almost every hour, according as the day is clear or cloudy, as the sun is in the east, or south, or west, as my eye is in one part of the room or in another" (Reid, *An Inquiry*, 146). Obviously, Coleridge shared this perspective, for on his rambles, in addition to recording the static Euclidean geometric figures, he pays attention to the fluid variations and modifications in the visual scene before him. For instance, when Coleridge, in November 1799, gazed upon a Lakeland view, he noted how the physical sight of its various landmarks altered during the course of a walk: "We pass thro' the wood, road ascending – now over it & see nothing else – & now the whole violet Crag rises & fronts me – Then the waters near the upper end of Crummock the archipelago of tiniest Islands ... & two near the opposite shore – Buttermere comes upon us, a fragment of it – the view enclosed by a huge Concave Semicircle" (*CN* 1:537; f. 39). Several years later, in August 1802, he displayed a similar perspective: "As I proceed a few yards, the view is completely altered, and a round smooth rises up beyond the Sea Ness, & bisects the distance" (*CN* 1:1225; f. 28). And on Wednesday, June 29, 1803, he diagrammed the shifting figure of the setting sun that revealed a "number of black Orbs all as in a mirror – when the Sun dipped they followed the Shape, ◯, now semicircles, now ⌒, and now almost to points" (*CN* 1:1405; f. 48).

[47] According to Reid, a person finds his way in a physical environment by obeying Euclidean principles primarily because of what he learns from his kinesthetic and tactile experiences.

figure presented to the eye"; hence, the need for what he termed "a geometry of visibles." He believed that each of these two modes has different properties – even though both are valid. No longer, therefore, can these two forms of perception be under the umbrella of the single system of Euclidean geometry. Their structure and orientation are different, so must mathematically be taken into account. Hence the need to consider an alternate geometry that is distinct from Euclid's. Reid explains this want:

> Nothing shows more clearly our indisposition to attend to visible figure and visible extension than this, that although mathematical reasoning is no less applicable to them, than to tangible figure and extension, yet they have entirely escaped the notice of mathematicians. While the figure and the extension, which are objects of touch, have been tortured ten thousand ways for twenty centuries and a very noble system of science has been drawn out of them; not a single proposition do we find with regard to the figure and extension which are the immediate objects of sight! (*An Inquiry*, 185–86)

Reid's sensitivity to the difference between the visual experience and the conception of the abstract Euclidean figure has, I suggest, some affinity to Coleridge's own alertness to the distinction between what the bodily eye perceives and what the intellect intuitively comprehends. As Coleridge explained in his *Logic*, "the points, lines, and surfaces of Euclidean geometry are not bodies nor parts of bodies, but acts of the mind" (*CC* 13:76); they are forms which one knows intuitively. In other words, there are two systems of organizing space: one, centered in the rotating eye; the other, intellectual, rooted in the mind, and "wholly abstracted from all outward realities" (*CC* 13:75). Though not necessarily consciously replicating Reid's observations, Coleridge loosely approximates Reid's understanding of this insight when in many of his notebook entries he records both the fluctuating, visual physical experiences that emerge before his eyes and the abstracted Euclidean figures that reside in the mind. For instance, recognizing their dissimilarity, yet mutual validity, Coleridge, while on a walk in Germany, summons both modes to describe what he sees. When depicting the scene, as was his tendency, he combines the phenomenological and the abstract to offer a more complete depiction of what he is witnessing. As Kant intimates, only through such a union can knowledge arise:[48]

---

[48] At this point, one is reminded of Kant and his concept of the synthesis between experience and mind that creates the possibility of intuition – that intuitions belong to the perceiving mind and are akin to sensations. As Jeremy Gray points out: "Knowledge ... arises, according to Kant, from two

> A valley on the right semicircle stretching to an immense length – to the side of the Left Semicircle the arc, woody Hills, the higher lot firs with intermixture of yellow green Beeches – below & flowing down the Hill into a valley a fine flood trees. The town of ____ from here begin the description ____ far off on my right hand & close by my left ____ <near the River> / two greeneries the latter a parallelogram, walled on three sides by silver Birches, on the 4th by firs – the high proud Hills of Fir & <Beech soaring from> behind – (*CN* 1:417; f. 28)

Unlike Reid, however, Coleridge clearly never took the time, nor was he inclined, to formalize, mathematically, a geometry that systematized either the physiological experience of vision or the position of the real object as seen by the eye. It goes without saying that Coleridge, infatuated with the aesthetic and emotional dimensions of what he beheld, did not want to be confined to the limiting boundaries of such formulations. Reid, on the other hand, was interested. Keenly attentive to the discipline of mathematics, Reid dedicated himself to diagramming and classifying the angles, lines, and figurative structure of this phenomenon. To do this, his "geometry of visibles," generally speaking, positioned the eye at the center of a sphere.[49] From Reid's point of view, every visible figure has geometrical properties that are indistinguishable from a figure drawn on a sphere. According to his understanding, rather than being outside and, hence, looking down on the surface of an area (as one does in plane Euclidean geometry), one's eye centers itself in the midst of a sphere, from which position it rotates and looks up, down, below, and around toward a projection of objects.[50] Essentially, the geometry of visibles is the geometry of this single, interior point of view. Reid summarizes:

> Supposing the eye placed in the centre of a sphere, every great circle of the sphere will have the same appearance to the eyes as if was a straight line. For the curviture [*sic*] of the circle being turned directly toward the eye, is not perceived by it. And for the same reason, any line which is drawn in a plane of a great circle of the sphere, whether it be in reality straight or curved, will appear straight to the eye. (Reid, *An Inquiry*, 187)

---

fundamental sources: our capacity to receive representations, and our power of knowing an object through those representations by the spontaneous generation of concepts" (*Ideas of Space*, 82). Gray also points out that Kant was not committed to a geometry based upon the parallel postulate, which "he was prepared to hold in abeyance" (75). Apparently Kant corresponded about the fact that geometry is possible with or without the parallel postulate. He maintained that there are several theorems independent of this postulate which together form the body of "absolute geometry."

[49] It should be pointed out that spherical geometry was no stranger to a student of Euclid. It was well known at the time, and would have been especially studied by students in the Royal Mathematical School at Christ's Hospital who were being trained to become naval officers and navigate the seas.

[50] It is perhaps interesting to note here that in Plato's cave, the individual, who is released from looking only at shadows of the Idea, is able to turn their neck and look all around.

Though certainly not literally replicating Reid's mathematical orientation, Coleridge's descriptions of the landscape at times evoke the spirit of Reid's understanding, for in addition to expressing a sensitivity to both the Euclidean and physiological experience of perception, Coleridge often represented the physical act of seeing by placing the observer's rotating eye in the midst of an encompassing, arc-like landscape so that individuals gaze out to what is up, above, behind, below, and around them, as if in the midst of an amphitheater.[51] This stance reflects Coleridge's tendency, discussed in Chapter 1, to reject the cartographic imagination that requires one to be exterior to and separated from where one stands. Instead, Coleridge habitually removes himself from this elevated vantage point and locates himself *within* the interior spaces of the very scene he is observing. Unlike the picturesque observer, he descends from such landmarks as the Penrith Beacon. As a result, in many of his notebook entries, Coleridge regards a prospect by placing his eye as if it were in the center of the surrounding spherical landscape so that he can gaze at the various particulars projected onto his field of vision – though, as I have already noted, Coleridge, when he does this, certainly does not entertain the rules attending spherical geometry.[52]

Throughout the notebooks kept during his rambling days, there are many examples of this orientation. For instance, in August 1800, Coleridge lies down on the side of a hill in order to position his eye in the midst of the scene and register all that appears in the encompassing surroundings, from "the central part of the Bow ⌒⋀."[53] This is a perspective that recalls a May entry from the previous year in which Coleridge follows his eye as it freely rotates and views what is above, below, around, to the left and to the right of its gaze:

> *Above* [italics mine] us a tremendous Rock black & yellow, called Rehburg – / <Little Trees, an inch high, like weeds in the road> ... Now on all sides Firs, nothing but Firs (Violet tone) *below, above, around*

---

[51] One is reminded of Coleridge's portrait of firs growing on the side of hills that "rise one above the other, like Spectators in an [Amphitheatre –]" (*CL* 1:505).
[52] In Reid's system, the truths of spherical geometry and the truths of visible geometry are equivalent.
[53] Coleridge writes that he lay on the hill's slope so that he could

> look at the central part of the Bow ⌒⋀: a fine effect of the crags laying as I did on my face sideways to look at them / it looked in this way like a strange City where nothing was left but the Churches & Steeples – Churches & steeples with green spaces betwixt them – standing at the East & looking down it – you see its outlet the center of an inverted arch, & you look over upon that dead red clay chasm called Brandel head Gill, on that part of Carrock which ascends from [the] Skiddaw side. (*CN* 1:798; f. 23)

> [italics mine] us – Saw the little dancing Cataracts thro' the First in various Parts of the vale or deep Bason *below* [italics mine] – & now from the very high Hill *above* [italics mine] us, from the very Top, came down a very considerable Stream, dancing over the Rocks, & seen ever & anon thro-the Breaks of the Fir boughs – till towards the Bottom it became nakedly visible. – *Over* [italics mine] the high opposite Hill a round naked Hill, very much Hill, looked in upon us over the distance. (*CN* 1:412; f. 25)

Similarly, in September 1800 he positions himself in the midst of an inverted arch and records what he sees above and behind him, as well as and under his feet:

> Over Force Crag in a Green Ascent, making an inverted Arch at its summit – over the arch on the right I see the *wall*-crags I before described – / now I turn myself round – On my left Derwentwater etc on my right the Hill Crags & Sail – in front Coombes – that immediately fronting is a Ness quite grey-white & naked – / under my feet a precipice walled as deeply & strikingly as that leading to Crummock Water / (*CN* 1:805; f. 54)[54]

A year later, twice referring to the curvature of a spherical triangle, Coleridge seems almost consciously to place himself within Reid's sphere:

> I seemed to think that these high green mountains, so furrowed, delved, & wrinkled with Torrents are still wilder than craggy Mountains / the Mountains were all detached, a great Beauty! – One I shall never forget / in shape resembling a Schoolboy's Top, or rather presenting to the eye two sides of a spherical Triangle / as I looked back, on my left, at the extremity of this side of the Triangle, a curving wall of green Highland, & over it from the distance a ⌒ mountain. At the extremity of the other side another mountain from the distance, but of wild & fantastic outline / but the Mountain itself, the spheric Triangle, so very vast, so high, so worn & marked / – (*CN* 1:1482; ff. 40, 41)

---

[54] An August 1802 entry displays a similar perspective:
> leave the Great road & go up by the Irt, thro' a stony Road, behind me a beautiful view of the Sea and low-lands on the Shore seen in the most impressive of all ways, viz, thro' an inverted arch formed by the rough Fells before me, the huge enormous mountains of Wast dale all bare & iron-red – and on them a *forest* of cloud-shadow, all motionless / a low Ridge intercepts the Lake from *the eye* [italics mine] – to my right & to my left rough strong Common with great ~~Green~~ Knots, raggedly cloathed with underwood / No view of River / unless it be Sea ward / Mem. beautiful shadow of the Fern upon the lichened Stone which it overcanopied. (*CN* 1:1212; f. 9)

### Coleridge and the Curvature of Space

As the above passages demonstrate, Coleridge is notably alert to the curvature of the landscape he beholds – to its "bow," its "inverted Arch [es]," and its "curving." He attends to a hill that "folds in . . . a long *Ellipse*" and another, on his left, that "folds" in "a segment of a circle" (*CN* 1:1225; f. 29). He delights in the "curve of wild Mountain land behind" Lord Ballantyne's estate (*CN* 1:1457; f. 12) as well as in the "curvature" of "10 rain channels" floating down the bank of Grasmere Lake (*CN* 1:1487; f. 46). While rambling, Coleridge remarks on the River Sark "that winds like the <convex> edge of a crescent of sand / then rolls dark over its red brown Stones, a peat-moss River with a 1000 leisurely circles & ellipses of foam" / (*CN* 1:1433; f. 6); he gazes at a "green ellipse of grassiness" (*CN* 1:1439), and focuses on the "long gentle under curve of an Ellipse" at the "bottom of the Lake" (*CN* 1:1462; f. 16). Furthermore, Coleridge takes pleasure in noticing the "gentle curve" of a dip that resembles "the under half of an ellipse 〜‿‿‿" (*CN* 1:1228; f. 32). And eventually on his way to Malta in 1804, he draws attention to "the arc of Heaven" (*CN* 2:2009; f. 37) and to "the ellipses & semicircles of the bellying Sails" (*CN* 2:2012; f. 39).

These arcs and bends, so integral to Coleridge's appreciation of a landscape, peripherally recall the Continental geometers' sensitivity to the curvature of space – to measuring one's surroundings by considering a scene's spherical and elliptical structures and being sensitive to lines that curve away or curve toward one another. In particular, the work of Karl Friedrich Gauss (1777–1855) comes to mind. During Coleridge's lifetime, Gauss was a respected mathematician (trained at the University of Göttingen) who was sensitive to this orientation. His ideas are now considered to be a key to the development of non-Euclidean geometry.

The part of Gauss's career that is of interest here is his surveying work that led to his questioning of Euclid and discovering discrepancies between Euclid's calculation of triangulation and the uneven angles that result from acknowledging the curvature of the earth's surface. After his student years at the University of Göttingen in the late 1790s, Gauss worked as a surveyor for the King of Hanover and, starting in 1821, spent months in the field conducting, with his heliotrope, a geodetic survey. During that time, Gauss, alert to the intrinsic curvature of the earth's surface, discovered discrepancies or an unevenness in the angles when calculating the land's triangulation – a divergence that eventually led to his negation and refutation of Euclid's model and his ensuing belief that a new geometry was possible.[55]

One important landmark in Gauss's survey was the Brocken, the third highest peak (3,742 feet) among the Harz Mountains – the very one, coincidentally, which Coleridge, while studying at the University of Göttingen, had climbed with a group of friends in May 1799, just two decades before Gauss was determining the base line of the area's triangulation.[56] It goes without saying that Gauss's field books noting his measurements of the Brocken and Coleridge's accounts of his ascent are notably different – even though there are marginal similarities, for, as I have earlier observed, Coleridge often adopted the surveyor's habit of counting his paces, noting the "various angles," and remarking, for instance, on "a *Slope* of Greenery ... exactly 170 Strides in diameter" (*CL* 1:500). Coleridge, however, did not confine himself, like Gauss, to these measurements and, most particularly, was not interested in transforming these calculations into a static, abstracted two-dimensional map. Coleridge was not studying a landscape just to establish its borders. Rather, he was intent on reaching beyond such restraints so as to admit and cherish the complex surging, roaring, scattering, and stretching landmarks that unsettled, if not violated, a map's certainty and network of boundaries. Although attracted to the Euclidean geometric figure and the posture of a surveyor, he, when jotting down entries in his notebooks, also desired to capture a scene's ever-flowing particulars. As a result, in a May 19, 1799 letter about his climb, Coleridge, after dismissing a prospect's "abrupt & grand outlines," turns his attention to the hills' gradations of

---

[55] For a discussion of Gauss's relationship to Euclidean geometry during the period of his surveying, see Ernst Breitenberger's essay "Gauss's Geodesy and the Axiom of Parallels," *Archives for History of Exact Sciences* 31 (Spring 1984): 273–89. Breitenberger points out that, although Gauss was still convinced of the validity of Euclid's geometry, he did, as a result of his calculations, reveal how the intrinsic curvature of the earth's surface resulted in slight discrepancies when fitting the smaller triangles inside the larger triangles. He was disturbed that the triangles' angles did not always add up to 180 degrees (as in Euclid). They either exceeded or were less than 180 degrees. In his article, Breitenberger suggests that Gauss, so beholden to Euclidean training, was convinced he had made a mistake when measuring the angles of his triangles. For a more inclusive discussion of Gauss's contribution to non-Euclidean geometry, to the idea that a new geometry is possible, see "Gauss's Contribution" in Jeremy Gray's *Ideas of Space*, 74–81.

[56] The friends who climbed with Coleridge were Charles and Frederic Parry, John Chester, Charles Bellas Greenough (a geographer and geologist), Clement Carlyon (a physician), and "the Son of Professor Blumenbach; an intelligent & well informed young man, especially in Natural History" (*CL* 1:497). For an essay on this Harz tour, see Maximiliaan van Woudenberg's "Revisiting the Harz Tour of Coleridge and the 'Carlyon-Parry-Greenation' in May 1799," *Romanticism* 27.1 (2021): 16–27. The article examines the tour in the context of current geological and mineralogical explorations.

color as well as their flowing, animated contours – to their curving, lingering, rising, sinking, frolicking, and surging, all of which unsettle and disrupt the carefully measured calculations of a surveyor.[57] Coleridge writes to Thomas Poole:"On the left and curving round till they formed the front view, Hills here green with leafy Trees, here still iron-brown, dappled as it were with coming Spring & lingering Winter; not (like the single Hill) of abrupt & grand outlines, but rising & sinking yet on the whole still rising, in a *frolic Surginess*" (*CL* 1:510). Similarly, in a letter to his wife about the climb, Coleridge celebrates a particular scene's unruly motions that contrast with its moments of stillness. In the following passage, he tosses in dashes to replicate the irregular breathlessness accompanying his own excited response to what he sees – dynamics, of course, foreign to a surveyor's report, yet familiar in Coleridge's notebook entries:

> We clomb down into the vale, & stood at the bottom of the Cascade, & climbed up again by it's side / – The rocks over which it plunged were unusually wild in their shape, giving fantastic resemblances of men & animals – & the fir-boughs by the side were kept almost in a *swing*, which unruly motion contrasted well with the stern Quietness of the huge Forest-sea every where else. (*CL* 1:502–03)

Significantly, throughout these descriptions, Coleridge, like Gauss and his fellow mathematicians, is alert to the bending of the earth's surface – the "winding" – of what he beholds. In another letter recounting the ascent of the Brocken, Coleridge sees himself in a swirling world. Turning and turning, he enters the "fourth Curve of the Vale" and "perceives all at once" that "the Verdure [has] vanished! All the Beech Trees were leafless / & so were the silver Birches, whose boughs always, winter & summer, hang so elegantly!" Further on in the letter he resumes his portrayal of this twisting and circling:

> & now we came to a most beautiful Road that *winded* [italics mine] on the breast of the Hill, from whence we looked down into a deep deep Valley or huge Bason full of Pines. & Firs, the opposite Hills full of Pines & Firs, & the Hill above us on whose breast we were *winding* [italics mine], likewise full of Pines & Firs. – The Valley or Bason on our Right Hand into which we looked down is called the Vale of Rauschenbach, that is, the Valley of the Roaring Brook – & *roar* it did, indeed, most solemnly! (*CL* 1:501–02)

---

[57] It is interesting to note that George Adams in his *Geometrical and Graphical Essays* remarks that "within the limits of an ordinary survey, the curvature of the earth's surface is so inconsiderable, that it's surface may be safely considered by the land surveyor as a plane. In a large extent, as a province, or a kingdom, the curvature of the earth's surface becomes very considerable, and due allowance must be made for it" (194).

## Conclusion: A Wild Geometry

Throughout these accounts of his climbing the Brocken, Coleridge's appreciation for the complexity of the scenes at which he gazes is both recognizable and alluring. It is an intricacy that at times challenged his powers of description, so that in a May 19, 1799 letter to his wife, he expresses how inadequate he felt while trying to replicate the shifting shapes of the hills that had emerged before his eyes:

> It were idle in me to attempt by words to give their projections & their retirings & how they were now in Cones, now in roundnesses, now in tonguelike Lengths, now pyramidal, now a huge Bow, and all at every step, varying the forms of their outlines; / or how they now stood abreast, now ran aslant, now rose up behind each other / or now, as at Harzburg, presented almost a Sea of huge motionless waves / too multiform for Painting, too multiform even for the Imagination to remember them / yea, my very sight seemed *incapacitated* by the novelty & Complexity of the Scene. (*CL* 1:513)

At these moments, the static cones, circles, and paradigms associated with Euclidean models are not adequate. They are not ends in themselves, for these set geometric shapes can only abstract the intricacies and fluctuations of what appear before Coleridge's sight.

As a consequence, Coleridge, though still recognizing and paying homage to his mathematical training, finds that he must breach its limits and, compellingly, introduce a "wild" geometry that breaks out of the set forms associated with Euclid. He must attend to the rocks that are "unusually *wild* [italics mine] in their shape," to a plunging waterfall, to a brook that "roars," and to the tree boughs swinging in "unruly motion" (*CL* 1:503). In his own, yet enigmatic way, then, Coleridge modifies Euclid and becomes unwittingly or unintentionally yet another of his "rivals." Though he does not participate in a mathematician's precise, numerical, and technical methods, he peripherally keeps company with those, such as Gauss, who at the same time as being beholden to the ancient geometer also recognize Euclid's shortcomings. Just as Euclid's rivals were to, Coleridge still walks with Euclid; yet, at the same time, recognizes that there are alternate ways of understanding the spatial organization of the physical world. He, therefore, occasionally gazes upon "strange" parallels made by "greenish black-spotted lichens" and "jagged circles" imprinted on a "flat pink-colour'd stone" (*CN* 1:227; f. 36), upon squares that resemble circles " looking boldly open" (*CN* 1:1175; f. 28), and upon a portrait of the head of Christ that resembles "a triangle with a curve-base" (*CN* 2:2480; f. 34) or a tower in Sicily that "struggles" between being "a Triangle & semi circle" (*CN* 2:2690; f. 89). In his idiosyncratic way, Coleridge ruptures the limits of the old geometry and embraces the possibility of another – in his case a wild, roaring, ever moving geometry.[58] To illustrate this course it is helpful to recall an October 10, 1800 notebook entry jotted down hastily, on the spot, when Coleridge had returned from Germany and was once more walking and climbing in the Lakes. The passage describes a series of waterfalls falling over a rocky, steep precipice. To catch the intricate fury of the scene, Coleridge combines his sensitivity to Euclidean forms and the habit of measuring like a surveyor with the wild organic shattering, dashing, fluctuating forms of the falling water. In such a way, he modifies and extends the boundaries of what he has been taught so as to embrace another dimension. With this turn, he obliquely joins those who sought to reach beyond a Euclidean geometry. The October 1800 entry that follows illustrates this impulse:

> when I went over & descended to the bottom, there I only saw the real; *Fall*, & the Curve of the steep slope & retracted – It is indeed so seen a fine thing – it falls parallel with a fine black rock for 30 feet, & is more shattered, more completely atomized & white than any I have ever seen – the pool likewise is formed by a few high large stones, and not a yard in breadth, of course as white as the fall itself – / Standing at the bottom you have no view of the Precipice on the right of which the Dash comes down – the Fall of the Dash is in a Horse-shoe Bason of its own wildly peopled with small ashes standing out of the rocks. / Crossed the stream close by the white pool, stood on the other side, in a complete Spray-*rain* / Here it assumes, I think, a still finer appearance – You see the vast ruggedness & angular points & upright Cones of the black rock – The fall assumes a variety & complexity – ~~some~~ parts rushing in wheels, other parts perpendicular, some in white horse-tails – white ~~on~~ toward the right edge of the black two or three leisurely Fillets have escaped out of the Turmoil / Turning your back on the Waterfall you look over ~~into~~ up an ~~Bassenthwaite~~ arc off the Top In short, go *close* to it and tis well worth

---

[58] In his study of non-Euclidean geometry and the Scottish Enlightenment, *Literature after Euclid: The Geometric Imagination in the Long Scottish Enlightenment* (Philadelphia: University of Pennsylvania Press, 2016), Matthew Wickman proposes that Gilpin's "concept of the picturesque is after a fashion, non-Euclidean. Or rather, it is late Euclidean." Wickman advocates that "without formalizing new paradigms, it opens the limits of the old geometry in its practice if not, yet, in its theory" (103). I suggest, however, that the raw wildness and immediacy of Coleridge's descriptions are far more radical and robust than Gilpin's. And it goes without saying that Coleridge's are infinitely more daring, disruptive, and organic than the possible alternate geometries propagated by the nineteenth-century proponents of a non-Euclidean geometry.

seeing / About 20 yards the Beck forms two other Waterfalls, both pleasing, & both singular – N.B. The precipice, which of course when you are at the bottom loses its perpendicularity, has a row of fine pyramidal rocks on its top of it – I ought to say, appears when you are the second Waterfall to have them – for only one is on the Top – /Ascend / and over this wch I have been describing as if it were the only yet another far finer, & above that another / they are the finest Water furies, I ever beheld / (*CN* 1:825; ff. 60–61)

The complexity of such scenes often frustrated Coleridge and made him doubt his descriptive powers. In a May 17$^{th}$, 1799 letter written to his wife after climbing the Brocken, Coleridge registered this concern. He deliberated on the fact that each "thing" is "individual" and, therefore, cannot rely on set expressions:

In Nature all things are individual; but a Word is but an arb[itrary Character] for a whole Class of Things; so that the same description may in almost all cas[es be applied] to twenty different appearances – & in addition to the difficulty of the Thing itse[lf I neither] am or ever was a good Hand at description. – I see what I write / but alas [! I cannot] write what I see. (*CL* 1:503)

In spite of his uncertainty, Coleridge did succeed in catching the individuality of what he saw. By supplementing and extending the Euclidean idiom, he created particular and compelling portrayals of his ever-evolving surroundings. In the end both the established geometric figures and this wilder geometry worked for him; each was mutually valid.[59] As a result, Euclid not only provided the traditional scaffolding that allowed Coleridge to organize, build, and display his thoughts but also offered Coleridge, whether in youth or age, a place from which to depart. Both geometries were Coleridge's companions.

---

[59] This combination reminds one of a passage he wrote in a November 1799 notebook entry soon after returning from Germany. While scrambling once more in the Lakes, Coleridge pays attention both to "the simple & tame Beauty" of a lower Lake as well as to "the wild betongued savage mountained upper Lake." In the same entry he also notes both the "pastoral River" and the "precipitous huge Bank" of "the steep Mountain" (*CN* 1:510; f. 49). Here the wild and the tame exist together.

# Afterword
## An Organic Geometry

> The Moon ~~in a/n amber Halo~~ rushing onward thro' the coursing clouds – like an indignant Warrior thro' a fleeing Army – but the amber Halo in which she moves – ⊖ a circle of Hope, what she leaves behind ⌒ her has not lost the radiance as it is melting away into oblivion – while still the other semi-circle ⌒ forms and catches the rich Light at her approach and heralds her ongress. – (*CN* 3:4037; f. 44)

Like so many of Coleridge's descriptions, the 1810 notebook entry quoted above comes to life through the motions and mutations of what it portrays. Like other passages in his journals, it traces the ever-changing shapes that populate the natural world. It recalls the rhythms of other entries that, for instance, follow the sun's varying reflections (*CN* 2:2052; f. 20) or monitor the swarming insects as they spiral, coil, uncoil, elongate, and contract "on the side of the Waves" in the Bay of Gibraltar (*CN* 2:2070; f. 30). Furthermore, it brings back a memory of Coleridge watching a flock of starlings that are continuously expanding and contracting from one geometric figure to another – from squares to globes, to orbs, ellipses, and to concave semicircles (*CN* 1:1589; f. 56). In these and numerous other depictions, nothing stays the same; all is fluid and in the state of becoming. The shape of the birds' collective soaring will never remain still but continue and evolve. It will always be in the process of metamorphosing from one shape to another. One soon realizes that Coleridge preferred to observe a scene by following its alterations through time.[1] Kathleen

---

[1] In Chapter 4, where I discuss the poetry, I point out that much of his nature poetry follows the becoming of a scene or the forming of an experience. Each line is another step that occurs in a sequence of particulars and movements that add up to the whole of the poem.

M. Wheeler's understanding of Coleridge's commitment to a living, pulsating, mutable world is most appropriate:

> All forms are open-ended and in the process of change, growth, and development. Forms and unities are never static and fixed as in structuralism. New forms, shapes, parts, wholes, and unities are constantly growing out of old ones. Hence, a work of art does not have fixed parts and a static whole or unity. It has the character of living things, things that are in growth, change, development, evolution without any final aim.[2]

But, as this book discusses, Coleridge's impulse to honor a landscape's evolving and becoming was not his only means of understanding what he saw. As this book has suggested, Coleridge was also enthusiastically dedicated to, and reliant upon, the more static, intuited geometric forms – the triangles, circles, ellipses, and parallelograms associated with Euclid's *Elements* – all of which allowed him to survey and more fully grasp what appeared before his gaze. In his descriptions, therefore, both these established figures and a scene's fluctuating particulars populated his notebook pages. They sat side by side on the notebook page to help him portray the shape and movements of what he saw on his rambles. As I have discussed, his use of these two seemingly contradictory modes – the abstract and the organic – was not necessarily paradoxical. Indeed, both helped Coleridge grasp the abundance and vitality of a landscape.

In this "Afterword" I want briefly to take a bold step further and propose that very occasionally, rather than maintaining its traditional function, the geometric figure, in Coleridge's hands, changes character and begins to exhibit organic qualities so that it becomes a living, growing being in its own right, without the prompting of its natural surroundings. The result is that in several notebook entries, geometric figures occasionally depart from their usual, settled appearance. They seem to reject the permanence of their cold, static ideal realm and exhibit traits that turn them into denizens of a moving, changing, vibrant, yet vulnerable world – an alteration that, of course, disrupts the traditional separation between the abstract, ideal form and the phenomenological particulars of the senses. And this change embraces a perspective that counters a section from Mark Akenside's *The Pleasures of the Imagination*, in which the poet celebrates the immutable, certain geometric forms "sequestered far from sense":

---

[2] Kathleen M. Wheeler, *Romanticism, Pragmatism and Deconstruction* (Oxford: Blackwell, 1993), 199.

> Such is the rise of forms
> Sequestered far from the sense and every spot
> Peculiar in the realms of space and time;
> Such is the throne which man for truth amid
> The paths of mutability hath built,
> Secure, unshaken still; and whence he views
> In matter's mouldering structures, the pure forms
> Of triangle or circle, cube, or cone,
> Impassive all; whose attributes nor force
> Nor fate can alter. There he first conceives
> True being, and the intellectual world
> The same this hour and ever. [3]

In the conclusion to Chapter 5, I suggest that from time to time Coleridge seems to have separated himself from what was once called the "old geometry" in order to include geometric figures that do not necessarily conform to the long-established and accepted truths of Euclid's system.[4] One consequence, I propose, is that Coleridge occasionally substitutes his own geometry and embraces a "wild geometry" that "rivals" the long-established school of Euclidean thought.[5] At these moments, instead of calling upon the traditional, immutable forms, Coleridge recognizes a more turbulent geometry and presents fluctuating, evolving, almost irrational geometric shapes that turn their backs on the settled, "abrupt & grand outlines" (*CL* 1:510) found in the master's *Elements*. In so doing, he intermittently identifies rocks that are "unusually wild in their shape" (*CL* 1:503); he acknowledges squares that resemble circles as well as triangles with curved bases, and he grants that there are forms that "struggle" between being "a Triangle & semi circle" (*CN* 2:2690). The consequence is that these geometric figures begin to simulate the organic world by taking on its becoming and even its vulnerability – they "struggle" (*CN* 2:2690; f. 89). Rather than being steady and fully realized, their shapes are in the midst of a transition from one form into another: from a square to a circle. Just as the moon, described in the entry quoted at the head of this "Afterword," moves from one shape to another, and just as the profile of the swarming insects or starlings elongates and contracts, these figures never actually resolve into a lasting form. In this manner, these

---

[3] Coleridge quotes these lines in *Logic* in the section entitled "On the Mathematical or Intuitive and Logical or Discursive Synthesis *a priori*" (*CC*, 13:199).

[4] At these moments, Coleridge seems to be qualifying his usual understanding that Man's "universal Principles, as far as they are Principles and universal, necessarily suppose uniform and perfect Subjects, which are to be found in the *Ideas* of pure Geometry and (I trust) in the *Realities* of Heaven, but never, never, in Creatures of Flesh and Blood" (*CC* 4:133).

[5] One is reminded here of Edward Muir's observations that the summits of mountains "belong to a different order. They are bold and regular and yet unexpected in their shape, as if they were the result of a wild geometry" (quoted in Wickman, *Literature after Euclid*, 96–97).

sporadically wild and often savage geometric images almost lose touch with their abstract, intuited, more permanent selves to join a realm that registers the mutations, accidents, and uncertainties of an organic presence. They start to domicile within a spatial three-dimensional world and join an environment ruled by time. They step out of and over the boundary of established classification. In a way, they reflect Coleridge's concept of a line in Nature, which is in "constant and continuous evolution" and which registers the motion of a landscape.[6]

On these occasions, Coleridge invites the possibility of something less determined and sure. Coleridge's rather sloppily drawn diagrams are evidence of this mode. Note for instance the difference between the neat and precise ("dry bones") published triangle printed in Joseph Cottle's *Reminiscences of Samuel Taylor Coleridge and Robert Southey* (see Chapter 4 of this book) and Coleridge's handwritten version of it in his original letter (see *CL* 3:23).[7] Coleridge's diagrammatic sketch slips, leans, slopes, and falters as if it were a living entity rather than a determined set, long-recognized figure. The very lines of this diagram seem to breathe. In general, during these moments Coleridge modifies and catches the permanent figure in the state of transition, in the act of becoming – one can sense the hand in the process of drawing the triangle's lines. In a way, when he breaks through these boundaries, he is no longer treating the geometric figure as a tame, rational entity but rather as an almost subjective figure that participates in the irregular, unpredictable motions of the natural world.[8]

Perhaps these unstable structures are yet another expression of Coleridge's sense of the limitations of geometry and his antipathy to confining form. But more likely they are yet another expression of his sensitivity to the sense of a vibrant richness in the surroundings he enjoyed when rambling. Moreover, they reflect his tendency to resolve dualities – to interfuse the nature of experience with the abstract – and to insist that "reality" is the intermingling of both the particular and the abstract as well as the interpenetration of opposing energies. The resulting wild geometric figures are products of this dialectical tension and a demonstration of what Thomas McFarland refers to as the "organically

---

[6] One of the aphorisms that appears in *Aids to Reflection* asserts that "Nature is a Line in constant and continuous evolution. Its *beginning* is lost in the Super-natural: and *for our understanding*, therefore, it must appear as a continuous line without beginning or end" (*CC* 9:268). Coleridge's sense of a landscape in motion prompts him to admit that "there is something enigmatically attractive and imaginative in the generation of curves, and in the whole geometry of motion" (*CC* 11.1:940).
[7] Coleridge referred to the "dry bones of the diagram" in an issue of *The Watchman* (*CC* 2:33).
[8] In *The Watchman*, Coleridge speaks of the "Geometrician, who *tames* [italics mine] into living and embodied uses the proud presentation of Truth" (*CC* 2:33).

interfused quality of [Coleridge's] learning."⁹ More significantly, though, perhaps these living geometric forms draw close to being an emblem of the primary imagination that allows the active mind to synthesize disparate parts in order to create a new reality that resides neither in an absolute subject nor in the object.¹⁰

---

⁹ Thomas McFarland, *Coleridge and the Pantheistic Tradition* (Oxford: Clarendon Press, 1969), xxix.
¹⁰ In *Coleridge's Figurative Language*, Tim Fulford suggests: "what we know through the evidence of the senses is in fact a synthesis of the manifold of sense impressions and the active power of understanding to shape them into coherence" (104).

# *Bibliography*

Adams, George. *Geometrical and Graphical Essays Containing a Description of the Mathematical Instruments Used in Geometry, Civil and Military Surveying Levelling and Perspective, with Many New Problems, Illustrations of Each Branch*. London: R. Hindmarsh, 1791.
Aikin, J[ohn]. *An Essay on the Application of Natural History to Poetry*. London: J. Johnson, 1777.
Andrews, Kerri and Tim Fulford, guest eds. "Romantic Walking." *Romanticism* 27.1 (2021). Special issue.
Andrews, Malcolm. *The Search for the Picturesque: Landscape Aesthetics and Tourism in Britain, 1760–1800*. Aldershot: Scolar Press, 1990.
Baker, Harold D. "Landscape as Textual Practice in Coleridge's Notebooks." *ELH* 59.3 (1992): 651–70.
Ball, W. W. Rouse. *History of the Study of Mathematics at Cambridge*. Cambridge: Cambridge University Press, 1889.
 *A Short Account of the History of Mathematics*. London: Macmillan, 1908.
Barrow, Isaac. *The Usefulness of Mathematical Learning Explained and Demonstrated: Being Mathematical Lectures Read in the Public Schools at the University of Cambridge*. London: Printed for Stephen Austen, 1734.
 ed. *Euclide's Elements: The Whole Fifteen Books Compendiously Demonstrated: with Archimedes' Theorems of the Sphere and Cylinder Investigated by the Method of Indivisibles*. London: J. Redmayne, 1772.
Barrow-Green, June. "Models of Geometric Surfaces." In *The London Mathematical Society and Sublime Symmetry* [produced in conjunction with the De Morgan Foundation for the exhibition "Sublime Symmetry: The Mathematics behind William De Morgan's Ceramic Designs"]. London: London Mathematical Society, 2017, 18–20.
Bartrum, William. *Travels through North and South Carolina, Georgia, East & West Florida*. Philadelphia: James & Johnson, 1791.
Bate, Walter Jackson. *Coleridge*. Cambridge, MA: Harvard University Press, 1969.
Bayne-Powell, Rosamond. *Travellers in Eighteenth-Century England*. London: John Murray, 1951.
Beddoes, Thomas. *Observations on the Nature of Demonstrative Evidence, with an Explanation of Certain Difficulties Occurring in the Elements of Geometry and Reflection on Language*. London: J. Johnson, 1793.

Bender, John and Michael Marrinan. *The Culture of the Diagram.* Stanford, CA: Stanford University Press, 2010.
Best, Stephen and Sharon Marcus. "Surface Reading: An Introduction." *Representations* 108 (Fall 2009): 1–21.
Bicknell, Richard and Robert Woof. *The Discovery of the Lake District 1750–1810.* Grasmere and Wordsworth Museum, 1982.
Blumenbach, Johann Friedrich. *A Manual of the Elements of Natural History.* Trans. R. T. Gore. London: W. Simpson & R. Marshall, 1825.
Blunden, Edmund. "Coleridge's Notebooks." *A Review of English Literature* 7.1 (January 1966): 25–30.
Bowles, William Lisle. *The Poetical Works of William Lisle Bowles.* Vol. 1. Ed. and rev. George Gilfillan. Edinburgh: James Nichol, 1855.
Breitenberger, Ernst. "Gauss's Geodosy and the Axiom of Parallels." *Archives for History of Exact Sciences* 31 (Spring 1984): 273–89.
Byrne, Oliver. *The First Six Books of the Elements of Euclid: In Which Coloured Diagrams and Symbols are Used Instead of Letters for the Greater Ease of Learners.* London: William Pickering, 1847.
Cajori, Florian. "Attempts Made during the Eighteenth and Nineteenth Centuries to Reform the Teaching of Geometry." *American Mathematical Monthly* 17.10 (October 1910): 181–201.
Carlson, Julia S. *Romantic Marks and Measures: Wordsworth's Poetry in Fields of Print.* Philadelphia: University of Pennsylvania Press, 2016.
Cervantes, Gabriel and Dahlia Porter. "Walking with John Howard: Itinerary and Romantic Reform." *Romanticism* 27.1 (2021): 4–15.
Chambers, Ephraim. *Cyclopaedia: or, An Universal Dictionary of the Arts and Sciences.* 2 vols. London: James & John Knopton, John Darby, and others, 1729.
*Christ's Hospital Recollections of Lamb, Coleridge, and Leigh Hunt.* Ed. R. Brimley Johnson. London: George Allen, 1890.
Clayson, Allan. *Wish You Were Here: Coleridge's Holidays at Ramsgate 1819–1833.* Ramsgate, Kent: A. & C. Clayson, 2001.
Coleridge, Samuel Taylor. *Collected Letters of Samuel Taylor Coleridge.* 6 vols. Ed. Earl Leslie Griggs. Oxford: Oxford University Press, 1956–71 [*CL*].
  *The Collected Works of Samuel Taylor Coleridge.* General Editor Kathleen Coburn. 16 vols. Princeton, NJ: Princeton University Press, 1971–2002 [*CC*].
  *The Complete Poetical Works of Samuel Taylor Coleridge.* 2 vols. Ed. Ernest Hartley Coleridge. Oxford: Oxford University Press, 1957 [*CP*].
  MS notebooks. British Library, Add. MSS 47496–47502.
  MS notebooks. Victoria University Library, University of Toronto, E. J. Pratt Library.
  *The Notebooks of Samuel Taylor Coleridge.* Ed. Kathleen Coburn. 5 vols. Princeton, NJ: Princeton University Press, 1957–2002 [*CN*].
Colley, Ann C. *The Search for Synthesis in Literature and Art: The Paradox of Space.* Athens: University of Georgia Press, 1990.
*The Connoisseur* 57 (1774).

Cooley, W. D. "Elementary Geometry." *Nature* 4 (1871): 485–86.
*The Elements of Geometry Simplified and Explained.* London: William and Morgate, 1860.
Cottle, Joseph. *Reminiscences of Samuel Taylor Coleridge and Robert Southey.* New York: Wiley and Putnam, 1843.
*The Country Spectator.* [Ed. Thomas Fanshaw Middleton.] London: Gainsborough, 1793.
Crilly, Tony. "The Rise and Fall of the Mathematical Tripos." In *Mathematics in Victorian Britain.* Ed. Raymond Flood, Adrian Rice, and Robin Wilson. Oxford: Oxford University Press, 2011, 17–84.
Crocker, A. *The Elements of Land Surveying for the Use of Schools and Students.* London: Richard Phillips, 1806.
Cudworth, Ralph. *The True Intellectual System of the Universe.* 4 vols. London: Richard Priestley, 1820.
Cunn, Samuel. *An Appendix to the English Translation of Commandine's Euclid.* London: Tho. Woodward, 1725.
Daniels, Norman. "Thomas Reid's Discovery of Non-Euclidean Geometry." *Philosophy of Science* 39.2 (June 1976): 219–34.
De Certeau, Michael. *The Practice of Everyday Life.* Trans. Steven F. Rendall. Berkeley: University of California Press, 1984.
Denniss, John. *Figuring It Out: Children's Arithmetical Manuscripts 1680–1880.* Oxford: Huxley Scientific Press, 2012.
Despeaux, Sloan Evans. "A Voice for Mathematics." In *Mathematics in Victorian Britain.* Ed. Raymond Flood, Adrian Rice, and Robin Wilson. Oxford: Oxford University Press, 2011, 155–76.
Dix, Thomas. *A Treatise on Land-Surveying, in Seven Parts.* 5th ed. London: Whittaker, Treacher, and Co., 1829.
Dixon, Josie. "The Notebooks." In *The Cambridge Companion to Coleridge.* Ed. Lucy Newlyn. Cambridge: Cambridge University Press, 2002, 75–88.
Dodgson, Charles. *Euclid and His Modern Rivals.* London: Macmillan, 1879.
*A New Theory of Parallels.* 3rd ed. London: Macmillan, 1890.
Eddy, Matthew Daniel. "The Nature of Notebooks: How Enlightenment Schoolchildren Transformed the Tabula Rasa." *Journal of British Studies* 57.2 (March 29, 2018): 275–307.
"The Elements of Navigation Perform'd by Charles Shea Educated in the Royal Mathematical School Christ's Hospital, 1802." MS. Christ's Hospital Museum Archives.
Enfield, William. *The History of Philosophy.* 2 vols. London: J. F. Dove, 1891 [1791].
Euclid. *The Elements of Euclid: The First Six Books Together with the Eleventh and Twelfth.* Ed. Robert Simson. Glasgow: Robert and Andrew Foulis, 1756.
*The Elements of Euclid; The First Six Books Together with the Eleventh and Twelfth.* Ed. Robert Simson. 16th ed. London: F. Wingrave, 1814.

Fara, Patricia. *Erasmus Darwin: Sex, Science, and Serendipity*. Oxford: Oxford University Press, 2012.

Fielding, Theodore Henry and J. Walton. *A Picturesque Tour of the English Lakes*. London: William Clowes, 1821.

Fowler, D. H. *The Mathematics of Plato's Academy: A New Reconstruction*. Oxford: Oxford University Press, 1987.

Frend, William. *Principles of Algebra*. 2 vols. London: Robinson, 1796.

Fulford, Tim. *Coleridge's Figurative Language*. Houndmills, Basingstoke: Macmillan, 1991.

"Virtual Topography: Poets, Painters, Publishers and the Reproduction of Landscape in the Early Nineteenth Century." *Romanticism and Victorianism on the Net* (May 2010): 57–58.

Gascoigne, John. "Mathematics and Meritocracy: The Emergence of the Cambridge Mathematical Tripos." *Social Studies of Science* 14.4 (November 1, 1984): 551–72.

Gilpin, William. *Observations, Relative Chiefly to Picturesque Beauty 1786*. Poole: Woodstock Books, 1996.

*Remarks on Forest Scenery, and Other Woodland Views*. Vol. 1. London: R. Blamire, 1791.

Gonzalez, Jonathan. "'Peripateticating among the mountains': Robert Southey and the Aesthetics of Pedestrian Motion." *Romanticism* 27.1 (2021): 75–87.

Goslee, Nancy Moore. *Shelley's Visual Imagination*. Cambridge: Cambridge University Press, 2011.

Gray, Jeremy. *Ideas of Space: Euclidean, Non-Euclidean, and Relativistic*. Oxford: Clarendon Press, 1979.

*Plato's Ghost: The Modernist Transformation of Mathematics*. Princeton, NJ: Princeton University Press, 2008.

Gray, Thomas. *Journal of a Visit to the Lake District*. Ed. William Roberts. Liverpool: Liverpool University Press, 2001.

Green, William. *The Tourist's New Guide Containing a Description of the Lakes, Mountains, and Scenery in Cumberland, Westmorland, and Lancashire, with Some Account of Their Bordering Towns and Villages*. 2 vols. Kendal: R. Lough, 1819.

Griggs, E. L. "Samuel Taylor Coleridge and Opium." *Huntington Library Quarterly* 17.4 (August 1954): 357–78.

Hankinson, Alan. *Coleridge Walks the Fells: A Lakeland Journey Retraced*. Cumbria: Ellenbank Press, 1991.

Hazlitt, William. "My First Acquaintance with Poets." In *The Complete Works of William Hazlitt in Twenty-One Volumes*. Vol. 17. Ed. P. P. Howe. London: J. M. Dent, 1931–34.

Hewitt, Rachel. *Map of a Nation: A Biography of the Ordnance Survey*. London: Granta, 2011.

Hodgson, James. *A System of the Mathematics: Volume 1. Containing the Euclidian Geometry, Plane, and Spherical Trigonometry, the Projection of the Sphere, Both*

*Orthographic and Stereographic, Astronomy, the Use of the Globe and Navigation*. London: Thomas Page, William and Fisher Mount, 1723.

Holmes, Richard. *Coleridge: Early Visions*. New York: Viking, 1990.

House, Humphrey. *Coleridge: The Clark Lectures 1951–52*. London: Rupert Hart-Davis, 1967.

Housman, John. *A Descriptive Tour, and Guide to the Lakes, Caves, Mountains, and Other Natural Curiosities in Cumberland, Westmorland, Lancashire, and a Part of the West Riding of Yorkshire*. Carlisle: F. Jollie, 1800.

Hucks, Joseph. *A Pedestrian Tour through North Wales, in a Series of Letters*. Ed. Alan R. Jones. Tydeman, Cardiff: University of Wales Press, 1979 [1795].

Hutchinson, William. *An Excursion to the Lakes in Westmoreland and Cumberland; with a Tour through Part of the Northern Counties, in the Years 1773 and 1774*. London: J. Wilkie, 1776.

*History and Antiquities of Cumberland*. Carlisle: G. Jolliffe, 1794.

Ingold, Timothy. *Being Alive: Essays in Movement, Knowledge and Description*. London: Routledge, 2011.

*Lines: A Brief History*. London: Routledge, 2009.

*The Perception of the Environment: Essays on Livelihood, Dwelling and Skills*. London: Routledge, 2000.

Jarvis, Robin. *Romantic Writing and Pedestrian Travel*. Houndmills, Basingstoke: Palgrave, 1997.

Jenkins, Alice. *Space and the March of Mind*. Oxford: Oxford University Press, 2007.

Johnson, L. M. *Wordsworth's Metaphysical Verse: Geometry, Nature, and Form*. London: University of Toronto Press, 1982.

Jones, Clifford. *The Sea and the Sky: The History of the Royal Mathematical School of Christ's Hospital*. Horsham: Christ's Hospital, 2015.

Kandinsky, Wassily. *Kandinsky: Complete Writings on Art*. Vol. 1: *1901–1921*, vol. 2: *1922–1943*. Ed. Kenneth C. Lindsay and Peter Vergo. London: Faber and Faber, 1982.

Kelley, Theresa M. "Spirit and Geometric Form: The Stone and the Shell in Wordsworth's Arab Dream." *Studies in English Literature* 22 (1982): 563–82.

Kirby, William and William Spence. *An Introduction to Entomology: or Elements of the Natural History of Insects with Plates*. Vol. 2. London: Longman, Hurst, Rees, Orme and Brown, 1817.

Klee, Paul. *Pedagogical Sketchbook*. Trans. Sibyl Moholy-Nagy. New York: Praeger, 1972.

*The Thinking Eye*. Ed. Jerry Spiller. London: Lund Humphries, 1961.

Langan, Celeste. *Romantic Vagrancy: Wordsworth and the Simulation of Freedom*. Cambridge: Cambridge University Press, 1995.

Leadbetter, Gregory. "Poets in a Transnatural Landscape: Coleridge, Nature, Poetry." *Romanticism* 27.1 (2021): 46–62.

Lefebure, Molly. "First of the Fellwalkers." In *Cumberland Heritage*. London: Victor Gollancz, 1970.

Leighton, Angela. *On Form: Poetry, Aestheticism, and the Legacy of a Word*. Oxford: Oxford University Press, 2007.
Leslie, John. *Elements of Geometry, Geometric Analysis, and Plane Trigonometry*. Edinburgh: James Ballantyne, 1809.
Lodge, Sara. *Inventing Edward Lear*. Cambridge, MA: Harvard University Press, 2019.
*The London Mathematical Society and Sublime Symmetry* [in conjunction with the De Morgan Foundation for the exhibition "Sublime Symmetry: The Mathematics behind William De Morgan's Ceramic Designs"]. London: London Mathematical Society, 2017.
Long, Richard. *Selected Statements & Interviews*. Ed. Ben Tufnell. London: Haunch of Venison, 2007.
Love, John. *Geodaesia or the Art of Surveying and Measuring of Land Made Easy*. London: G. G. J.& J. Robinson, 1792.
Macfarlane, Robert. *Old Ways: A Journey on Foot*. New York: Penguin Books, 2013.
*Mathematics in Victorian Britain*. Ed. Raymond Flood, Adrian Rice, and Robin Wilson. Oxford: Oxford University Press, 2011.
Mawman, Richard Joseph. *An Excursion to the Highlands of Scotland and the English Lakes*. London: Printed for J. Mawman, 1805.
Mayer, Andreas. *The Science of Walking: Investigating Locomotion in the Long Nineteenth Century*. Trans. Tilman Skowroneck and Robin Blanton. Chicago: University of Chicago Press, 2020.
McFarland, Thomas. *Coleridge and the Pantheistic Tradition*. Oxford: Clarendon Press, 1969.
Middleton, Thomas Fanshaw. *The Country Spectator*. London: Gainsborough, 1793.
Miller, J. Hillis. *Topographies*. Stanford, CA: Stanford University Press, 1995.
Morkteft, Amitrouche. "The Euclid Debate." In *Mathematics in Victorian Britain*. Ed. Raymond Flood, Adrian Rice, and Robin Wilson. Oxford: Oxford University Press, 2011, 321–34.
Newcomb, Simon. "The Fundamental Definitions and Propositions of Geometry, with Especial Reference to the Syllabus of the Association for the Improvement of Geometrical Training." *Nature* 21.535 (January 29, 1880): 293–95.
Nicholson, Jovan. *Winifred Nicholson in Cumberland*. Kendal: Abbot Hall Art Gallery, 2016.
Noyes, Russell. *Wordsworth and the Art of Landscape*. New York: Haskell House Publishers, 1973.
Otley, Jonathan. *A Concise Description of the English Lakes and Adjacent Mountains with General Directions to Tourists; Notes of the Botany, Mineralogy, and Geology of the District; the Floating Island and Derwent Lake; and the Black Lead Mine in Borrowdale*. 5th ed. Keswick: published by the author, 1834.
Paley, Morton D. *Samuel Taylor Coleridge and the Fine Arts*. Oxford: Oxford University Press, 2008.

"Particulars of Christ's Hospital 1787." MS. Christ's Hospital Museum Archives.
Pennant, Thomas. *British Zoology*. 4 vols. London: Benjamin White, 1796.
  *Tour in Wales*. Vol. 1. London: Wilkie and Robinson, 1810.
Plato. *Timaeus*. Ed. J. Warrington. London: Dent, 1965.
Plumptre, James. *The Lakers*. London: W. Clarke, 1798.
Pope, Alexander. *Essay on Man*. Ed. Henry Morley. London: Cassell & Company, 1891.
Price, Uvedale. *On the Picturesque*. Ottley: Woodstock Books, 2000 [1796].
Radcliffe, Ann. *A Journey Made in the Summer of 1794 through Holland and the Western Frontier of Germany, with Return Down the Rhine: To Which Are Added, Observations during a Tour to the Lakes of Lancashire, Westmoreland, and Cumberland*. Dublin: William Potter, 1795.
Rambler, A. [Joseph Budworth]. *A Fortnight's Ramble to the Lakes in Westmoreland, Lancashire, and Cumberland*. London: Hookham and Carpenter, 1792.
Readman, Paul. *Storied Ground: Landscape and the Shaping of English National Identity*. Cambridge: Cambridge University Press, 2018.
Réaumur, R. A. F. de. *Mémoires pour server à l'histoire des insects*. Paris: De l'imprimerie royal, 1738.
Reid, Thomas. *An Inquiry into the Human Mind: On the Principles of Common Sense*. 7th ed. Edinburgh: Anderson and Macdowall, and James Robertson, 1818.
Robertson, J. *The Elements of Navigation Containing the Theory and Practice with the Necessary Tables, and Compendium for Finding the Latitude and Longitude at Sea*. 2 vols. 5th ed. Revised by William Wales, Master of the Royal Mathematical School, Christ's Hospital, London. London: C. Nourse, 1806.
Ruddick, William. "'As Much Diversity as the Heart That Trembles': Coleridge's Notes in the Lakeland Fells." In *Coleridge's Imagination: Essays in Memory of Peter Lauer*. Ed. Richard Garvis, Lucy Newlyn, and Nicholas Roe. Cambridge: Cambridge University Press, 1985, 88–101.
Saccheri, Gerolamo. *Euclid Vindicated from Every Blemish*. Ed. G. B. Halsted and L. Allegri. Heidelberg: Birkhäuser, 2014.
Schneider, Ben Ross, Jr. *Wordsworth's Cambridge Education*. Cambridge: Cambridge University Press, 1957.
Simpkins, Diana M. "Early Editions of Euclid in England." *Annals of Science* 22.4 (December 1966): 225–49.
Solomon, Alex. "The Novel and the Bowling Green: Toby Shandy's Diagrammatic Realism." *Philological Quarterly* 95.2 (2016): 269–91.
Stedall, Jacqueline. *The History of Mathematics: A Very Short Introduction*. Oxford: Oxford University Press, 2012.
  "The Pathway to Knowledge and the English Euclidean Tradition." In *Robert Recorde: The Life and Times of a Tudor Mathematician*. Ed. Gareth Ffowc Roberts and Fenny Smith. Cardiff: University of Wales Press, 2012, 57–72.

Stillinger, Jack. *Coleridge and Textual Instability: The Multiple Versions of the Major Poems*. New York: Oxford University Press, 1974.
Sullivan, Joseph. *A Tour through Parts of England, Scotland, and Wales in 1778*. Dublin: Jenkins, White, Byrne, Marchbank, and Davis, 1785.
Talbot, B. *The Compleat Art of Land-Measuring or, a Guide to Practical Surveying*. London: T. and W. Lowndes, 1784.
Taylor, Thomas. *The Philosophical and Mathematical Commentaries of Proclus; Surnamed, Plato's Successor, on the First Book of Euclid's Elements*. Vol. 1. London: Printed for the author, 1788.
Thewall, John. *The Peripatetic*. Ed. Judith Thompson. Detroit: Wayne State University Press, 2001 [1793].
Thom, Walter. *Pedestrianism: Or an Account of the Performances of Celebrated Pedestrians during the Last and Present Century; with a Full Account of Captain Barclay's Public and Private Matches and an Essay on Training*. Aberdeen: D. Chalmers and Co., 1813.
Todhunter, Isaac. *The Elements of Euclid for the Use of Schools and Colleges*. Rev. ed. London: Macmillan, 1882.
*The University Magazine*. January, February, and March 1795.
Walker, A. [Adam]. *Remarks Made in a Tour from London to the Lakes of Westmoreland and Cumberland in the Summer of 1791 ... to Which is Annexed a Sketch of the Police, Religion, Arts, and Agriculture of France Made in an Excursion to Paris in 1785*. London: G. Nicol and C. Dilly, 1792.
Walker, Carol Kyros. *Breaking Away: Coleridge in Scotland*. New Haven, CT: Yale University Press, 2002.
Walker, Dave and Kerry. *Wordsworth and Coleridge: Tour of the Lake District*. Fleetwood, Lancashire: David Walker, 1997.
Walton, John K. and Jason Wood, eds. *The Making of a Cultural Landscape: The English Lake District as Tourist Destination, 1750–2010*. New York: Routledge, 2016.
Warner, Richard. *A Second Walk through Wales, in August and September 1798*. Bath: R. Crutwell, 1799.
*A Walk through Wales in August 1797*. Bath: R. Crutwell, 1798.
Warren, John. *A Treatise on the Geometrical Presentation of the Square Roots of Negative Quantities*. Cambridge: J. Smith, 1828.
Werner, Stephen. *Blueprint: A Study of Diderot and the Encyclopédic Plates*. Birmingham, AL: Summa Publications, 1993.
West, Thomas. *A Guide to the Lakes in Cumberland, Westmorland and Lancashire*. 3rd ed. London: B. Law and Kendal: William Pennington, 1784.
*A Guide to the Lakes in Cumberland, Westmorland, and Lancashire*. 8th ed. Kendal: William Pennington, 1802.
Whalley, George. "The Bristol Library Borrowings of Southey and Coleridge, 1793–8." *The Library: A Quarterly Review of Bibliography*. Ed. F. C. Francis. Fifth Series, 4. London: Oxford University Press, 1950, 114–32.
Wheeler, Kathleen M. "Coleridge's Theory of Imagination: A Hegelian Solution to Kant?" In *The Interpretation of Belief: Coleridge, Schleiermacher and*

*Romanticism*. Ed. David Jasper. Houndmills, Basingstoke: Macmillan, 1986, 16–40.
  *The Creative Mind in Coleridge's Poetry*. Cambridge, MA: Harvard University Press, 1981.
  "Irony and Dramatic Art in Plato's *Meno*." In *Ironie in Philosophie, Literatur und Recht*. Ed. Bärbel Frischmann. Würzburg: Königshausen & Neuman, 2014, 37–54.
  *Romanticism, Pragmatism, and Deconstruction*. Oxford: Blackwell, 1993.
Whiston, William. *The Elements of Euclid with Select Theorems out of Archimedes*. 11th ed. Dublin: R. Jackson, 1791.
Wickman, Matthew. *Literature after Euclid: The Geometric Imagination in the Long Scottish Enlightenment*. Philadelphia: University of Pennsylvania Press, 2016.
Wilberforce, William. *Journey to the Lake District from Cambridge 1799*. Ed. C. E. Wrangham. Stocksfield: Oriel Press, 1983.
Wilkinson, Joseph, Rev. *Select Views in Cumberland, Westmorland and Lancashire*. London: R. Acherman, 1810.
Wilson, James Maurice. *Elementary Geometry Books I–V Containing the Subject of Euclid's First Six Books Following the Syllabus of Geometry Prepared by the Geometrical Association*. 4th ed. London: Macmillan, 1878.
  *A Lecture on Mathematical Teaching, Especially Geometry*. Rugby: W. Billington, 1870.
Wimsatt, W. K. "The Structure of Romantic Nature Imagery." In *The Verbal Icon: Studies in the Meaning of Poetry*. Lexington: University of Kentucky Press, 1954, 103–16.
Wordsworth, Dorothy. *The Grasmere Journal*. In *Journals of Dorothy Wordsworth*. Vol. 1. Ed. E. de Selincourt. New York: The Macmillan Company, 1941, 37–189.
  *Recollections of a Tour Made in Scotland (1802)*. In *Journals of Dorothy Wordsworth*. Vol. 1. Ed. E. de Selincourt. New York: The Macmillan Company, 1941, 191–422.
Wordsworth, William. *The Prelude: The Four Texts (1798, 1799, 1805, 1850)*. Ed. Jonathan Wordsworth. London: Penguin Books, 1995.
Woudenberg, Maximiliaan van. "Revisiting the Harz Tour of Coleridge and the 'Carlyon-Parry-Greenation' in May 1799." *Romanticism* 27.1 (2021): 16–27.
Young, Arthur. *A Six Month's Tour through the North of England*. London: W. Strahan, 1771.

# Index

*a priori* intuition, 7, 106, 108
abstraction, power of, 7, 69, 103–6, 108–9, 112, 144
Adams, George, 107
Aikin, John, 142
Akenside, Mark, 177
Allardice, Captain Robert Barclay, 15
Allsop, Thomas, 150
Allston, Washington
    Coleridge's translation of, 6, 55, 66–67
Alps, the, 18, 24
Andrews, Malcolm, 17
Aristotle, 2, 161
Association for the Improvement of Geometrical Training, 157
attention, power of, 7, 103, 104, 106

Ball, W. W. Rouse, 94
Barker, Thomas, 33
Barrow, Isaac, 3, 96
Batty, John, 15
Beaumont, Lady, 16
Beaumont, Sir George, 16, 28
    Coleridge's translation of, 6, 62–66, 79
"Beck in Winter, A" (Coleridge), 114, 121–22
Beddoes, Thomas, 108, 157, 158
Bicknell, Peter, 17
Bowles, William Lisle, 122–24
Boyer, James, 46, 85, 134
Brocken, the, 10, 20, 171–73
Budworth, Joseph, 18, 25

Carlson, Julia S., 31
cartographic imagination, 33, 168
cartography, 31–32, 71
Cayley, Arthur, 163
Chester, John, 23
Christ's Hospital School, 1, 7, 40, 42, 45, 83–89, 93, 100–1, 123, 129, 134–35, 154
*Christabel* (Coleridge), 117

Claude glass, 27–28, 105
Coburn, Kathleen, 23, 32, 57, 60, 77
Coleridge, Ernest Hartley, 136
Coleridge, George, 16, 88–89
Coleridge, Samuel Taylor, 127
    and alternative paradigms, 163–72
    attraction to the transient, 110
    boots of, 6, 45–50
    critique of geometric models, 82–108, 178
    and the curvature of space, 170–72
    as Euclid's rival, 10, 173, 178
    and geometric figures. *See* poetry: and the geometric figure
    and the geometric idiom. *See* geometric idiom
    and geometric figures in the landscape. *See* landscape: geometric figures in
    and the Geometry of Visibiles, 164–70
    at Greta Hall, 23, 81, 150
    and lineal organization of poetry, 125–27, *See also* poetry: and the geometric figure
    and maps, 5, 32–33, 67
    opium addiction of, 16, 23, 147
    organic geometry of, 177–80
    and patterns of a poem's lines, 8, 126, 129
    peripatetic rhythms of his verse, 8, 115–25
    and physical contact with the earth, 9, 142
    at Ramsgate, 149–50
    rhythm of his walking, 8, 117
    Scottish excursion of, 16–17, 22, 24, 29, 33, 41, 44, 47–49, 53, 80–81, 105, 111
    sense of wellbeing of, 12, 16
    sensibility of fluidity and vitality, 82, 135
    sensitivity to motion, *See also* motion, lines of
    sensitivity to the organic, 35, 37, 55, 76, 141, 143
    sensuous appreciation of, 3–5, 7, 9, 69, 82–83, 106, 108–11, 137, 139, 142
    spatial orientation of, 12–13, 126, 173
    as surveyor, 6, 42–45, 49, 66, 78, 119, 171–72, 174

and the teaching of geometry, 82, 152
and tread of his feet, 2, 5, 8, 13, 40–45, 49, 115–16, 121, 125, 143, 149–50, 169
walking and composing poetry, 8, 119, 121, 125
Welsh excursion of, 15, 17–18, 20
Coleridge, Sara, 47, 148
Cooley, W. D., 158
Costobadie, Jacob de, 90
Cottle, Joseph, 135, 138, 179
Crocker, Abraham, 153
Cruikshank, Mary, 138
Cudworth, Ralph, 100

Darwin, Erasmus, 98
De Morgan, Augustus, 163
"Devonshire Roads" (Coleridge), 121
diagrammatic culture, 71
diagrammatic sketches, 1, 6, 8, 52, 56, 73, 179
diagrams, geometric, 6, 76, 86
Dodgson, Charles L., 162–65

*Elements* (Euclid), 2–4, 7, 110, 152–54, 159
*Elements of Geometry, The* (Billingsley), 3
Enfield, William, 100
"Eolian Harp, The" (Coleridge), 126
*Epitome of Geometry* (Allingham), 3
Euclid
 fifth postulate of, 160
 first proposition of, 88, 91
Euclid debate, the, 162–63
Euclidean culture, 95
Euclidean geometry, 1–4
 in art, 5–6
 and patterns of a poem's lines, 8
*Euclid's Elements of Geometry* (Barrow), 3
*Euclid's Elements of Geometry* (Leeke and Serle), 3
*Euclid's Elements of Geometry* (Rudd), 3
Evans, Anne, 90
Evans, Mary, 90
experiential, the, 109

"First Proposition in the First Book of Euclid, Poetically Rendered, The" (anonymous), 92
forms
 geometric, 4, 7, 10, 52, 77, 79, 82, 100, 111, 131, 166, 173, 177–80
 Platonic, 106, 110
 poetical, 128
Frend, William, 91
"Frost at Midnight" (Coleridge), 9, 114, 133–35, 137, 144
Fulford, Tim, 135

Gauss, Karl Friedrich, 10, 170–73
geometric caterpillar, 6, 43, 78
geometric figures
 absence of in Coleridge's poetry, 132, 142
 in the landscape. *See* landscape: geometric figures in
 and the organic world, 178–79
 pattern and form of, 5, 79, 132
 in Plato, 106
 and poetry, 8, 131–33, 135
geometric idiom
 Coleridge's early awareness of, 83
 Coleridge's use of, 5–7, 9, 12, 50, 102, 131, 152
 and fluidity, 111–13
 in landscapes, 52, 77, 79
 and the organic, 3, 5
 and perception, 1
 practicality of, 2
 and sensibility to fluidity, 82
geometric perspective, 4, 7, 115
geometry
 as middle situation, 100
 as temper of mind, 83
 wild, 159, 173–75
Gillman, James, 149–50, 152
Gilpin, William, 27, 67–69, 82
Godwin, Charles, 141
Grand Tour, 18
Gray, Jeremy, 159
Gray, Thomas, 26
Griggs, E. L., 147
*A Guide to the Lakes* (West), 18, 25

Harz Mountains, 10, 20, 171
Hazlitt, William, 22, 23
Heberden, William, 93
Housman, John, 67
Hucks, Joseph, 18, 20
Hutchinson, Sara, 23, 30, 39, 41, 49
Hutchinson, William, 32, 68

imagination, spatial, 6, 12, 74
Ingold, Timothy, 30, 41, 52
*Inquiry into the Human Mind: On the Principles of Common Sense, An* (Reid), 10, 83, 164
interspaces, 33
*Introduction to Entomology, An* (Kirby and Spence), 79

Jarvis, Robin, 30, 38, 115, 117, 128
Jebb, John, 94
Jesus College, 42, 89–91, 95, 101
John Hersee Collection, 43, 155

Kandinsky, Wassily, 5–6, 73, 75–76
Kant, Immanuel
  and experience and the mind, 166
  and intuited knowledge, 7, 106, 108
Klee, Paul, 5–6, 73–76
"Kubla Khan" (Coleridge), 126

Lake District, 17, 19–20, 24, 26, 28–29, 44, 54, 58, 81, 150
Lamb, Charles, 136–37, 139–40, 148
landscape
  appreciation of, 3
  as continuous process, 31
  descriptions of, 7–8
  geometric figures in, 9–10, 81–82, 105, 109–11
  identification of body in, 40
  interspaces in, 33
  lines of motion in, 6, 31, 34, 36–37, 40, 49, 64, 70, 73, 103, 172, 179
  measurement of, 1–2, 5–6
  motion in, 36
  organic nature of, 35, 37, 55, 76, 141, 143
  perception of, 5
  recording of, 5
laudanum, 17
Lear, Edward, 71
Legendre, Adrien-Marie, 161
Leslie, John, 103
"Lewti" (Coleridge), 116
"Life" (Coleridge), 116
*Life and Opinions of Tristram Shandy, Gentleman* (Sterne), 70
"Lines: Composed while climbing the Left Ascent of Brockley Coomb, Somersetshire, May 1795" (Coleridge), 8, 119
"Lines: To a Beautiful Spring in a Village" (Coleridge), 115–16
"Lines written at Shurton Bars" (Coleridge), 115–16
Long, Richard, 49, 73
Love, John, 153

Macfarlane, Robert, 49
Malta, 11, 45, 55, 59, 63, 80, 170
*A Manual of the Elements of Natural History* (Blumenbach), 78
mathematical copybooks, 42–43, 154
Mathematical Tripos, 94
mathematics
  as language of pattern and form, 9
  meaning, patterns of, 5
Mendip Hills, 24
metaphor, organic. *See* landscape: organic nature of

"Metrical Feet: Lessons for a Boy" (Coleridge), 118
Middleton, Thomas Fanshaw, 93, 95
models, wooden geometric, 83–107, 158
motion
  circular, 135
  geometry of, 101, 111
  lines of, 1, 6, 8, 54–57, 66, 77, 87, 115, 125–28, 131

Napoleonic Wars, 18
nature poetry, 2, 5, 8–9, 50
Nether Stowey, 22–23, 109, 138
Newton, John, 90
Newton, Sir Isaac, 93–94
Newton, Thomas, 101
Nicholson, Winifred, 73
non-Euclidean geometry, 10, 83, 159–60, 162, 164–65, 170
notebooks (Coleridge), 1, 5–6, 8, 9, 28, 31, 35–36, 41, 42, 49, 52, 55, 56, 59, 60, 61, 77, 79, 80, 168

"On Bala Hill" (Coleridge), 116
Otley, Jonathan, 25
Ottmann, Henri, 73

Paley, Morton D., 62–65
paradigms, Euclidean, 98
*The Pathway to Knowledge* (Recorde), 2–3
*Pedestrianism or an Account of the Performances of Celebrated Pedestrians during the last and present Century* (Thom), 15
Pennant, Thomas, 19
"Perspiration: A Travelling Eclogue" (Coleridge), 39, 115
"Picture or the Lover's Resolution, The" (Coleridge), 127
picturesque, the, 5, 26–28, 34, 38, 68–69
Plato, 2, 96, 100–1, 106
Platonic idea, 7, 106, 108
Platonists, Cambridge, 100–1
Plotinus, 79, 100
poetry, and the geometric figure 8–9, 133–42
Poole, Thomas, 172
Poussin, Nicolas, 28
Powell, Foster, 15
Price, Uvedale, 68
Proclus, 2, 95, 100
"Proposition the first and Problem the first" (Coleridge), 88
Pythagoras, 100–1

Quantock Hills, 22

Rambler, A. *See* Budworth, Joseph
"Recollection" (Coleridge), 127

# Index

Reid, Thomas, 10, 83, 164–69
*Remarks on Forest Scenery* (Gilpin), 82
*Reminiscences of Samuel Taylor Coleridge and Robert Southey* (Cottle), 138, 179
"River Charwell, The" (Bowles), 122
"River Wainsbeck" (Bowles), 122
Rosa, Salvatore, 26, 28
Royal Mathematical School, 84, 86, 154

Senate House examinations, 93
Shea, Charles, 43, 154–55
Simson, Robert, 153
Solomon, Alex, 77
"Songs of the Pixies" (Coleridge), 117
"Sonnet II" (Dermody), 129–31
"Sonnet On Quitting School for College" (Coleridge), 120
"Sonnet: To the River Otter" (Coleridge), 109, 114–15, 122, 124–25, 127–29, 131
Sotheby, William, 116, 142–43
Southey, Robert, 15, 20, 22–24, 32, 39, 146
space, curvature of, 10, 170–73
Stedall, Jacqueline, 2–3
Sterne, Laurence, 6, 69–71, 76
surveying, 6, 11, 42–44, 54, 95, 126, 153, 170

Taylor, Thomas, 2, 95, 100
"This Lime-Tree Bower My Prison" (Coleridge), 9, 42, 114, 136, 138–42
*Timaeus* (Plato), 106
"To a Young Friend On his proposing to domesticate with the Author" (Coleridge), 120
"To the Rev. W. L. Bowles" (Coleridge), 123
"To the River Itchin" (Bowles), 122, 124
Todhunter, Isaac, 163
topography, 9

tourists, picturesque, 29–30
tyranny of the eye, 13

*University Magazine, The* (Cambridge), 89, 91–92
University of Cambridge, 1, 7, 89–95
University of Göttingen, 100, 170–71
University of Leicester Library, 43, 155

vestibule of thought, 7
Victoria University Library, 55, 59

Wakefield, Gilbert, 92
Wales, William, 85
Walker, A., 70
walking, 4, 8
  culture of, 5
  excursions, 1, 5–6
  and health, 15, 21, 25
Walton, John K., 17
Warner, Rev. Richard, 19
Wedgwood, Thomas, 11, 21, 40, 45
West, Thomas, 18, 67
Wheeler, Kathleen M., 176–77
Whiston, William, 96
Wilberforce, William, 19, 29
Wilkinson, Joseph, 28
Wilson, James Maurice, 157, 161–62
Wood, Jason, 17
Woof, Robert, 17
Wordsworth, Dorothy, 13, 22, 26, 47, 111
Wordsworth, William, 19–20, 22–23, 73, 98
  cartographic perspective of, 31
  *Prelude, The*, 86, 93, 101, 109
  Scottish excursion, 29, 48

"Youth and Age" (Coleridge), 145–52

# CAMBRIDGE STUDIES IN ROMANTICISM

*General Editor*
JAMES CHANDLER, *University of Chicago*

1. *Romantic Correspondence: Women, Politics and the Fiction of Letters*
   MARY A. FAVRET
2. *British Romantic Writers and the East: Anxieties of Empire*
   NIGEL LEASK
3. *Poetry as an Occupation and an Art in Britain, 1760–1830*
   PETER MURPHY
4. *Edmund Burke's Aesthetic Ideology: Language, Gender and Political Economy in Revolution*
   TOM FURNISS
5. *In the Theatre of Romanticism: Coleridge, Nationalism, Women*
   JULIE A. CARLSON
6. *Keats, Narrative and Audience*
   ANDREW BENNETT
7. *Romance and Revolution: Shelley and the Politics of a Genre*
   DAVID DUFF
8. *Literature, Education, and Romanticism: Reading as Social Practice, 1780–1832*
   ALAN RICHARDSON
9. *Women Writing about Money: Women's Fiction in England, 1790–1820*
   EDWARD COPELAND
10. *Shelley and the Revolution in Taste: The Body and the Natural World*
    TIMOTHY MORTON
11. *William Cobbett: The Politics of Style*
    LEONORA NATTRASS
12. *The Rise of Supernatural Fiction, 1762–1800*
    E. J. CLERY
13. *Women Travel Writers and the Language of Aesthetics, 1716–1818*
    ELIZABETH A. BOHLS
14. *Napoleon and English Romanticism*
    SIMON BAINBRIDGE
15. *Romantic Vagrancy: Wordsworth and the Simulation of Freedom*
    CELESTE LANGAN

16. *Wordsworth and the Geologists*
   JOHN WYATT

17. *Wordsworth's Pope: A Study in Literary Historiography*
   ROBERT J. GRIFFIN

18. *The Politics of Sensibility: Race, Gender and Commerce in the Sentimental Novel*
   MARKMAN ELLIS

19. *Reading Daughters' Fictions, 1709–1834: Novels and Society from Manley to Edgeworth*
   CAROLINE GONDA

20. *Romantic Identities: Varieties of Subjectivity, 1774–1830*
   ANDREA K. HENDERSON

21. *Print Politics: The Press and Radical Opposition in Early Nineteenth-Century England*
   KEVIN GILMARTIN

22. *Reinventing Allegory*
   THERESA M. KELLEY

23. *British Satire and the Politics of Style, 1789–1832*
   GARY DYER

24. *The Romantic Reformation: Religious Politics in English Literature, 1789–1824*
   ROBERT M. RYAN

25. *De Quincey's Romanticism: Canonical Minority and the Forms of Transmission*
   MARGARET RUSSETT

26. *Coleridge on Dreaming: Romanticism, Dreams and the Medical Imagination*
   JENNIFER FORD

27. *Romantic Imperialism: Universal Empire and the Culture of Modernity*
   SAREE MAKDISI

28. *Ideology and Utopia in the Poetry of William Blake*
   NICHOLAS M. WILLIAMS

29. *Sexual Politics and the Romantic Author*
   SONIA HOFKOSH

30. *Lyric and Labour in the Romantic Tradition*
   ANNE JANOWITZ

31. *Poetry and Politics in the Cockney School: Keats, Shelley, Hunt and Their Circle*
   JEFFREY N. COX

32. *Rousseau, Robespierre and English Romanticism*
   GREGORY DART

33. Contesting the Gothic: Fiction, Genre and Cultural Conflict, 1764–1832
   JAMES WATT

34. Romanticism, Aesthetics, and Nationalism
   DAVID ARAM KAISER

35. Romantic Poets and the Culture of Posterity
   ANDREW BENNETT

36. The Crisis of Literature in the 1790s: Print Culture and the Public Sphere
   PAUL KEEN

37. Romantic Atheism: Poetry and Freethought, 1780–1830
   MARTIN PRIESTMAN

38. Romanticism and Slave Narratives: Transatlantic Testimonies
   HELEN THOMAS

39. Imagination under Pressure, 1789–1832: Aesthetics, Politics, and Utility
   JOHN WHALE

40. Romanticism and the Gothic: Genre, Reception, and Canon Formation, 1790–1820
   MICHAEL GAMER

41. Romanticism and the Human Sciences: Poetry, Population, and the Discourse of the Species
   MAUREEN N. MCLANE

42. The Poetics of Spice: Romantic Consumerism and the Exotic
   TIMOTHY MORTON

43. British Fiction and the Production of Social Order, 1740–1830
   MIRANDA J. BURGESS

44. Women Writers and the English Nation in the 1790s
   ANGELA KEANE

45. Literary Magazines and British Romanticism
   MARK PARKER

46. Women, Nationalism and the Romantic Stage: Theatre and Politics in Britain, 1780–1800
   BETSY BOLTON

47. British Romanticism and the Science of the Mind
   ALAN RICHARDSON

48. The Anti-Jacobin Novel: British Conservatism and the French Revolution
   M. O. GRENBY

49. *Romantic Austen: Sexual Politics and the Literary Canon*
   CLARA TUITE

50. *Byron and Romanticism*
   JEROME MCGANN AND JAMES SODERHOLM

51. *The Romantic National Tale and the Question of Ireland*
   INA FERRIS

52. *Byron, Poetics and History*
   JANE STABLER

53. *Religion, Toleration, and British Writing, 1790–1830*
   MARK CANUEL

54. *Fatal Women of Romanticism*
   ADRIANA CRACIUN

55. *Knowledge and Indifference in English Romantic Prose*
   TIM MILNES

56. *Mary Wollstonecraft and the Feminist Imagination*
   BARBARA TAYLOR

57. *Romanticism, Maternity and the Body Politic*
   JULIE KIPP

58. *Romanticism and Animal Rights*
   DAVID PERKINS

59. *Georgic Modernity and British Romanticism: Poetry and the Mediation of History*
   KEVIS GOODMAN

60. *Literature, Science and Exploration in the Romantic Era: Bodies of Knowledge*
   TIMOTHY FULFORD, DEBBIE LEE AND PETER J. KITSON

61. *Romantic Colonization and British Anti-Slavery*
   DEIRDRE COLEMAN

62. *Anger, Revolution, and Romanticism*
   ANDREW M. STAUFFER

63. *Shelley and the Revolutionary Sublime*
   CIAN DUFFY

64. *Fictions and Fakes: Forging Romantic Authenticity, 1760–1845*
   MARGARET RUSSETT

65. *Early Romanticism and Religious Dissent*
   DANIEL E. WHITE

66. *The Invention of Evening: Perception and Time in Romantic Poetry*
   CHRISTOPHER R. MILLER

67. *Wordsworth's Philosophic Song*
   SIMON JARVIS

68. *Romanticism and the Rise of the Mass Public*
   ANDREW FRANTA

69. *Writing against Revolution: Literary Conservatism in Britain, 1790–1832*
   KEVIN GILMARTIN

70. *Women, Sociability and Theatre in Georgian London*
   GILLIAN RUSSELL

71. *The Lake Poets and Professional Identity*
   BRIAN GOLDBERG

72. *Wordsworth Writing*
   ANDREW BENNETT

73. *Science and Sensation in Romantic Poetry*
   NOEL JACKSON

74. *Advertising and Satirical Culture in the Romantic Period*
   JOHN STRACHAN

75. *Romanticism and the Painful Pleasures of Modern Life*
   ANDREA K. HENDERSON

76. *Balladeering, Minstrelsy, and the Making of British Romantic Poetry*
   MAUREEN N. MCLANE

77. *Romanticism and Improvisation, 1750–1850*
   ANGELA ESTERHAMMER

78. *Scotland and the Fictions of Geography: North Britain, 1760–1830*
   PENNY FIELDING

79. *Wordsworth, Commodification and Social Concern: The Poetics of Modernity*
   DAVID SIMPSON

80. *Sentimental Masculinity and the Rise of History, 1790–1890*
   MIKE GOODE

81. *Fracture and Fragmentation in British Romanticism*
   ALEXANDER REGIER

82. *Romanticism and Music Culture in Britain, 1770–1840: Virtue and Virtuosity*
   GILLEN D'ARCY WOOD

83. *The Truth about Romanticism: Pragmatism and Idealism in Keats, Shelley, Coleridge*
   TIM MILNES

84. *Blake's Gifts: Poetry and the Politics of Exchange*
   SARAH HAGGARTY

85. *Real Money and Romanticism*
   MATTHEW ROWLINSON

86. *Sentimental Literature and Anglo-Scottish Identity, 1745–1820*
   JULIET SHIELDS

87. *Romantic Tragedies: The Dark Employments of Wordsworth, Coleridge, and Shelley*
   REEVE PARKER

88. *Blake, Sexuality and Bourgeois Politeness*
   SUSAN MATTHEWS

89. *Idleness, Contemplation and the Aesthetic*
   RICHARD ADELMAN

90. *Shelley's Visual Imagination*
   NANCY MOORE GOSLEE

91. *A Cultural History of the Irish Novel, 1790–1829*
   CLAIRE CONNOLLY

92. *Literature, Commerce, and the Spectacle of Modernity, 1750–1800*
   PAUL KEEN

93. *Romanticism and Childhood: The Infantilization of British Literary Culture*
   ANN WEIRDA ROWLAND

94. *Metropolitan Art and Literature, 1810–1840: Cockney Adventures*
   GREGORY DART

95. *Wordsworth and the Enlightenment Idea of Pleasure*
   ROWAN BOYSON

96. *John Clare and Community*
   JOHN GOODRIDGE

97. *The Romantic Crowd*
   MARY FAIRCLOUGH

98. *Romantic Women Writers, Revolution and Prophecy*
   ORIANNE SMITH

99. *Britain, France and the Gothic, 1764–1820*
   ANGELA WRIGHT

100. *Transfiguring the Arts and Sciences*
   JON KLANCHER

101. *Shelley and the Apprehension of Life*
   ROSS WILSON

102. *Poetics of Character: Transatlantic Encounters 1700–1900*
   SUSAN MANNING

103. *Romanticism and Caricature*
   IAN HAYWOOD

104. *The Late Poetry of the Lake Poets: Romanticism Revised*
   TIM FULFORD

105. *Forging Romantic China: Sino-British Cultural Exchange 1760–1840*
   PETER J. KITSON

106. *Coleridge and the Philosophy of Poetic Form*
   EWAN JAMES JONES

107. *Romanticism in the Shadow of War: Literary Culture in the Napoleonic War Years*
   JEFFREY N. COX

108. *Slavery and the Politics of Place: Representing the Colonial Caribbean, 1770–1833*
   ELIZABETH A. BOHLS

109. *The Orient and the Young Romantics*
   ANDREW WARREN

110. *Lord Byron and Scandalous Celebrity*
   CLARA TUITE

111. *Radical Orientalism: Rights, Reform, and Romanticism*
   GERARD COHEN-VRIGNAUD

112. *Print, Publicity, and Popular Radicalism in the 1790s*
   JON MEE

113. *Wordsworth and the Art of Philosophical Travel*
   MARK OFFORD

114. *Romanticism, Self-Canonization, and the Business of Poetry*
   MICHAEL GAMER

115. *Women Wanderers and the Writing of Mobility, 1784–1814*
   INGRID HORROCKS

116. *Eighteen Hundred and Eleven: Poetry, Protest and Economic Crisis*
   E. J. CLERY

117. *Urbanization and English Romantic Poetry*
STEPHEN TEDESCHI

118. *The Poetics of Decline in British Romanticism*
JONATHAN SACHS

119. *The Caribbean and the Medical Imagination, 1764–1834: Slavery, Disease and Colonial Modernity*
EMILY SENIOR

120. *Science, Form, and the Problem of Induction in British Romanticism*
DAHLIA PORTER

121. *Wordsworth and the Poetics of Air*
THOMAS H. FORD

122. *Romantic Art in Practice: Cultural Work and the Sister Arts, 1760–1820*
THORA BRYLOWE

123. *European Literatures in Britain, 1815–1832: Romantic Translations*
DIEGO SIGALIA

124. *Romanticism and Theatrical Experience: Kean, Hazlitt and Keats in the Age of Theatrical News*
JONATHAN MULROONEY

125. *The Romantic Tavern: Literature and Conviviality in the Age of Revolution*
IAN NEWMAN

126. *British Orientalisms, 1759–1835*
JAMES WATT

127. *Print and Performance in the 1820s: Improvisation, Speculation, Identity*
ANGELA ESTERHAMMER

128. *The Italian Idea: Anglo-Italian Radical Literary Culture, 1815–1823*
WILL BOWERS

129. *The Ephemeral Eighteenth Century: Print, Sociability, and the Cultures of Collecting*
GILLIAN RUSSELL

130. *Physical Disability in British Romantic Literature*
ESSAKA JOSHUA

131. *William Wordsworth, Second-Generation Romantic: Contesting Poetry after Waterloo*
JEFFREY COX

132. *Walter Scott and the Greening of Scotland: The Emergent Ecologies of a Nation*
SUSAN OLIVER

133. *Art, Science and the Body in Early Romanticism*
   STEPHANIE O'ROURKE

134. *Honor, Romanticism, and the Hidden Value of Modernity*
   JAMISON KANTOR

135. *Romanticism and the Biopolitics of Modern War Writing*
   NEIL RAMSEY

136. *Jane Austen and Other Minds: Ordinary Language Philosophy in Literary Fiction*
   ERIC REID LINDSTROM

137. *Orientation in European Romanticism: The Art of Falling Upwards*
   PAUL HAMILTON

138. *Romanticism, Republicanism, and the Swiss Myth*
   PATRICK VINCENT

139. *Coleridge and the Geometric Idiom: Walking with Euclid*
   ANN C. COLLEY

For EU product safety concerns, contact us at Calle de José Abascal, 56–1°, 28003 Madrid, Spain or eugpsr@cambridge.org.

www.ingramcontent.com/pod-product-compliance
Lightning Source LLC
LaVergne TN
LVHW011821060526
838200LV00053B/3859